Killing Jesus

Also by Bill O'Reilly and Martin Dugard

Killing Lincoln

Killing Kennedy

Killing Patton

Killing Reagan

Killing the Rising Sun

Killing Jesus

A HISTORY

BILL O'REILLY

AND MARTIN DUGARD

ST. MARTIN'S GRIFFIN ⚞ NEW YORK

www.stmartins.com

Designed by Meryl Sussman Levavi

The Library of Congress has cataloged the Henry Holt edition as follows:

O'Reilly, Bill.
    Killing Jesus : a history / Bill O'Reilly, Martin Dugard.
       p. cm.
    ISBN 978-0-8050-9854-9 (hardcover)
    ISBN 978-0-8050-9855-6 (e-book)
    1. Jesus Christ—Crucifixion.   I. Dugard, Martin.   II. Title.
    BT450.O74 2013
    232.96—dc23

                                2013021752

ISBN 978-1-250-14220-7 (trade paperback)

First published by Henry Holt, an imprint of Henry Holt and Company, LLC

First St. Martin's Griffin Edition: March 2017

10 9 8 7 6 5 4 3 2 1

This book is dedicated to those

who love their neighbors as themselves

Killing Jesus

A NOTE TO READERS

IN THE BEGINNING . . .

To say that Jesus of Nazareth was the most influential man who ever lived is almost trite. Nearly two thousand years after he was brutally executed by Roman soldiers, more than 2.2 billion human beings attempt to follow his teachings and believe he is God. That includes 77 percent of the U.S. population, according to a Gallup Poll. The teachings of Jesus have shaped the entire world and continue to do so.

Much has been written about Jesus, the son of a humble carpenter. But little is actually known about him. Of course we have the Gospels of Matthew, Mark, Luke, and John, but they sometimes appear contradictory and were written from a spiritual point of view rather than as a historical chronicling of Jesus's life. Who Jesus actually was and what exactly happened to him are emotional subjects that often lead to contentious discussion.

In the writing of this fact-based book, Martin Dugard and I do not aim to suggest that we know everything about Jesus. But we know much and will tell you things that you might not have heard. Our research has uncovered a narrative that is both fascinating and frustrating. There are major gaps in the life of Jesus, and at times we can only deduce what happened to him based upon the best available evidence. As often as possible, we relied on classical works. Our primary sources are cited in the last pages of the book. As we did in our previous books, *Killing Lincoln* and *Killing Kennedy*, we will tell you when we don't know what happened or if we believe the evidence we are citing is not set in stone.

The Romans kept incredible records of the time, and a few Jewish historians in Palestine also wrote down the events of the day. The problem is that it wasn't until the last few months of Jesus's short life that he became the focus of establishment attention. Until then, he was just another Jewish man struggling to survive in a harsh society. Only his friends paid much heed to what Jesus was doing.

But those friends did pass much along verbally, and so we have the narrative of the Gospels. But this is not a religious book. We do not address Jesus as the Messiah, only as a man who galvanized a remote area of the Roman Empire and made very powerful enemies while preaching a philosophy of peace and love. In fact, the hatred toward Jesus and what happened because of it may, at times, overwhelm the reader. This is a violent story centered both in Judea and in Rome itself, where the emperors were also considered gods by their loyal followers.

Martin Dugard and I are both Roman Catholics who were educated in religious schools. But we are also historical investigators and are interested primarily in telling the truth about important people, not converting anyone to a spiritual cause. We brought this dedication and discipline to Abraham Lincoln and John F. Kennedy, and in these pages we will do the same with Jesus of Nazareth. By the way, both Lincoln and Kennedy believed Jesus was God.

To understand what Jesus accomplished and how he paid with his life, we have to understand what was happening around him. His was a time when Rome dominated the Western world and brooked no dissent. Human life was worth little. Life expectancy was less than forty years, and far less if you happened to anger the Roman powers that were. An excellent description of the time was written—perhaps with some bombast—by journalist Vermont Royster in 1949:

> There was oppression—for those who were not the friends of Tiberius Caesar . . . what was man for but to serve Caesar?
>
> There was persecution of men who dared think differently, who heard strange voices or read strange manuscripts. There was enslavement of men whose tribes came not from Rome, disdain for those who did not have the familiar visage. And most of all, there was contempt for human life. What, to the strong, was one man more or less in a crowded world?
>
> Then, of a sudden, there was a light in the world, and a man from Galilee saying, Render unto Caesar the things that are Caesar's and unto God the things that are God's.
>
> And the voice from Galilee, which would defy Caesar, offered a new kingdom in which each man could walk upright and bow to none but his God . . . so the

light came into the world and the men who lived in darkness were afraid, and they tried to lower a curtain so that man would still believe that salvation lay with the leaders.

But it came to pass for a while in diverse places that the truth did set men free, although the men of darkness were offended and they tried to put out the light.

And these men succeeded (at least in the short term). Jesus was executed. But the incredible story behind the lethal struggle between good and evil has not been fully told. Until now. At least, that is the goal of this book. Thank you for reading it.

BILL O'REILLY
Long Island, New York

BOOK

I

The World of Jesus

CHAPTER ONE

BETHLEHEM, JUDEA

MARCH, 5 B.C.

MORNING

THE CHILD WITH THIRTY-SIX YEARS TO LIVE IS BEING hunted.

Heavily armed soldiers from the capital city of Jerusalem are marching to this small town, intent on finding and killing the baby boy. They are a mixed-race group of foreign mercenaries from Greece, Gaul, and Syria. The child's name, unknown to them, is Jesus, and his only crime is that some believe he will be the next king of the Jewish people. The current monarch, a dying half-Jewish, half-Arab despot named Herod, is so intent on ensuring the baby's death that his army has been ordered to murder every male child under the age of two years in Bethlehem.* None of the soldiers knows what the child's mother and father look like, or the precise location of his home, thus the need to kill every baby boy in the small town and surrounding area. This alone will guarantee the extermination of the potential king.

It is springtime in Judea, the peak of lambing season. The rolling dirt road takes the army past thick groves of olive trees and shepherds tending their flocks. The soldiers' feet are clad in sandals, their legs are bare, and they wear the skirtlike *pteruges* to cover their loins. The young men sweat profusely beneath the plates of armor on their chests and the tinned bronze attic helmets that cover the tops of their heads and the sides of their faces.

The soldiers are well aware of Herod's notorious cruelty and his penchant for killing anyone who would try to threaten his throne. But there is no moral debate about the right or wrong of slaughtering infants.† Nor do the soldiers question whether they will have the nerve to rip a screaming child from his mother's arms and carry out the execution. When the time comes, they

---

*There were actually two cities named Bethlehem, and both can make a claim for being the true site of the Nativity. The city of King David's birth is located just a few miles from Jerusalem. Archaeological investigations have shown that it was either a very small village or relatively uninhabited at the time of Jesus's birth. The second location is in Galilee, four miles from Nazareth. Supporters of that site believe that Mary's full-term pregnancy would have made it very difficult for her to walk a hundred miles to the other location. Supporters of the traditional site point to the biblical prophecy that Jesus would be born in the City of David, which is the Bethlehem located near Jerusalem. The fact that Mary and Joseph brought Jesus to the temple in Jerusalem eight days after his birth, and then again on the fortieth day, would seem to tip the scales in favor of the traditional site.

†Genocide was replete throughout the Classical world. "He slits the wombs of pregnant women; he blinds the infants," goes an ancient Assyrian poem. Genocide often was considered ethically justifiable if the killing was done to inflict revenge or thwart an aggressor.

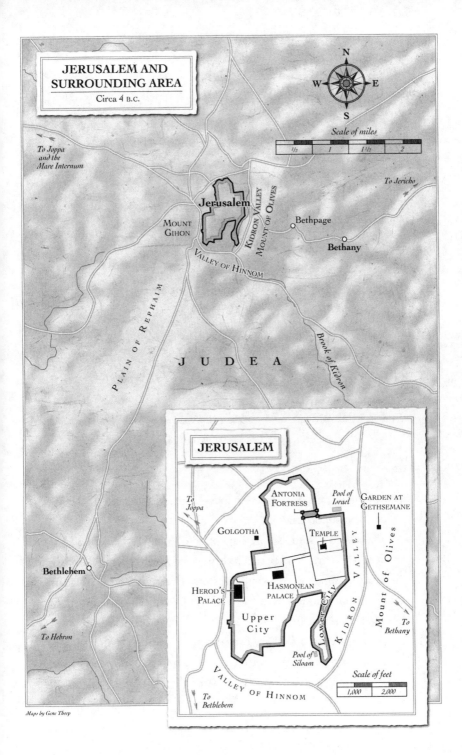

JERUSALEM AND
SURROUNDING AREA
Circa 4 B.C.

N
W   E
S

Scale of miles
½   1   1½   2

To Joppa
and the
Mare Internum

To Jericho

Jerusalem

MOUNT
GIHON

KIDRON VALLEY
MOUNT OF OLIVES

Bethpage

Bethany

VALLEY OF HINNOM

PLAIN OF REPHAIM

JUDEA

Brook of Kidron

Bethlehem

To Hebron

JERUSALEM

To
Joppa

ANTONIA
FORTRESS

Pool of
Israel

GARDEN AT
GETHSEMANE

GOLGOTHA

TEMPLE

HASMONEAN
PALACE

HEROD'S
PALACE

Upper
City

Lower City

KIDRON VALLEY

Mount of Olives

To
Bethany

Pool of
Siloam

Scale of feet
1,000   2,000

VALLEY OF HINNOM

To
Bethlehem

Herod's Slaughter of the Innocents

will follow orders and do their jobs—or risk being immediately killed for insubordination.

The sword's blade is how they plan to dispatch the babies. All soldiers are armed with the Judean version of the razor-sharp *pugio* and *gladius* preferred by the Roman legions, and they wear their weapons attached to the waist. Their method of murder, however, will not be restricted to the dagger or sword. Should they wish, Herod's soldiers can also use a skull-crushing stone, hurl the baby boys off a cliff en masse, or just wrap their fists around the infants' windpipes and strangle them.

The cause of death is not important. What matters most is one simple fact: king of the Jews or not, the infant must die.

✝✝✝

Meanwhile, in Jerusalem, King Herod gazes out a palace window toward Bethlehem, anxiously awaiting confirmation of the slaughter. In the cobbled streets below him, the Roman-appointed king sees the crowded bazaars, where vendors sell everything from water and dates to tourist trinkets and roast lamb. The walled city of some eighty thousand residents packed into less than a single square mile is a crossroads of the eastern Mediterranean. With one sweep of his eyes, Herod can see visiting Galilean peasants, brightly dressed Syrian women, and the foreign soldiers he pays to wage his battles. These men fight extremely well but are not Jews and don't speak a word of the Hebrew language.

Herod sighs. Back in his youth, he would never have stood in a window and worried about the future. A great king and warrior such as he would have ordered that a bridle be thrown over his favorite white charger so that he might gallop to Bethlehem and murder the child himself. But Herod is now a man of sixty-nine. His massive girth and incessant medical problems make it physically impossible for him to leave his palace, let alone mount a horse. His bloated face is wreathed in a beard that extends from the bottom of his chin to just below his Adam's apple. On this day, he wears a royal purple Roman-style mantle over a short-sleeved white silk tunic. Normally Herod prefers soft leather leggings that have been stained purple. But today even the gentlest bristle of fabric against his inflamed big toe is enough to make him cry out in pain. So it is that Herod, the most powerful man in Judea, hobbles through the palace barefoot.

Herod the Great overseeing the Temple expansion

But gout is the least of Herod's ailments. The king of the Jews, as this nonpracticing convert to the religion likes to be known, is also suffering from lung disease, kidney problems, worms, a heart condition, sexually transmitted diseases, and a horrible version of gangrene that has caused his genitals to rot, turn black, and become infested with maggots—thus the inability to sit astride, let alone ride, a horse.

Herod has learned how to live with his aches and pains, but these warnings about a new king in Bethlehem are scaring him. Since the Romans first installed him as ruler of Judea more than thirty years ago, Herod has foiled countless plots and waged many wars to remain king. He has murdered anyone who would try to steal his throne—and even executed those only suspected of plotting against him. His power over the locals is absolute. No one in Judea is safe from Herod's executions. He has ordered deaths by hanging, stoning, strangulation, fire, the sword, live animals, serpents, beating, and a type of public suicide in which victims are forced to hurl themselves off tall buildings. The lone form of execution in which he has not engaged is crucifixion, that most slow and humiliating of deaths, where a man is flogged and then nailed naked upon a wooden cross in plain sight of the city walls. The Romans are the masters of this brutal art, and they almost exclusively practice it. Herod would not dream of enraging his superiors in Rome by appropriating their favorite form of murder.

Herod has ten wives—or *had*, before he executed the fiery Mariamme for allegedly plotting against him. For good measure, he also ordered the deaths of her mother and of his sons Alexander and Aristobulus. Within a year, he will murder a third male offspring. Small wonder that the great Roman emperor Caesar Augustus was rumored to have openly commented, "It is better to be Herod's pig than to be his son."

But this newest threat, though it comes from a mere infant, is the most dangerous of all. For centuries, Jewish prophets have predicted the coming of a new king to rule their people.* They have prophesied five specific occurrences that will take place to confirm the new Messiah's birth.

The first is that a great star will rise.

The second is that the baby will be born in Bethlehem, the small town where the great King David was born a thousand years before.

The third prophecy is that the child must also be a direct descendant of David, a fact that can easily be proven by the temple's meticulous genealogical records.

Fourth, powerful men will travel from afar to worship him.

Finally, the child's mother must be a virgin.†

What troubles Herod most deeply is that he knows the first two of these to be true.

He might be even more distressed to learn that all five have come to pass. The child is from the line of David; powerful men have traveled from afar to worship him; and his teenage mother, Mary, swears that she is still a virgin, despite her pregnancy.

He also does not know that the child's name is Yeshua ben Joseph—or Jesus, meaning "the Lord is salvation."

---

*The Jewish homeland was first known as Israel, a "promised land" that God offered to his followers. The northern portion of this kingdom fell in 722 B.C. to the Philistines, while the Babylonians later conquered the southern half. The Roman conquest in 63 B.C. led to the area around Jerusalem being referred to as Judea. The whole region, including Galilee, was administratively part of the Roman province of Syria, and the terms *Israel* and *Palestine* were not used in Jesus's time. *Israel* was once again put into use when the independent Jewish state was founded on May 14, 1948—almost four thousand years after the first Jews crossed into the Promised Land.

†In order, the prophecies are Numbers 24:17, Micah 5:2–5, Jeremiah 23:5 and Isaiah 9:7, Psalms 72:10–11, and Isaiah 7:13–14.

Herod first learns about Jesus from the travelers who have come to worship the baby. These men are called Magi, and they stop at his castle to pay their respects en route to paying homage to Jesus. They are astronomers, diviners, and wise men who also study the world's great religious texts. Among these books is the Tanakh,* a collection of history, prophecy, poetry, and songs telling the story of the Jewish people. The wealthy foreigners travel almost a thousand miles over rugged desert, following an extraordinarily bright star that shines in the sky each morning before dawn. "Where is the one who has been born the king of the Jews?" they demand to know upon their arrival in Herod's court. "We see his star in the east and have come to worship him."†

Amazingly, the Magi carry treasure chests filled with gold and the sweet-smelling tree resins myrrh and frankincense. These priests are learned, studious men. Theirs is a life of analysis and

---

*There are three dominant texts in the Jewish tradition: the Tanakh, the Torah, and the Talmud. The Tanakh constitutes the canonical collection of Jewish Scriptures and appears to have been compiled five hundred years before the birth of Christ. The Tanakh is also known as the Jewish Bible, while Christians refer to it as the Old Testament. The Torah is comprised of the first five books of the Tanakh: Genesis, Exodus, Leviticus, Numbers, and Deuteronomy. The Talmud was written almost six hundred years later, after the fall of the Temple in A.D. 70. Rabbinical teachings, commentaries, and philosophies were compiled so that they might be passed on in written, rather than oral, form.

†In 1991, *The Quarterly Journal of the Royal Astronomical Society* (volume 32, pages 389–407) noted that Chinese astronomers had observed a long-tailed, slow-moving comet in their skies during March of 5 B.C. This *sui-hsing*, or "star," hung in the Capricorn region for more than seventy days. This same comet would have been visible in the skies over Persia, home of the Magi, in the hours just before dawn. Due to the earth's orbital motion, the comet's light would have been directly in front of the Magi during their journey— hence, they would have truly followed the star.

reason. Herod can conclude only that either the Magi are out of their minds for risking the theft of such a great fortune in the vast and lawless Parthian desert or they truly believe this child to be the new king.

A furious Herod summons his religious advisers. As a secular man, he knows little about Jewish prophecies. Herod insists that these high priests and teachers of religious law tell him exactly where to find the new king.

The answer comes immediately: "In Bethlehem, in Judea."

The teachers whom Herod is interrogating are humble men. They wear simple white linen caps and robes. But the bearded Temple priests are a far different story. They dress elaborately, in white-and-blue linen caps with a gold band on the brow, and blue robes adorned in bright tassels and bells. Over their robes they wear capes and purses adorned in gold and precious stones. On a normal day their garb distinguishes them from the people of Jerusalem. But even in his dissipated state, King Herod is the most regal man in the room by far. He continues to hector the teachers and priests. "Where is this so-called king of the Jews?"

"Bethlehem, in the land of Judah." They quote verbatim from the words of the prophet Micah, some seven centuries earlier. "Out of you will come a ruler who will be the shepherd of my people Israel."

Herod sends the Magi on their way. His parting royal decree is that they locate the infant, then return to Jerusalem and tell Herod the child's precise location so that he can venture forth to worship this new king himself.

The Magi see through this deceit. They never come back.

So it is that time passes and Herod realizes he must take

action. From the windows of his fortress palace, he can see all of Jerusalem. To his left rises the great Temple, the most important and sacred building in all Judea. Perched atop a massive stone platform that gives it the appearance of a citadel rather than a simple place of worship, the Temple is a physical embodiment of the Jewish people and their ancient faith. The Temple was first built by Solomon in the tenth century B.C. It was leveled by the Babylonians in 586 B.C., and then the Second Temple was built by Zerubbabel and others under the Persians nearly seventy years later. Herod recently renovated the entire complex and expanded the Temple's size to epic proportions, making it far larger than that of Solomon's. The Temple and its courts are now a symbol not just of Judaism but of the evil king himself.

So it is ironic, as Herod frets and gazes toward Bethlehem, that Jesus and his parents have already traveled to Jerusalem twice and paid visits to that great stone fortress, built atop the site where the Jewish patriarch Abraham nearly sacrificed his own son, Isaac. The first visit came eight days after Jesus's birth,* so that he might be circumcised. There the child was formally named Jesus, in keeping with the prophecy. The second visit came when he was forty days old. The baby Jesus was brought to the Temple and formally presented to God, in keeping with the laws of the

---

*The month of March coincides with Gospel descriptions of shepherds tending their flocks on the hillside, as this is also lambing season. December 25, which we now celebrate as the date of Jesus's birth, was chosen and named Christmas—a shortening of Christ's Mass, or the mass in honor of Jesus's birth—by the Romans once their empire became Christian in the fourth century. For the Romans, that date was once the conclusion of an orgiastic pagan holiday known as Saturnalia. Once they set aside their more lascivious ways, it made sense to replace that celebration with a day commemorating the birth of their new savior.

Jewish faith. His father, Joseph, a carpenter, dutifully purchased a pair of young turtledoves to be sacrificed in honor of this momentous occasion.

Something very strange and mystical occurred as Jesus and his parents entered the Temple on that day—something that hinted that Jesus might truly be a very special child. Two complete strangers, an old man and an old woman—neither of whom knew anything about this baby called Jesus or his fulfillment of prophecy—saw him from across the crowded place of worship and went to him.

Mary, Joseph, and Jesus were traveling in complete anonymity, avoiding anything that would draw attention to them. The old man's name was Simeon, and he was of the belief that he would not die until he laid eyes upon the new king of the Jews. Simeon asked if he might hold the newborn. Mary and Joseph agreed. As Simeon took Jesus into his arms, he offered a prayer to God, thanking him for the chance to see this new king with his own eyes. Then Simeon handed Jesus back to Mary with these words: "This child is destined to cause the falling and rising of many in Israel, and to be a sign that will be spoken against, so that the thoughts of many hearts will be revealed. And a sword will pierce your own soul, too."

At that very moment, a woman named Anna* also approached. She was an eighty-four-year-old widowed prophetess who spent all her waking hours in the Temple, fasting and

---

*Anna is referred to as a "prophetess" in the Gospel of Luke. This makes her the only female in the New Testament so honored. This designation meant she saw things that were hidden from ordinary people. This also means that she held a higher calling than Simeon, who is merely praised by the same author as being "righteous and devout." Luke also mentions the name of Anna's tribe, that of Asher, which makes her a rarity among New Testament characters.

praying. Simeon's words were still ringing in Mary's and Joseph's ears when Anna stepped forth and also praised Jesus. She loudly thanked God for bringing this very special baby boy into the world. Then she made a most unusual claim, predicting to Mary and Joseph that their son would free Jerusalem from Roman rule.

Mary and Joseph marveled at Simeon's and Anna's words, flattered for the attention as all new parents would be, but also unsure what all this talk about swords and redemption truly meant. They finished their business and departed from the Temple into the bustling city of Jerusalem, both elated and fearful for the life their son might be destined to lead.

†††

If only Herod had known that Jesus had been so close—literally, less than six hundred yards from his throne room—his torment could have been relieved. But Jesus and his parents were just three more bodies making their way through the noisy bazaars and narrow, twisting streets en route to the Temple that day.

It is a temple that will stand forever as a monument to Herod's greatness—or so he believes. Ironically, he is barely welcome inside its walls, thanks to his utter lack of devotion or faith and his ruthlessness in subjugating the Jewish people.

Beyond the Temple, on the far side of the Kidron Valley, rises the steep Mount of Olives, where shepherds tend their flocks on the grasses of the limestone-flecked hillsides. Soon will come the Passover feast, bringing with it tens of thousands of Hebrew pilgrims from all around Herod's kingdom, eager to pay good money to purchase those sheep for a sacrificial slaughter in the great Temple.

In many ways, the slaughter of the babies in Bethlehem is no different. They are being sacrificed for the good of Herod's rule—which is the same as saying they are being murdered in the name of the Roman Empire. Herod is nothing without Rome, a puppet who owes his kingdom completely to that brutal and all-powerful republic. It is his right and duty to propagate its oppressive ways. For Herod's kingdom is different from any other under Rome's iron fist. The Jewish people are an ancient civilization founded upon a belief system that is at odds with Rome's, which worships many pagan deities instead of the one solitary Jewish god.

Herod is the intermediary in this precarious relationship. The Romans will hold him accountable for any problems caused by an alleged new king of the Jews. They will not tolerate a ruler they have not themselves chosen. And if the followers of this new "king" foment revolution, it is certain that the Romans will immediately step in to brutally crush this voice of dissent. Better that Herod handle it himself.

Herod cannot see Bethlehem from his palace, but it is roughly six miles away, on the far side of some low green hills. He cannot see the blood flowing in its streets right now, nor hear the wails of the terrified children and their parents. As Herod gazes out from his palace, he does so with a clean conscience. Let others condemn him for murdering more than a dozen infants. He will sleep well tonight, knowing that the killings are for the good of his reign, the good of Judea, and the good of Rome. If Caesar Augustus hears of this slaughter, he will surely understand: Herod is doing what must be done.

✝✝✝

Jesus and his family barely get out of Bethlehem alive. Joseph awakes from a terrifying dream and has a vision of what is to come. He rouses Mary and Jesus in the dead of night and they escape. Herod's soldiers arrive too late. They butcher the babies in vain, fulfilling a prophecy made five hundred years earlier by the contrarian prophet Jeremiah.*

There are many more prophecies about the life of Jesus outlined in Scripture. Slowly but surely, as this child grows to manhood, those predictions will also come true. Jesus's behavior will see him branded as a revolutionary, known throughout Judea for his startling speeches and offbeat teachings. He will be adored by the Jewish people but will become a threat to those who profit from the populace: the high priests, the scribes, the elders, the puppet rulers of Judea, and, most of all, the Roman Empire.

And Rome does not tolerate a threat. Thanks to the examples of empires such as those of the Macedonians, Greeks, and Persians that came before them, the Romans have learned and mastered the arts of torture and persecution. Revolutionaries and troublemakers are dealt with in harsh and horrific fashion, in order that others won't be tempted to copy their ways.

So it will be with Jesus. This, too, will fulfill prophecy.

---

*The exact number of years that Jesus lived is widely debated, but the conclusion that he was born sometime in the spring of either 6 or 5 B.C. is based on clear historical evidence, as Herod the Great died in 4 B.C. The date of Jesus's death was on the fourteenth day of Nisan. The annual start of Passover is dependent upon lunar charts, so his death can be pinpointed to have occurred on a Friday in the years A.D. 27–30. History shows that Jesus was executed when Pilate and Caiaphas both ruled in Judea, which occurred A.D. 26–37, making the date of A.D. 30, and his age at the time of death, logical—though still the subject of great discussion.

All of that is to come. For now, Jesus is still an infant, cared for and loved by Mary and Joseph. He was born in a stable, visited by the Magi, presented with their lavish gifts, and is now on the run from Herod and the Roman Empire.*

---

*The most insightful facts, quotes, and stories about Jesus that we know come from the four Gospels of Matthew, Mark, Luke, and John. Many today challenge these writings, but thanks to scholarship and archaeology, there is growing acceptance of their overall historicity and authenticity. Many scholars believe that Matthew was written in Greek by the disciple and former tax collector, sometime between A.D. 50 and 70. Mark was written by John Mark, a close friend of Peter's who most likely learned of Jesus through the preaching of Peter. Matthew and Mark are incredibly similar, leading many to wonder if Matthew used Mark as a reference—or vice versa. Luke was a friend of Paul, the former Pharisee who became a convert to Christianity and preached even more zealously than the disciples. The Gospel of Luke was written for a Gentile audience, with a theme of salvation at its center. John was written by the disciple, and its focus is evangelism. John's Gospel is written in Greek, and is long believed to have been the last Gospel written. The Gospels of Matthew, Mark, and Luke are known as the Synoptic Gospels, due to the many ways in which they agree with one another. All four Gospels together are known as the Canonical Gospels, as they form the essential canon of the Christian faith. John wrote independently of the other Gospel writers, using his unique eyewitness testimony in the same manner as Matthew. If he did, indeed, write his Gospel last, then John would have had the final say on the life of Jesus—not just confirming what the others had written but adding the definitive chronology and sequence of events. The fact that John not only was there at every pivotal moment in Jesus's ministry, and thus able to describe many scenes with vivid first-person imagery, but was also Jesus's closest confidant among the disciples ("the disciple whom Jesus loved," he boasts in John 20:02, in yet another example of the disciples grappling for prestige and power in the eyes of their leader) only adds to the power of his narrative.

CHAPTER TWO

T HE DICTATOR WITH ONE HOUR TO LIVE RIDES ATOP THE shoulders of slaves. Julius Caesar sits comfortably inside his litter, dressed in his usual dapper fashion: a loose belt, a purple wool toga over a white silk tunic, and a wreath of oak leaves atop his head that attests to his heroism while also hiding the bald spot he so despises. Lately Caesar has developed a passion for wearing high red boots, but on this morning his feet are clad in sandals.

He is barely contemplating his upcoming meeting with the Roman Senate, for which he is already late. The thoughts most on his mind are rumors of a death—his own. But of course Caesar has no idea that the whispered gossip of his impending demise will prove all too true this time.

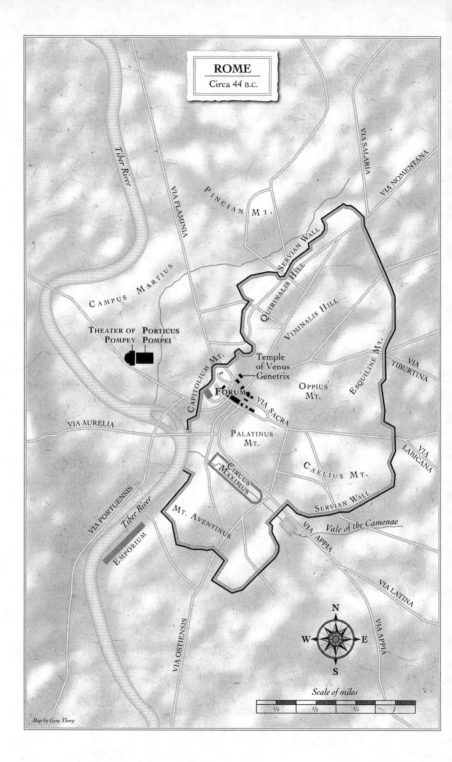

ROME

Circa 44 B.C.

Tiber River

VIA SALARIA

VIA NOMENTANA

VIA FLAMINIA

PINCIAN MT.

SERVIAN WALL

QUIRINALIS HILL

CAMPUS MARTIUS

VIMINALIS HILL

THEATER OF   PORTICUS
POMPEY   POMPEI

CAPITOLIUM MT.

Temple
of Venus
Genetrix

ESQUILINE MT.

VIA
TIBURTINA

FORUM

OPPIUS
MT.

VIA SACRA

VIA AURELIA

PALATINUS
MT.

VIA
LABICANA

CAELIUS MT.

CIRCUS
MAXIMUS

VIA PORTUENSIS

SERVIAN WALL

Tiber River

MT. AVENTINUS

Vale of the Camenae

VIA APPIA

EMPORIUM

VIA LATINA

VIA OSTIENSIS

VIA APPIA

N

W   E

S

Scale of miles

1/4   1/2   3/4   1

Julius Caesar is the most powerful man in the world, so mighty that he has not only changed the number of days per year but will soon have the month of his birth and the entire calendar renamed after himself. Today is the equivalent of Wednesday in the seven-day Jewish week. But the Romans use the eight-day cycle and give their days a letter rather than a name, so today is simply "G." They also believe in giving each sunrise a number, so now it is the fifteenth day of Martius in the year 44 B.C. on Caesar's brand-new Julian calendar.

Or, as it is also known, the Ides of March. And as the great Roman orator and lawyer Cicero will soon write, "The Ides changed everything."

The fifty-five-year-old Divus Julius—"Julius the God," as the Roman Senate will later proclaim him—is being carried through

Julius Caesar

Rome. The day is warm but not hot, and the people stand back in awe as Caesar passes by. He is a man of average height but extraordinary determination, having successfully conquered, invaded, or allied Rome with what will later be called Spain, Britain, France, Egypt, and Italy. Caesar is a study of conflict in his personal life, eating little and drinking even less, even as he spends money with abandon—such as when he commissioned the construction of a new villa, only to tear it down as soon as it was completed because he felt it wasn't perfect. And while many Roman men are wary of their sex drives, believing that too much sex will drain the virility from their bodies, Caesar has no such compunction. Calpurnia is his third wife, but he has had many mistresses, including the ambitious Cleopatra of Egypt.

Now, reclined in his litter, the well-muscled warrior statesman contemplates the subject of murder—his own. Friends, soothsayers, and even his beloved Calpurnia—whom he first bedded when he was forty and she was a sixteen-year-old virgin—have warned him that something terrible will happen today. It was Calpurnia who made Caesar late this morning. Last night she dreamed in most vivid fashion that he would be assassinated, and she begged him not to go to the Senate. Under normal circumstances, Caesar would have ignored her forebodings, but in the past few days informants have urgently warned him about a conspiracy to kill him. Given the choice of heeding those warnings or ignoring them, Caesar has chosen to brush them off—and even make light of them.

"What is the sweetest way to die?" asked Lepidus, Caesar's second in command, two nights earlier over dinner.

"The kind that comes without warning," the dictator shot back.

Caesar indulged Calpurnia's fears for much of this morning.

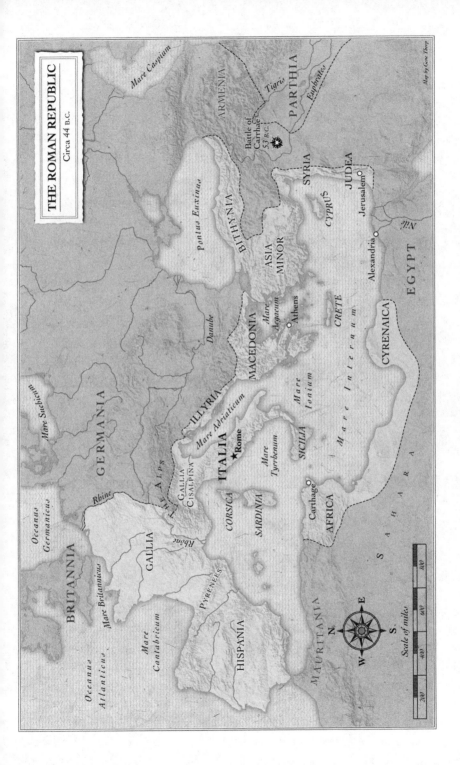

He even sent word that the Senate be dismissed. But then Decimus Brutus, the great general who had crushed the Venetian fleet during the Gallic Wars, arrived at Caesar's home and pleaded with him to ignore Calpurnia's nightmares. He reminded Caesar of his impending journey to Parthia, the land west of Judea where Rome's legions had suffered one of their most bruising defeats at the Battle of Carrhae nearly ten years earlier. Caesar's aim is to subjugate the Parthians—who hail from the mountainous deserts of the modern-day Middle East—and continue the expansion of Rome's global empire.

The scheduled departure is March 18, just three days away. Caesar could be gone for months, perhaps a year. So it's urgent that he meet with the Senate and clear up any unfinished business. Brutus also hints that there might be a nice surprise awaiting Caesar. A month ago the nine hundred members of the Senate named Caesar dictator for life. Now Brutus is intimating that they might also name Caesar king this morning, meaning that he will become the first monarch Rome has known in almost five hundred years.

The citizens of Rome have enjoyed a republic ever since Lucius Tarquinius Superbus was overthrown in 509 B.C., and they are so averse to the idea of an absolute ruler that the Latin word for "king," *rex*, is considered repugnant. But as Caesar draws closer and closer to his meeting with the Senate, he is sure that the people feel differently about him. He has long been devoted to keeping the masses happy. One way to do this is by ensuring that popular entertainment is available to one and all, distracting them from any issues they might have about their government. Right now, for instance, as Caesar's path to the Senate takes him from his home on the Via Sacra and out beyond the *pomerium*, Rome's sacred boundary, he can hear the roar of the crowds in the Theater of Pompey's grand arena as they gather to watch a blood-soaked gladiatorial battle.

The Theater of Pompey was built by, and named after, Caesar's greatest rival. The eleven-year-old columned structure is made of stone and concrete, unlike the wooden theaters that have long been a staple of Roman life. It is an enormous and complex work of architecture—so monumental, in fact, that in the entire seven-hundred-year history of Rome, there has never been a larger or more elaborate entertainment venue. One half is comprised of the *D*-shaped amphitheater where popular entertainments such as plays and gladiatorial competitions take place. Mock battles with elephants have been staged there, as well as very real combat between lions and men.

The garden area features lavish flower beds and arcades decorated with fountains and statuary and is partially covered to allow people escape from the rain or sun. Still another portion of this "theater" is the cool and quiet marble-floored great hall, where the Roman Senate meets. Caesar could have changed the facility's title after Pompey's execution, but demeaning his rival's memory would have served no useful political purpose. So it is that Pompey's name still adorns this magnificent structure and that a giant marble statue of the fallen general watches over the portico of the great hall, as if listening in on everything the Senate has to say.

The people of Rome joyfully mob Caesar's litter as the slaves carry him toward the Campus Martius, an open plain along the Tiber River where Roman legions assemble before marching off to war. Once, to ensure his popularity with those armies, Caesar gave each soldier his own personal slave, taken from the ranks of the Gauls they had just defeated in battle. The legionaries have never forgotten that gift and continue to reciprocate by showing

Caesar their unconditional support. So, unlike many rulers, Caesar is quite sure of his personal safety. He has even reassigned the two thousand soldiers who once served as his personal guards and is unafraid to walk freely through the streets of Rome, so that one and all can see that he is not a tyrant. "I would rather die," Caesar has noted, "than be feared."

As the journey comes to an end at Pompey's theater, Caesar spies a familiar face in the crowd. "The day which you warned me against is here," Caesar calls out to Spurinna, the fortune-teller who was bold enough to predict that a terrible fate would befall the empire's leader on this very day. Spurinna divined this knowledge by studying the raw livers of sacrificed sheep and chickens. The goddess Venus Genetrix is Caesar's personal deity, and he has dedicated a large temple in her honor, but on this morning Caesar has little use for religion or superstition. He wears a confident smile on his face—but it is one that quickly vanishes when Spurinna offers his reply.

"Yes," the Etruscan haruspex shouts over the clamor of the loyal people of Rome, who now press in around Caesar's litter. Spurinna is quite sure of his prediction and not at all fearful of being reprimanded for what he is about to say. "It is here, but it is not yet gone."

Caesar hears those words but does not respond. Gathering his purple toga to his body with his left arm, he steps from his litter, hoping to soon become king of Rome.

✝✝✝

But there will be no coronation. Instead, a team of assassins waits for Caesar inside the Senate. These killers are not soldiers or angry citizens but self-styled "Liberators" comprised of dozens of Caesar's closest friends and trusted allies, men of regal bearing and upbringing whom he trusts completely and with whom he has shared many a meal and battlefield victory. These rogue senators are uneasy about Caesar's ever-growing power and his desire to be king. Such a promotion would ensure not only Caesar's authority for life but also that it be passed down through his will to the heir of his choice. That Caesar publicly refused a crown when his good friend Marc Antony recently tried to place one upon his head does not appease them. With these thoughts, along with nagging doubts that they might not have the guts to follow through on their assassination plan, the rebel senators have waited in their Senate seats all morning, freshly sharpened *pugiones* concealed beneath the thick folds of their togas.

The Liberators are in the minority—just sixty men among nine hundred—and if they lose their nerve, there is every chance they will be imprisoned, executed, or exiled. Caesar is known to be a benevolent man, but he is also quick to exact revenge, such as the time he ordered the crucifixion of a band of pirates who had kidnapped him. "Benevolent" in that instance meant executioners dragging the razor-like steel of a *pugio* across each pirate's windpipe before nailing him to the cross, so that his death might be quicker.

Some of the senators, such as general and statesman Decimus Junius Brutus Albinus, have fought in battle and are well acquainted with the act of killing. Brutus, as he is known, was the one sent to Caesar's home to lure him to the Senate when it appeared he might not show up this morning. It was Caesar who named Brutus to the position of praetor, or magistrate. But Brutus's family has a long tradition of rejecting tyrants, beginning in 509 B.C. with Junius Brutus, the man credited with overthrowing Tarquinius Superbus and ending the Roman monarchy. That act of rebellion was as cold-blooded as the murder the Liberators have planned for Caesar.

Other senators, such as the heavy-drinking Lucius Tillius Cimber and his ally Publius Servilius Casca Longus, have the soft and uncallused hands of elected officials. Wielding a killing blade will be a new sensation for them.

Murdering Caesar is the boldest—and most dangerous—of ideas. He is not like other men. In fact, he has become the greatest living symbol of Roman power and aggression. Caesar has so completely consolidated his hold on Roman politics that the only likely outcome of this murder will be anarchy, and perhaps even the end of the Roman Republic.

†††

This is hardly the first time someone has wanted Julius Caesar dead. The one million inhabitants of the city of Rome are reactive and unpredictable. Caesar is known by everyone and admired by most. Since the age of fifteen, when his father suddenly died while putting on his shoes one morning, Caesar has endured one challenge after another in order to make himself a success. But each contest has made him stronger, and with each hard-won triumph his legend—and his power—has grown.

But in terms of sheer glory, legend, and impact, no moment will ever match the morning of January 10, 49 b.c. Caesar is a great general now, a fifty-year-old man who has spent much of the last decade in Gaul, conquering the local tribes and getting very rich in the process. It is dusk. He stands on the north side of a swollen, half-frozen river known as the Rubicon. Behind him stand the four thousand heavily armed soldiers of the Legio XIII Gemina, a battle-hardened group that has served under him for the last nine years. Rome is 260 miles due south. The Rubicon is the dividing line between Cisalpine Gaul and Italy—or, more germane to Caesar's current situation, between freedom and treason.

The population of Gaul has been devastated by Caesar's wars. Of the four million people who inhabited the region stretching from the Alps to the Atlantic, one million have been killed in battle and another million taken into slavery. After capturing Uxellodunum, a town along the Dordogne River near modern-day Vayrac, Caesar cut off the hands of every man who'd fought against him. And during his epic siege of Alesia, in the hills near what is now called Dijon, he surrounded the fortress with sixty thousand men and nine miles of fierce fortifications. All this could be viewed from above, from tall towers erected by Caesar's engineers, allowing the Roman archers to rain arrows down on the enemy forces. In order to break out of the besieged town, the trapped Gauls would have to find a way through this killing zone.

When food began running out, the Gauls, under the legendary general Vercingetorix, allowed their women and children to exit the city so that the Romans might feed them. This was an act of dubious kindness, for it likely meant a life of slavery, but it was better than letting them starve to death inside the city. However, Caesar would not allow these innocents to cross over into the Roman lines. As their husbands and fathers looked on from within the city walls, unable to invite them back inside for lack of food, the women and children remained stuck in the no-man's-land between armies, where they lived on grass and dew until they slowly perished from starvation and thirst. Adding insult, Caesar refused to allow their bodies to be collected for burial.

But Caesar's greatest atrocity—and the one for which his enemies in the Roman Senate have now demanded that he stand trial as a war criminal—was committed against the Germanic Usipetes and Tenchtheri tribes in 55 B.C. These hostile invaders had slowly begun moving across the Rhine River into Gaul, and it was believed that they would soon turn their attentions south, toward Italy. From April to June of 55 B.C., Caesar's army traveled from its winter base in Normandy to where marauding elements of the Germanic tribes were aligning themselves with Gauls against Rome. These "tribes" were not small nomadic communities but an invading force with a population half the size of Rome's, numbering almost five hundred thousand soldiers, women, children, and camp followers.

Hearing of Caesar's approach, the Germans sent forth ambassadors to broker a peace treaty. Caesar refused, telling them to turn around and go back across the Rhine. The Germans pretended to go along with Caesar's demands, but a few days later they reneged on their word and launched a surprise attack. As Caesar's cavalry watered their horses along what is now the Niers River, eight hundred German horsemen galloped directly toward them, with intent to kill. The German tactics were peculiar—and terrifying. Rather than wage battle atop their mounts, they leapt from their horses and used their short spears or battle swords to slit open the bellies of the Roman steeds, killing the animals, and sending the now foot-bound legions fleeing in panic.

Caesar considered the attack an act of duplicity because it came during a time of truce. "After having sued for peace by way of stratagem and treachery," he would later write, "they had made war without provocation." In a dramatic show of force, Caesar launched a counterattack of his own. Placing his disgraced cavalry at the rear of his force, he ordered the legions to trot double-time the eight miles to the German camp. This time it was the Romans who had the element of surprise. Those Germans who stood their ground were slaughtered, while those who tried to run were hunted down by the disgraced Roman cavalry, who were bent on proving their worth once more. Some Germans made it as far as the Rhine but then drowned while trying to swim the hundreds of yards to the other side.

But Caesar didn't stop there. His men rounded up all remaining members of the German tribes and butchered them—old men and women, wives, teenagers, children, and toddlers—yielding a killing ratio of eight Germans for each legionary. Generally, the Roman soldiers are educated men. They can recite poetry and enjoy a good witticism. Many have wives and children of their own and could never imagine such barbarous cruelty being visited on those they love. But they are legionaries, trained and disciplined to do as they are told. So they used the steel of their blades and the sharpened tips of their spears to pierce body after body after body, ignoring the screams of terrified children and the wails and pleas for mercy.

Caesar's revenge began as an act of war but soon turned into a genocide that killed an estimated 430,000 people. And just to show the Germans living on the other side of the Rhine that his armies could go anywhere and do anything, Caesar ordered his engineers to build a bridge across that previously impregnable river. This they accomplished in just ten short days. Caesar then crossed the Rhine and launched a brief series of attacks, then withdrew and destroyed the bridge.

Rome is a vicious republic and gives no quarter to its enemies. But these brutal offenses were too much, even for the heartless Roman leadership in the Senate, who called for Caesar's arrest. Cato, a statesman renowned not just for his oratory but also for his long-running feud with Caesar, suggested the general be executed and his head given on a spike to the defeated Germans. The

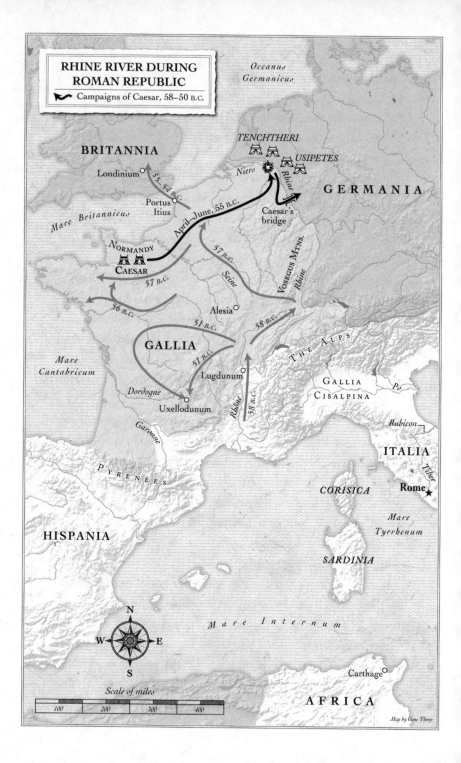

charges against Caesar were certainly not without merit. But they stemmed as much from political rivalry as from the slaughter on the banks of the Rhine. One thing, however, is clear: Caesar's enemies wanted him dead.

✝✝✝

In 49 B.C., nearly six years after that massacre, Gaul is completely conquered. It is time for Caesar to return home, where he will finally stand trial for his actions. He's been ordered to dismiss his army before setting foot into Italy.

This is Roman law. All returning generals are required to disband their troops before crossing the boundary of their province, in this case the Rubicon River. This signals that they are returning home in peace rather than in the hopes of attempting a coup d'état. Failure to disband the troops is considered an act of war.

But Caesar prefers war. He decides to cross the Rubicon on his own terms. Julius Caesar is fifty years old and in the prime of his life. He has spent the entire day of January 10 delaying this moment, because if he fails, he will not live to see the day six months hence when he will turn fifty-one. While his troops play dice, sharpen their weapons, and otherwise try to stay warm under a pale winter sun, Caesar takes a leisurely bath and drinks a glass of wine. These are the actions of a man who knows he may not enjoy such creature comforts for some time to come. They are also the behavior of man delaying the inevitable.

But Caesar has good reason to hesitate. Pompey the Great, his former ally, brother-in-law, and builder of Rome's largest theater, is waiting in Rome. The Senate has entrusted the future of the Republic to Pompey and ordered him to stop Caesar at all costs. Julius Caesar, in effect, is about to begin a civil war. This is as much about Caesar and Pompey as it is about Caesar and Rome.

To the winner goes control of the Roman Republic. To the loser, a certain death.

Caesar surveys his troops. The men of Legio XIII stand in loose formation, awaiting his signal. Each carries almost seventy pounds of gear on his back, from bedroll to cooking pot to three days' supply of grain. On this cold winter evening, they wear leather boots and leggings and cloaks over their shoulders to keep out the chill. They will travel on foot, wearing bronze helmets and chain mail shirts. All protect themselves with a curved shield made of wood, canvas, and leather, along with two javelins—one lightweight, the other heavier and deadlier. They are also armed with double-edged "Spanish swords," which hang from scabbards on their thick leather belts, and the requisite *pugiones*. Some men are kitted out with slingshots, while others are designated as archers. Their faces are lined and weathered from years of sun and wind, and many bear the puckered scars from where an enemy spear plunged into their bodies or the long purple scar tissue from the slash of an enemy sword cutting into biceps or shoulder. They are young, mostly between seventeen and twenty-three years of age, but there are some salt-and-pepper beards among them, for any male Roman citizen as old as forty-six can be conscripted into the legions. Young or old, they have endured the rugged physical training that makes the stamina of legionaries legendary. New recruits march for hours wearing a forty-five-pound pack, all the while maintaining complicated formations such as the wedge, hollow square, circle, and *testudo*, or "tortoise." And all Roman legionaries must learn how to swim, just in case battle forces them to cross a river. Any moment of failure during this rigorous training means the sharp thwack of a superior's staff across one's back.

Once a conscript's four months of basic training are finished, rigorous conditioning and drilling remain part of his daily life. Three marches of more than twenty miles in length while wearing a heavy pack are required from every man each month. When the long miles in formation are done, the legionary's unit is required to build a fortified camp, complete with earthen ramparts and trenches.

So it is that the tough, loyal, muscled men of Legio XIII are drilled in the art of battle strategy, intuitively able to exploit an enemy's strengths and weaknesses, and proficient in every weapon of their era. They live off the land, pooling their supplies of grain and any meat they can forage. They have built roads and bridges, delivered mail, collected taxes, served as police, endured the deep winters of Gaul, known the concussive sting of a slingshot-hurled rock bouncing off their helmets, and even played the role of executioner, driving nails through the hands and feet of escaped slaves and deserters from their own ranks who have been captured and condemned to crucifixion. The oldest among them can remember the uprising of 71 B.C., when seven thousand slaves, led by a rebel named Spartacus, revolted, were captured, and were crucified in a 240-mile line of crosses that stretched almost all the way from Naples to Rome.

It is Caesar to whom these men have sworn their allegiance. They admire how he leads by example, that he endures the same hardships and deprivations during a campaign that they do. He prefers to walk among the "comrades," as he calls his troops, rather than ride a horse. Caesar is also well known throughout the ranks for his habit of rewarding loyalty and for his charisma. His men proudly boast of the many women he has had throughout Gaul, Spain, and Britain, and they even make fun of his thinning hair by singing songs about "our bald whoremonger." Likewise, Caesar gives his legions free rein to chase women and gamble when

Caesar crossing the Rubicon

they are off duty. "My men fight just as well when they are stinking of perfume," he says.

But in the end, the legionaries fight, first and foremost, for one another. They have trained together, cooked meals together, slept in the same cramped leather tents, and walked hundreds of miles side by side. No thought is more unbearable than letting down their *commilito* ("fellow soldier") on the field of battle. They call one another *frater* ("brother"), and the highest honor a legionary can earn is the wreath of oak leaves known as the *corona civica*, awarded to those who risk their lives to save a fallen comrade. That Julius Caesar wears such a crown is testimony to his soldiers that their commander is not a mere figurehead, but a man who can be trusted to wage war with courage and distinction.

But while it is Caesar who will lead the legion into battle, it is his men who will engage the enemy. Theirs is not a compassionate profession, and these are not compassionate men. They are legionaries, tasked with doing the hard, ongoing work of keeping Rome the greatest power in the world.

In the growing darkness, Caesar now addresses his army, reminding them of the significance of crossing from one side of the Rubicon to the other. "We may still draw back," he tells them, though all within earshot know that the moment for retreat has long since passed. "But once across that little bridge, we shall have to fight it out."

Legio XIII is not Caesar's favorite—that would be the Tenth. But, like his other troops, those soldiers are still scattered throughout Gaul. Waiting for them would ruin his plans for a lightning-fast march straight into the heart of Rome.

Julius Caesar may be nervous as the temperature continues to drop and men shiver in the dampness, but any fear is offset by the awareness that each and every soldier in Legio XIII is a killing machine.

Problem is, so are the men they will be fighting. Caesar is about to pit Roman against Roman, legionary against legionary, *frater* against *frater*.

The time has come. Caesar stands alone, gazing over to the other side of the Rubicon. His officers huddle a few feet away, awaiting his orders. Torches light their faces and those of Legio XIII.

"*Alea iacta est*," Caesar says to no one in particular, quoting a line from the Greek playwright Menander: "The die is cast."

Caesar and his legion cross into Italy.

✝✝✝

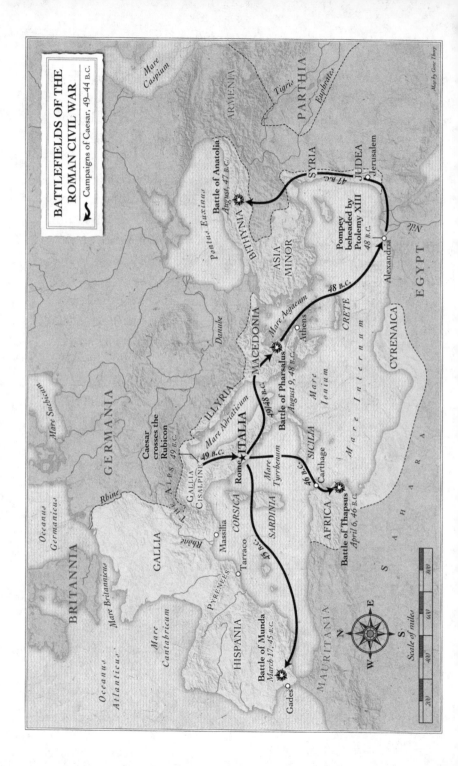

BATTLEFIELDS OF THE
ROMAN CIVIL WAR

⌒ Campaigns of Caesar, 49–44 B.C.

Map by Gene Thorp

What follows is not just a Roman civil war, but also the first world war in history. The entire Mediterranean rim soon becomes a battleground, its plains and deserts filled with legionaries, its seas brimming with warships conveying these men from one land to another. The fighting is brutal, often hand to hand. The fate awaiting prisoners of war is torture and death, leading many to commit suicide when a battle has been lost rather than submit to the victors. Caesar takes Rome within two months, only to find it abandoned. Merely capturing Rome is not enough. He must have total victory. Pompey has fled, and Caesar gives chase across the Mediterranean, to Egypt.

As he wades ashore to meet with Ptolemy XIII, the teenage king of Egypt, Pompey—the great general, architect, builder, and prodigious lover who was married five times, and who was three times given the privilege of riding in triumph through the streets of Rome after epic battlefield conquests in his youth—is stabbed through the back with a sword, and then stabbed several more times for good measure. Not wanting his murderers to see his expression at the moment death arrives, Pompey pulls the hem of his toga up over his face. His murderers quickly cut off his head, and leave his corpse on the sand to be picked apart by shorebirds. Thinking it will please Julius Caesar, the Egyptians bring him Pompey's severed skull. But Caesar is devastated. He weeps, and then demands that the rest of the body be retrieved so that it might be given a proper Roman burial.

But Pompey's murder is not the end of the war, for his outraged allies and sons soon take up his cause. In the end, Caesar will win the civil war and take control of the Roman Republic, much to the joy of its common citizens, who revere him. Yet four years of conflict will pass before that day arrives. In the meantime, Julius Caesar will command his legions in locales ranging from Pharsalus, in central Greece; to Thapsus, in Tunisia; to the plains of Munda, in present-day southern Spain,* and his legend will only grow larger.

Caesar's conquests, however, are not only on the battlefield.

†††

The year is 48 B.C. A civil war is taking place in Egypt at the same time as the civil war in Rome. On one side is the twenty-one-year-old Cleopatra. On the other is her thirteen-year-old brother, Ptolemy XIII, who is being advised by a conniving eunuch named Potheinos. Ptolemy has succeeded in driving Cleopatra from her palace in the seaside capital at Alexandria. The troubles in Italy then intervene when Caesar chases Pompey to Alexandria. It is Potheinos, thinking to ally himself with Caesar, who has Pompey beheaded on the Egyptian beach just moments after the Roman is assassinated while coming ashore to align himself strategically with Ptolemy XIII.

But Caesar is disgusted by Potheinos's barbarous act, for he had planned to be lenient toward Pompey. "What gave him the most pleasure," the eminent historian Plutarch will one day write of Caesar, "was that he was so often able to save the lives of fellow citizens who had fought against him."

Caesar moves into Egypt's royal palace for the time being. But he fears that Potheinos will attempt to assassinate him, so he stays up late most nights, afraid to go to sleep. One such evening, Caesar retires to his quarters. He hears a noise at the door. But rather than Potheinos or some other assassin, a young woman walks into the

---

*Upon defeating King Pharnaces of Pontus at Munda, Caesar famously stated, "*Veni, vidi, vici*"—"I came. I saw. I conquered."

room alone. It is Cleopatra, though he does not yet know that. She has slipped into the palace through a waterfront entrance and navigated its stone corridors without being noticed. Her hair and face are covered, and her body is wrapped in a thick dark mantle. Beguiled, Caesar waits for this stranger to reveal herself.

Slowly and seductively, Cleopatra shows her face, with her full lips and aquiline nose. She then lets her wrap drop to the marble floor, revealing that she is wearing nothing but a sheer linen robe. Caesar's dark eyes look her body up and down, for he can now clearly see much more than the outline of Cleopatra's small breasts and the sway of her hips. The lust between them is not one-sided. In that moment of revealing, one historian will write of Cleopatra, "her desire grew greater than it had been before."

Cleopatra knows well the power of seduction, and she is about to bestow upon Caesar her most precious gift—intending, of course, to gain a great political reward. The bold gambit pays off immediately. That night, she and Caesar begin one of the most passionate love affairs in history, a political and romantic entanglement that will have long-lasting effects on the entire world. Before the morning sun rises, Caesar decides to place Cleopatra back on the Egyptian throne—just as she had hoped. For Caesar, this means he is now aligned with a woman who owes her reign to the legacy of Alexander the Great, the omnipotent Macedonian conqueror he so admires. The confluence of his growing dynasty and Cleopatra's is a powerful aphrodisiac. They speak to each other in Greek, although Cleopatra is said to be fluent in as many as nine tongues. Each is disciplined, sharp-witted, and charismatic. Their subjects consider them benevolent and just, and both can hypnotize a crowd with their oratorical skills. Cleopatra and Egypt need Caesar's military might, while Caesar

Cleopatra, paramour of Caesar and, later, Marc Antony

and Rome need Egypt's natural resources, particularly her abundant grain crops. It could be said that Caesar and Cleopatra make the perfect couple, were it not for the fact that Julius Caesar is already married.

Not that this has stopped Caesar in the past. He has had three wives, one of whom died in childbirth, another whom he divorced for being unfaithful, and now Calpurnia. He sleeps with the wives of friends, often thereby gleaning information about colleagues. The love of his life is Servilia Caepionis, mother of the treacherous Marcus Junius Brutus—whom many believe to be Caesar's illegitimate son.

But Caesar's most notorious affair was not with a woman. It is widely rumored that, in his youth, he had a yearlong affair with

King Nicomedes IV of Bithynia.* The sneering nickname "Queen of Bithynia" still follows Caesar.

Lacking from Caesar's many dalliances has been an heir. The number of his bastard offspring scattered throughout Gaul and Spain is legendary, but he had only one legitimate child, Julia—who, ironically, married Caesar's rival Pompey—and she has long since died in childbirth. Calpurnia, Caesar's current wife, has been unable to give him a child.

Cleopatra gives birth to a son on June 23, 47 B.C. She names him Philopator Philometor Caesar—or Caesarion for short. A year later, Cleopatra travels to Rome, where she and the child live as a guest of Caesar and Calpurnia's at Caesar's Trastevere villa. When Caesar is forced to return to war, Cleopatra and the child remain behind with Calpurnia, who, not surprisingly, despises the Egyptian woman. But Caesar has ordered her to stay in Rome, even as rumors swirl throughout the city about her and Caesar possibly getting married one day. Caesar has not helped matters by having a statue of a naked Cleopatra erected in the Temple of Venus, portraying her as a goddess of love.

For reasons known only to him, Caesar allows Caesarion to use his name but refuses to select him as heir. Instead, his will states that upon his death his nephew Octavian will become his adopted son and legal heir.

Cleopatra is a shrewd and ruthless woman. She knows that she will lose her hold on Egypt should her relationship with Caesar end. She has quietly begun to plot a betrayal—an Egyptian overthrow of Rome. It all depends on Caesarion's being named Julius Caesar's rightful heir and successor—and that means somehow getting Caesar to change his will.

---

*Modern-day northwest Turkey.

Or maybe there is another way: should Caesar be named king of Rome, he will need a queen of royal birth to consummate a true royal marriage. So Cleopatra's plan is simple: continue pushing Caesar to accept the crown of king of Rome. Then they will marry, and her son will rule as legal heir when Caesar dies.

Everything seems to be going Cleopatra's way. It's clear that the Senate is about to name Caesar as king. This will all but ensure their marriage and the removal of Octavian as a threat to Caesarion's eventual claim to the thrones of both Egypt and Rome.

Caesar, the master statesman, is being outmaneuvered by a woman less than half his age, and with no army at her disposal. Thousands of men have died in Rome's civil war, all in an attempt to control the Roman Republic. But Cleopatra is on the verge of accomplishing the same feat solely through seduction.

It's all so brilliant. So perfect. Then, of course, comes the Ides of March. Not only will there not be a Roman Republic by the time the battle for succession comes to an end, but there will no longer be a Caesarion, either.

Nor, for that matter, will there be a Cleopatra.

†††

The "friend" who has stepped forward to engage Julius Caesar in conversation as he climbs down from his litter and enters the Senate chamber is Popilius Laenas, a man descended from a centuries-long line of landowning Roman noblemen known for their cruelty and treachery. So, as the conspirators look on from a distance, unable to hear what Popilius is saying, they are justifiably worried. Only moments before, Popilius had wished Marcus Brutus good luck in the conspiracy, but perhaps that was all a ruse. The Liberators can see that his conversation with Caesar is earnest and friendly. Their stomachs churn with fear that Popilius is informing Caesar of their plot. "Not being able to hear what he said, but guessing by what themselves were conscious of . . . and, looking upon one another, agreed from each other's countenances that they should not stay to be taken, but should all kill themselves [instead of Caesar]," the historian Plutarch will write of this moment.

Popilius ends his conversation by kissing the hands of Divus Julius and walking away from the Theater of Pompey. Caesar does not seem to be agitated. Relieved, they settle back into their seats to await his arrival.

The great statue of Pompey glowers down on Caesar as he glides into the Senate. Cassius, who, along with Brutus, is the lead assassin, turns to the statue of Pompey and prays, hoping to invoke courage from Caesar's former enemy.

The entire Senate rises as Caesar enters the chamber. They have been conducting state business all morning and now watch as he takes his seat in a gilded throne. Almost immediately, a large group of them walk toward Caesar, led by Lucius Tillius Cimber. There is nothing ominous in their behavior, for it is common for senators to approach Caesar with personal petitions— and, indeed, Caesar can clearly see the scroll Tillius holds in one hand, but not the dagger he clutches in the other.

It is easy enough for Caesar to guess what Tillius wants. The brother of the veteran senator has been sent into exile, and the petition is most likely a request for a pardon.

The group of senators mill around Caesar's chair, their numbers growing by the second, until he is ringed by a small mob. They lean down to offer kisses of respect on his head and chest, which has the effect of pressing the dictator even farther down into his seat.

Caesar grows furious at their aggressive behavior and rises violently to his feet.

The murder of Julius Caesar

This is the moment the assassins have been waiting for. Tillius grabs the top of Caesar's robe and wrenches it down past his shoulders, pinning the dictator's arms to his sides. At the same time, the Liberator named Publius Servilius Casca Longus—"Casca"—plunges his dagger into Caesar's shoulder. The thrust is feeble, and the wound draws little blood, but the sudden flash of pain as he is stabbed makes Caesar cry out. "Villain Casca," Caesar says in Latin while firmly grabbing the handle of Casca's dagger, "what do you do?"

As he turns to face his attacker, Caesar sees not one knife, but sixty. He feels not one stab wound, but dozens. Each of the senators has pulled a *pugio* from beneath his toga. Caesar sees the faces of enemies, but even more faces are those of friends, including Decimus Brutus and that of another Brutus—Marcus, the arrogant forty-one-year-old Stoic who is also rumored to be Caesar's son. The conspirators thrust their sharpened blades into the defenseless Caesar, hacking at him again and again. Such is the depth of their frenzy that many of the senators mistakenly stab one another, and all are soon covered in blood.

Meanwhile, Caesar attempts to fight back.

But then Marcus Brutus delivers the most arrogant thrust. Instead of aiming for the heart or the great artery of the neck, the bastard son Marcus plunges his blade deep into Caesar's groin. It is an act of murder, but also an act of emasculation, meant to humiliate the man who would not claim Marcus as his own. Blood drenches Caesar's tunic, flowing down the pale skin of his bare legs as he collapses back onto the throne.

"You, too, my boy?" Caesar says despairingly, staring at Marcus.

Not wanting anyone to see the death mask that will soon cross his face, Caesar pulls the fringe of his toga up over his head. A great pool of blood oozes across the marble floor as Caesar's limp body slides from his throne and comes to rest at the foot of Pompey's statue.

Head covered, death arrives. Only after he dies does Julius Caesar achieve the ultimate power he so desired, when the Roman Senate posthumously deifies him as Divus Julius.

Julius the God is quite mortal, as his murder clearly shows.

CHAPTER THREE

PHILIPPI, NORTHERN GREECE
OCTOBER 23, 42 B.C.
MORNING

T HE SON OF GOD THINKS HIMSELF IMMORTAL.* HE IS ALSO
fighting a very bad cold.

Gaius Julius Caesar Octavianus, or Octavian, as he is also
known, has been sick for what seems like forever. The fact that
his army is camped next to an enormous swamp certainly hasn't
helped matters. This young man who has affected the title Divi
Filius ("son of god") now pulls his cloak tightly around his shoulders and intently studies the cloudless blue sky, hoping for some

---

*Octavian (later known as Caesar Augustus) used the term *divi filius* as a
propaganda tool for most of his lifetime. Tens of millions of coins were issued
bearing his image and that title. One silver denarius issued in 38 B.C. even
portrayed Julius Caesar in profile, facing the profile of Octavian. Next to
Caesar is stamped the name DIVINE JULIUS and next to Octavian, DIVINE SON.

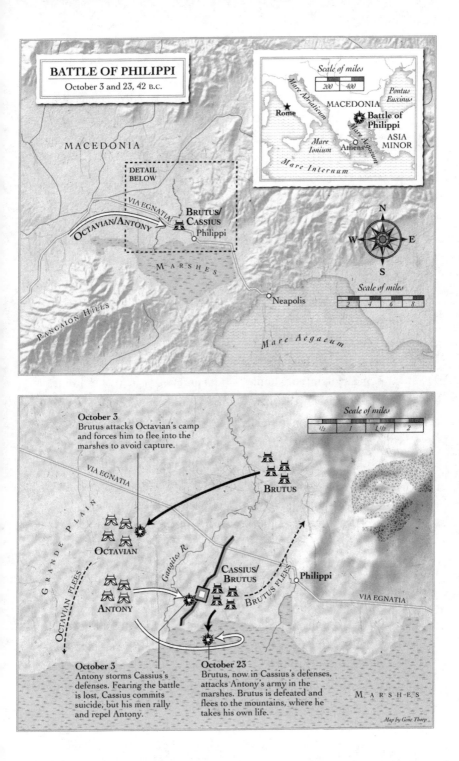

BATTLE OF PHILIPPI
October 3 and 23, 42 B.C.

Scale of miles
200   400

MACEDONIA

Pontus
Euxinus

Rome

Mare Adriaticum

Battle of Philippi

ASIA MINOR

Mare Ionium

Athens

Mare Internum

MACEDONIA

DETAIL BELOW

VIA EGNATIA

OCTAVIAN/ANTONY

BRUTUS/CASSIUS

Philippi

M A R S H E S

PANGAION HILLS

Neapolis

N
W   E
S

Scale of miles
2   4   6   8

Mare Aegaeum

October 3
Brutus attacks Octavian's camp and forces him to flee into the marshes to avoid capture.

Scale of miles
1/2   1   1 1/2   2

VIA EGNATIA

BRUTUS

GRANDE PLAIN

OCTAVIAN

OCTAVIAN FLEES

Gangites R.

CASSIUS/BRUTUS

ANTONY

BRUTUS FLEES

Philippi

VIA EGNATIA

October 3
Antony storms Cassius's defenses. Fearing the battle is lost, Cassius commits suicide, but his men rally and repel Antony.

October 23
Brutus, now in Cassius's defenses, attacks Antony's army in the marshes. Brutus is defeated and flees to the mountains, where he takes his own life.

M A R S H E S

Map by Gene Thorp

good news to offset the misery of his illness. Above him, two golden eagles fly in tight circles with talons extended, engaged in midair combat. The eagle is the symbol of the Roman legion, and to witness these great predators dueling on the eve of his own battle is surely an omen.

But an omen for whom: Octavian or the Liberators who killed his uncle?

Their two powerful armies, consisting of more than three dozen legions and two hundred thousand men combined, face each other across this flat Balkan plain. It is a broad expanse, anchored by low mountains on one side and the vast swamp behind Octavian on the other—a terrain best suited for either farming wheat or waging war. The smoke from a thousand cooking fires curls into the sky as both sides undertake last-minute preparations for the battle that will avenge the death of Julius Caesar, some eight hundred miles distant and two years past in Rome.

The scrape of steel blades on sharpening stones rings through the air. The legionaries set aside javelins and arrows as they choose their weapons for today. The fighting promises to be hand to hand and personal. So instead of spears, which are less useful in close quarters, the legionaries slip daggers and swords into sheaths. Hundreds of thousands of hardened legionaries on both sides of the lines gird their loins by tucking the hems of their cloaks into their belts, so that they won't trip while racing into combat. Cavalry horses stand patiently while saddles are thrown across their bare backs, knowing all too well what is about to transpire: mayhem.

Octavian's ally, the hard-drinking general, pedophile, and statesman Marc Antony, oversees the preparations, looking every bit the warrior: barrel-chested, gallant in appearance, and blessed with the thick, muscular thighs that are his one source of vanity.

Caesar Augustus, first ruler of the Roman Empire

Unlike Octavian, who will remain behind in camp during the fight, Marc Antony relishes the prospect of entering the battlefield and engaging the enemy with the same ferocity as his legions.

Octavian, on the other hand, is a sickly and pompous twenty-year-old with a large nose, a weak chin, and high, wide-set cheekbones framed by a mop of short hair and bangs that he compulsively brushes to one side. The adopted son of Caesar does not even command his own men. He has handed off that responsibility to another man his own age, a burly intellectual with an unlikely passion for geography named Marcus Vipsanius Agrippa.

Yet what Octavian lacks in physical strength he more than makes up for in cunning and audacity. Since learning that Julius Caesar's will named him the dictator's legal heir, Octavian has misappropriated vast public sums of money for his personal use, raised taxes, and decreed himself to be Divi Filius. He has ensured that the Liberators Marcus Brutus and Cassius, whose legions stand waiting on the other side of the battlefield, were declared enemies of the state. Their property was confiscated, and they fled Rome for their lives and raised an army in the hope of returning to Rome in triumph. Octavian and Marc Antony gave chase with their own legions, meeting up with the Liberators on this plain five long months ago. Both armies camped here throughout the summer, building palisades and other fortifications as they stared across at one another, waiting for this day. It was a miserable time for Octavian, who nursed one illness after another during those long, cold months.

Cassius was the first casualty, three weeks ago in the initial battle between the two forces. Fearing the campaign lost, he committed suicide rather than subject himself to the horrors of being taken prisoner. The cautionary tale of Marcus Licinius Crassus, a former general serving alongside Julius Caesar, would have made any man think twice about surrender. It was Crassus who, after being defeated by the Parthians at the Battle of Carrhae in 53 B.C., was killed by having molten gold poured down his throat.*

So Cassius fell upon his sword, thinking all was lost. But the Liberator was wrong. Shortly after he committed suicide, his legions reversed the flow of the battle and won the day.

---

*Another famous reminder not to be taken alive would come years later, when Rome's legions lost a decisive battle to the Germanic tribes at the Battle of Teutoburg Forest. Some of the Roman soldiers were forced inside wicker baskets and burned alive, while others were placed on altars and sacrificed to the German gods. The sound of their screams led Roman general Publius Quinctilius Varus to commit suicide. The Germans later severed the head from his body and sent it to Rome for burial. Ironically, Varus's father was aligned with the conspirators in the plot against Julius Caesar, and he killed himself on the battlefield at Philippi rather than be taken alive. Varus himself was infamous for crucifying two thousand Jews outside Jerusalem to quell the uprisings after the death of Herod the Great.

Octavian also nearly died that afternoon. His lines were over-run during Cassius's counterattack, and the young leader escaped only by hiding in a swamp while Cassius's legionaries plundered Octavian's camp before returning to their lines. Disgraced by his cowardice and that he had allowed more than fifteen thousand of his men to be slain, Octavian remained hidden for three days before sneaking back to his tent.

Now, three weeks later, the unmistakable blasts of brass *tubae* (trumpets) echo from one side of the plain to the other, a sound that makes the heart of every Roman legionary beat faster, for this is the call to battle.

On this morning, the coward will have his revenge. Octavian knows this because the fight between the two eagles has just been decided. The two majestic birds were not part of an orchestrated ritual and fought over the battlefield only by pure chance. But the eagle that approached from Marcus Brutus's side of the lines is now plummeting to earth, killed by the majestic bird of prey that flew into combat from Octavian's side.

It is an omen—a good one. And like his dead uncle Julius, the Divi Filius is a firm believer in omens.

† † †

Even two years after the fact, the death of Julius Caesar still affects almost every part of the world. It can be felt in Rome, where chaos continues to reign, and in Egypt, where Cleopatra has ruthlessly scrambled to maintain her toehold on power by murdering her own brothers. The shock waves are slow to reach Judea, but they will soon be keenly felt in the province of Galilee, in the village of Nazareth, where a builder named Jacob is raising a son called Joseph.

Jacob is a direct descendant of Abraham, the patriarch of the

Jewish faith, and of David, the greatest king Judea has ever known. Twenty-six generations separate Jacob from Abraham, and at least fourteen separate him from David. But while Abraham was extremely wealthy, and David and his son Solomon even more so, their lineage has fallen on hard times. The quiet and humble backdrop of Nazareth is a far cry from the great kingdoms enjoyed by those prior generations. It is a village of fewer than four hundred residents and three dozen homes, situated in a hollow formed by the rolling hills of southern Galilee. The tiny houses* are built from the soft limestone and other stone that litters the hills. As a builder, Jacob works with both foundation stone and oak from nearby forests to construct roofs and furniture. When work is scarce in Nazareth, there are always jobs to be found in the cosmopolitan city of Sepphoris, just an hour's walk away.

Like his father before him, Jacob trains Joseph to follow in his footsteps, teaching the boy not only how to build but also other vital skills, such as pressing wine and olive oil, terracing a hillside to grow the crops that will feed the family, and rerouting the local spring as a source of irrigation. But most important of all, Jacob raises his son up in the Jewish faith. For though the Greek, Arab, and Roman cultures have all made their mark on Nazareth over the centuries, the lineage of Jacob and their devotion to a one true

---

*The typical home in Nazareth was a single-family structure of one or two stories, built into the side of a limestone hill. The floors were made of dirt tamped down with ash and clay, while the walls were stones stacked on top of one another. Mud was smeared in the joints to keep out the elements. The roof was flat and made of wood, straw, mud, and lime. A bottom floor was reserved for storage, nighttime animal lodging, and a cooking fire, while the upper floor was for sleeping on thin mattresses stuffed with wool. A ladder led from one floor to the other. There were no indoor bathing or restroom facilities.

God has not changed since Abraham walked the earth two thousand years ago.

Even the great Julius Caesar did not attempt to alter Jewish tradition. The calculating dictator who believed in the divinity of Venus and who sought omens in the entrails of dead animals rather than through prayer, was, surprisingly, an ardent supporter of Judea and the Jewish way of life—if only because its location provided a natural buffer between Syria and Egypt. Caesar understood, as the Nazi Germans would two thousand years later, the importance of maintaining an empire by allowing local leaders to have some measure of control over their own destiny. In fact, the Nazis would one day borrow from the basic tenets of Roman occupation: a local official appointed to serve as a puppet ruler, a network of informants to flush out any pockets of rebellion, and the appearance that normal life was being maintained in spite of subjugation.

The death of Caesar has directly affected the backwater known as Judea, even if its citizens do not realize it. But the Battle of Philippi, an epic moment in history, will affect the area even more. When this battle is over, nothing for the Jews will be the same again.

†††

The battle is done. The fighting has been as bloody and intimate as many had feared, with men literally clawing at their opponents as they struggled to murder one another in hand-to-hand fighting. Blood flows from open wounds and from those awful marks on their bodies where men have lost arms, eyes, and hands. Many soldiers have been hamstrung, the large back muscle of their legs flayed open with a sword's blade, making it impossible for them to walk. These men will die a slow death on the battlefield.

Thousands upon thousands of dead bodies litter the earth between mountain and swamp, soon to be picked clean—first by the hordes of nearby citizens, who will fleece the dead of any signs of wealth, and then by the great buzzards and wolves, who will enjoy a rare feast.

Those alive from the losing army are now in chains but remain defiant. When Octavian appears, they jeer at him, showing gross disrespect.

The losing general, Marcus Brutus, is not among them—he has persuaded his slave to kill him with the single hard thrust of a two-foot-long sword. Brutus's head will be cut off and returned to Rome, even as the rest of the body is cremated where it fell.

As one and all knew before that first long blare of the *tubae*, this day, and this battle, will decide the fate of the Roman Republic.

And it has. That largely egalitarian institution will soon be no more, replaced by a despotic empire. And though it will take eleven long years before he stands atop that kingdom as its undisputed emperor, Octavian will know that moment of glory, just as he knows today's. He will reign for the rest of his life, growing crueler and more callous with every passing year. And just as Jacob of Nazareth is training Joseph to follow in his footsteps, the new emperor will teach his stepson, Tiberius, to reign with an iron fist, so when the day comes that *he* is named emperor, he will maintain his own ruthless hold on power—brooking no opposition, crushing any rebellion, and flogging, stripping, and publicly nailing to a cross any man who poses a threat to Rome.

That will include a humble carpenter.

But, on this day, another general walks among the vanquished and is not disrespected. Forty-one-year-old Marc Antony strides purposely through the carnage as men on both sides admire his strength.

Octavian and Marc Antony are the victors. But of course there can be only one ruler of this new empire. So, for the next decade, these two men will wage a long and bitter war for total control of Rome. The entire world will be affected by the outcome.

✝✝✝

The final battle takes place in 31 B.C., in Actium, just off the coast of Greece. Just before the fighting begins, one of Marc Antony's top generals, Quintus Dellius, defects to Octavian, bringing Antony's battle plans with him. When this leads to the destruction of his naval fleet, Marc Antony's nineteen legions and twelve thousand cavalry desert.* Now hunted and without an army, Antony flees to Egypt with his longtime lover the once-powerful queen Cleopatra, who chose to ally herself with the warrior rather than Octavian. Furious, Octavian gives chase, and Marc Antony kills himself with his sword to avoid being taken prisoner, dying in his lover's arms. Cleopatra soon follows him

---

*Actium is located at the modern-day city of Preveza, in western Greece, on the Ionian Sea. There are some who believe that Marc Antony was persuaded to give up his claims to the Roman Empire after ten long years of fighting and to retire to Egypt to be with Cleopatra. His forces had been decimated by malaria, and morale was at rock bottom. This theory holds that the Battle of Actium was designed to conceal his retreat. If this is true, Antony was performing one of the greatest ruses in history, committing some 230 war galleys, several thousand archers, and twenty thousand soldiers to the scheme. The entire battle was conducted at sea, ending before Antony's infantry could engage Octavian's onshore. Cleopatra, still clinging to her hope of ruling Rome, was present, but on a separate ship from Marc Antony's. Before the two lovers could escape, more than five thousand of Marc Antony's men were killed and almost two hundred ships were captured or sunk.

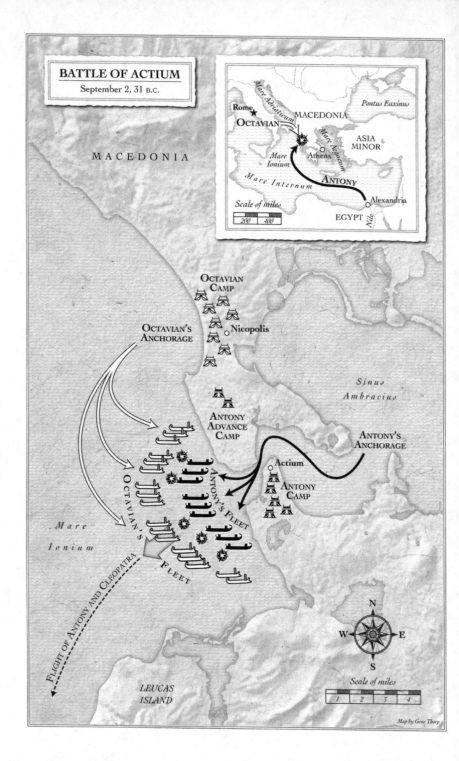

BATTLE OF ACTIUM
September 2, 31 B.C.

Pontus Euxinus

MACEDONIA

Rome

OCTAVIAN

Mare Adriaticum

Mare Aegaeum

ASIA
MINOR

Athens

Mare
Ionium

ANTONY

Mare Internum

Alexandria

Scale of miles

200   400

EGYPT

Nile

MACEDONIA

OCTAVIAN
CAMP

OCTAVIAN'S
ANCHORAGE

Nicopolis

Sinus
Ambracius

ANTONY
ADVANCE
CAMP

ANTONY'S
ANCHORAGE

Actium

ANTONY
CAMP

ANTONY'S FLEET

OCTAVIAN'S
FLEET

Mare
Ionium

FLIGHT OF ANTONY AND CLEOPATRA

N

W   E

S

LEUCAS
ISLAND

Scale of miles

1   2   3   4

Map by Gene Thorp

into death by drinking a poisonous blend of opium and hemlock.* She is thirty-nine years old.

To ensure he reigns as his uncle's undisputed heir, Octavian then
orders the murder of Caesarion, Julius Caesar's bastard child by
Cleopatra. The sixteen-year-old Caesarion escapes to India but is
lured back to Egypt by promises that he will be named the new
pharaoh. This proves to be a lie. Octavian's henchmen strangle
the teenage pretender, putting an end to the scheme Cleopatra
hatched when she first bedded Julius Caesar in those glorious
years before his assassination. The devious cycle is now complete.

So it is that the new Roman Empire is ruled by just one all-
powerful man who believes himself to be the son of god: Octavian, who will soon answer to a new name.

All hail Caesar Augustus.

---

*The legend that Cleopatra killed herself by letting a poisonous asp (or, some
say, an Egyptian cobra) bite her naked breast is just that, a legend. The blend
of opium and hemlock was also the poison used by the great philosopher
Socrates to end his life.

CHAPTER FOUR

JORDAN RIVER VALLEY, JUDEA
MARCH 22, A.D. 7
NOON

T HE CHILD WITH TWENTY-THREE YEARS TO LIVE IS MISSING.
The northeast road out of Jerusalem is dusty and barren, a desolate path leading steeply downhill through the city to the Jordan River and the rocky desert of Perea beyond. There is little shade and few places to take refuge from the sun. Mary and Joseph walk among a long line of pilgrims on their way back to Nazareth after the Passover festival in Jerusalem, a journey they are required by Jewish law to make each year. The couple leaves behind a city far different from when Jesus was born. King Herod is long dead, but rather than being better off—he was demented in his final hours, waving a knife and ordering the murder of yet another son—the Jewish people are actually worse for the tyrant's demise.

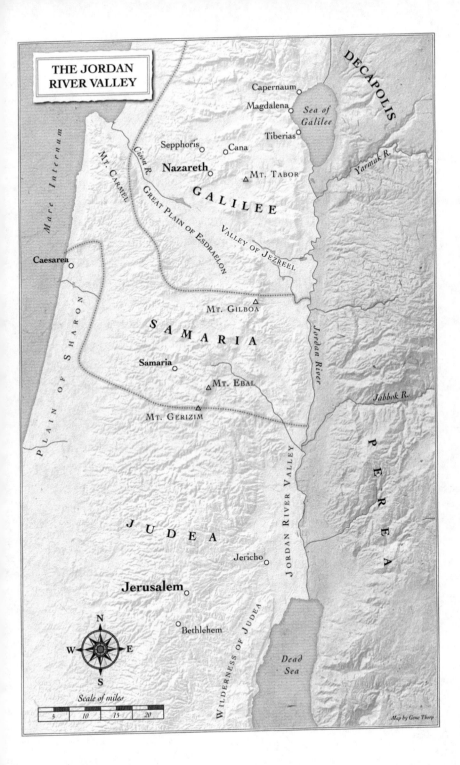

THE JORDAN
RIVER VALLEY

DECAPOLIS

Capernaum
Magdalena
Sea of Galilee
Tiberias

Sepphoris
Cana
Nazareth
MT. TABOR

G A L I L E E

Mare Internum

MT. CARMEL

Kison R.

GREAT PLAIN OF ESDRAELON

VALLEY OF JEZREEL

Yarmuk R.

Caesarea

MT. GILBOA

S A M A R I A

Samaria

MT. EBAL

MT. GERIZIM

Jordan River

Jabbok R.

PLAIN OF SHARON

P E R E A

J U D E A

Jericho

JORDAN RIVER VALLEY

Jerusalem

N
W E
S

Bethlehem

WILDERNESS OF JUDEA

Dead Sea

Scale of miles
5   10   15   20

Map by Gene Thorp

Intense rioting followed his passing in March of 4 B.C., and anarchy reigned once the people of Jerusalem realized that Herod's heir was a weak and ineffectual version of his father. But Archelaus, as the new king was known, struck back hard, showing that he could be as cruel as Herod. The slaughter came during Passover, the celebration of the night when the angel of death "passed over" the houses of the Jews while they were enslaved in Egypt during the time of the pharaohs, killing the firstborn sons of Egyptians instead. The holiday symbolizes the freedom from slavery that later followed, when Moses led the people out of Egypt in search of the homeland that God had promised them.

Passover is a time when Jerusalem is packed with hundreds of thousands of worshippers from all over the world, so it was horrific when Archelaus boldly asserted his authority by ordering his cavalry to charge their horses into the thick crowds filling the Temple courts. Wielding javelins and long, straight steel and bronze swords, Archelaus's Babylonian, Thracian, and Syrian mercenaries massacred three thousand innocent pilgrims. Mary, Joseph, and Jesus saw the bloodbath firsthand and were lucky to escape the Temple with their lives. They were also eyewitnesses to the crucifixion of more than two thousand Jewish rebels outside Jerusalem's city walls when Roman soldiers moved in to quell further revolts. In defiance of Jewish law,* the bodies were not taken down and buried, but left to rot or to be devoured by wild dogs and vultures as a symbol of what happens to those who defy the Roman Empire.

---

*Deuteronomy 21:22–23: "If a man guilty of a capital offense is put to death and his body is hung on a tree, you must not leave his body on the tree overnight. Be sure to bury him that same day, because anyone who is hung on a tree is under God's curse."

Rome soon inserted itself completely into Judean politics.* By
A.D. 6, Emperor Caesar Augustus deemed Archelaus unfit to reign
and exiled him to Gaul. Judea is now a Roman province, ruled by
a prefect sent from Rome. There are still Jewish rulers reigning
over other portions of Herod's former kingdom, but they are nothing more than figureheads and carry the title of tetrarch instead of
king. A tetrarch is a subordinate ruler in the Roman Empire. The
term refers to "fourths" and the fact that Herod the Great's kingdom of Judea was split into four unequal parts after his death.
Three of those parts went to his sons, one each to Herod and
Philip and two to Archelaus. Upon the exile of Archelaus in A.D. 6,
Rome sent prefects to be governors to oversee the land of the Jews.

Jerusalem is ruled by the local aristocracy and Temple high
priests, who mete out justice through the Great Sanhedrin, a
court comprised of seventy-one judges with absolute authority to
enforce Jewish religious law—though, in the case of a death sentence, they must get the approval of the Roman governor.

In this way, Emperor Caesar Augustus balances the needs of
his empire without insulting the Jewish faith. Nevertheless, he still
demands complete submission to his domain, a humiliation that
the Jews have no choice but to endure. This does not, however,
mean they have stopped rebelling. In fact, their region is the site of
more uprisings than any other part of the mighty Roman Empire,
a sprawling kingdom stretching the length of Europe, across the
sands of Parthia, and spanning almost the entire Mediterranean

---

*In Hebrew, "Jew" is *Yehudi* (יהודי), which originally meant a resident of
Yehuda (Judaea), which contained Jerusalem and the Temple. This later
came to mean a member of the religion of Yehuda, as mentioned in some of
the later prophets, and all through the scroll of Esther. The Jews came to be
called Hebrews (עברים), or the Sons of Israel. In Greek and Latin they were
Ioudaioi and *Iudaei*, respectively. In Hebrew they could be *Israel* or Sons of
Israel or *Yehudim*.

rim. The worst rebellion was in 4 B.C., when Jesus was just one year old. A rebel faction broke into the great palace fortress in Sepphoris, looted the royal armory, distributed its cache of weapons to the city's residents, and then attempted a takeover of the local government. Under the orders of Caesar Augustus, Publius Quinctilius Varus, the Roman governor of Syria, ordered his cavalry to slaughter the rebels, burn Sepphoris to the ground, and enslave its entire population of more than eight thousand residents.

The Jewish people have also begun boycotting the purchase of all Roman pottery. As passive and understated as the act may be, it serves as a daily reminder that despite their oppression, the Jews will never allow themselves to be completely trampled beneath the heel of Rome. For, while the Roman Republic kept its distance from Judean politics during the reign of Julius Caesar, the Roman *Empire* rules the Jews in an increasingly oppressive fashion.

For now, the thousands of observant worshippers filling the desolate road spilling down to the Jordan River can forget their gripes and fears about the Roman soldiers stationed in the barracks right next to the Temple. Passover is done. They have been stopped at the city gate to pay the publican yet another one of the exorbitant taxes that make their lives such a struggle—this time a tax on goods purchased in Jerusalem. Now they are headed home to Galilee. The pilgrims march in an enormous caravan to ensure protection from robbers, kidnappers, and slavers. A lucky few lead a donkey that carries their supplies, but most shoulder their own food and water. Mary and Joseph haven't seen the twelve-year-old Jesus since yesterday, but they are sure he is somewhere in the caravan, walking with friends or extended family.

This is not the easiest or shortest way home, though it is the safest. The most direct route means two days' less travel. But it leads due north, through Samaria, a region notorious for racial

hatred between the Samaritans and the Jews, and along mountain passes where murderous bandits give vent to that prejudice.

So the caravan is going around Samaria, on a path that can
only be described as treacherous. There are few inns or sources of
food and water, and the landscape alternates between desert and
rugged wilderness. But there is safety in numbers, and Mary and
Joseph's fellow travelers are hardly strangers, for they make this
journey together each year. The members of the caravan look
after one another and their families. If a child has wandered away
from his parents at nightfall, he is given a place to sleep and then
sent off to find his parents in the morning.

Mary and Joseph believe this is what has become of Jesus. He
is a bright and charismatic child who always gets along well with
others, so it was no surprise when he failed to sit with them at the
campfire last night. They fully trusted that he would turn up in
the morning.

But morning has come and gone. And as the noon sun looms
high overhead, Mary and Joseph realize that it has been a very
long time since they've seen Jesus.

They walk the length of the caravan in search of their lost boy,
growing more and more concerned by the moment, pleading
with fellow pilgrims for some clue as to their son's whereabouts.
But not a single person can remember seeing Jesus since the
moment the endless column of travelers left Jerusalem.

Mary and Joseph realize that not only have they lost their
child, but in all probability they have left him behind.

With no choice, they turn around and march back up the road.
They will walk all the way to Jerusalem and submit once more to
the Romans if need be. Nothing matters more than finding Jesus.

His destiny must be fulfilled, even if his worried parents have
no idea how horrific that destiny might be.

CHAPTER FIVE

Mary and Joseph's long walk back into Jerusalem in search of Jesus is finally complete. Now, somewhere among the merchants and soldiers and exotic travelers in this crowded, frenetic city, they must find him.

Meanwhile, the Son of God, as Jesus will refer to himself for the first time on this very day, listens with rapt fascination as a group of Jewish scholars shares insights about their common faith. The twelve-year-old Jesus of Nazareth sits in the shadow of the great Temple, on a terrace next to the Chamber of Hewn Stone, where the all-powerful Sanhedrin meets. Countless worshippers recently converged on this very spot during the Passover celebration, packing the terrace and the steps below so that they might hear the teachings of the sages and Temple priests. Despite

Jesus teaching in the Temple

the spiritual setting, the Jews were wary, knowing all the while that they were being closely watched for signs of unrest by the Roman troops of Emperor Caesar Augustus.

Now the pilgrims have begun their long trek home, and the soldiers have returned to their barracks in the nearby Antonia Fortress, allowing the worshippers in this religious citadel to resume their normal routines of prayer, fasting, worship, sacrifice, and teaching. It is a rhythm the child has never before experienced, and he enjoys it immensely. If anyone thinks it odd that a smooth-cheeked, simply dressed child from rural Galilee should be sitting alone among these gray-bearded rabbis, with their flowing robes and encyclopedic knowledge of Jewish history, they are not saying. In fact, the opposite is true: Jesus's understanding of complex spiritual concepts has astonished the priests and teachers. They listen to his words as he speaks and treat him like a savant, marveling to one another about his amazing gifts.

Jesus is quite aware that his parents have already begun the journey back to Nazareth. He is not an insensitive child, but his thirst for knowledge and his eagerness to share his insights are so great that it never crosses his mind that Mary and Joseph will be worried once they discover him missing. Nor does Jesus believe that his actions constitute an act of disobedience. The need to dig deeper into the meaning of God overwhelms every other consideration. Like all Jewish boys, when he begins puberty he will go from being considered a mere boy to being thought of as a full-fledged member of the religious community and thus accountable for his actions. But Jesus is different from other boys his age. He is not content merely to learn the oral history of his faith; he also feels a keen desire to debate its nuances and legends. So deep is this need that even now, days since his parents departed for home, Jesus is still finding new questions to ask.

†††

Meanwhile, Mary and Joseph frantically search the narrow streets and bazaars of the Lower City, fearing the worst for their boy. Jesus could have wandered away from the caravan and been abducted. Such things happen. Still, they believe he is in Jerusalem, no doubt scared and lonely and hungry. Perhaps the high priests have taken pity on him and allowed him to sleep at night in the Temple, with its many rooms. Or maybe he has been forced to curl up in an alley, shivering in the cold nighttime air. The most confounding thing about Jesus's disappearance is how uncharacteristic it is. He is normally an extremely well-behaved boy and not the sort to worry Mary and Joseph.

They enter the Temple through the southern doors and then climb the broad stone staircase leading up onto the Temple Mount. They find themselves standing on a large, crowded plaza, where they begin scanning the many worshippers for signs of their lost son.

But it's almost impossible to know where to look first. Twice as big as the Forum in Rome, the Temple Mount is a three-acre platform with walls stretching a quarter mile in length and looming 450 feet over the Kidron Valley below. Herod the Great built the entire structure in just eighteen months, atop the site where the former temples of Solomon and Zerubbabel once rose. The majority of the Mount is a vast open-air stone courtyard known as the Court of the Gentiles, which is open to Jew and Gentile alike. And it is here that Mary and Joseph now stand.

Seeing no sign of Jesus, they move to the center of the Mount. There, like a fifteen-story limestone-and-gold island, rises the Temple. This is not merely a place of worship but also a refuge from the repression of Roman occupation, a place where all Jews can speak freely and pray to God without fear. There are separate courtyards for men and women, rooms for priests to sleep when they are on duty, stairs and terraces from which those priests teach the Jewish faith, and altars where sheep, doves, and heifers are sacrificed. It is the first thing any visitor to Jerusalem sees as he comes up over the surrounding hills and gazes down upon the city.

The Temple is surrounded on four sides by a low wall that separates it from the Court of the Gentiles. Only Jews can cross from one side of the wall to the other. Just in case a Roman soldier or other Gentile should be tempted to step through the gates, a sign reminds them that they will be killed. FOREIGNERS! reads the inscription, DO NOT ENTER WITHIN THE GRILLE AND PARTITION SURROUNDING THE TEMPLE. HE WHO IS CAUGHT WILL ONLY HAVE HIMSELF TO BLAME FOR HIS DEATH WHICH WILL FOLLOW.

The threat is hollow. A Jew would be executed on the spot if he dared kill a trespassing legionary. And from time to time, Romans have even sent troops into the Temple to assert their authority. But the threatening sign does serve one purpose. The words are a reminder that this is a holy, inviolate place, built, according to tradition, in the precise location atop Mount Moriah where Abraham almost sacrificed Isaac, where King David chose to build the First Temple, and where God gathered dust to create Adam, the first man. There is no more profound or greater symbol of Jewish belief.

†††

Mary and Joseph step through the Temple gate, leaving the Court of the Gentiles behind. Now their task gets only more frustrating because Jesus could be inside any of the many rooms within the Temple—or in none. They pass through the colonnades of the Eastern Gate and into the Court of Women. At 233 feet long on each side, ringed by four lamp stands rising 86 feet tall, this square courtyard is capable of holding six thousand worshippers at a time. And at the height of Passover, just a few days earlier, there were certainly many crowded together. But now it is empty enough that Mary and Joseph can easily see that Jesus is not here.

The search becomes a process of elimination. Jesus is obviously not in the Chamber of the Lepers. The Chamber of the Hearth houses priests while they are on duty and contains just dormitories and offices, so that is unlikely. The Chamber of Hewn Stone is where the select council of high priests known as the Sanhedrin resides, so that, too, is probably out of the question. But Mary and Joseph are desperate and willing to look anywhere. They scour the Temple with the same frantic urgency with which they searched the bazaars and alleys of Jerusalem earlier in the day.

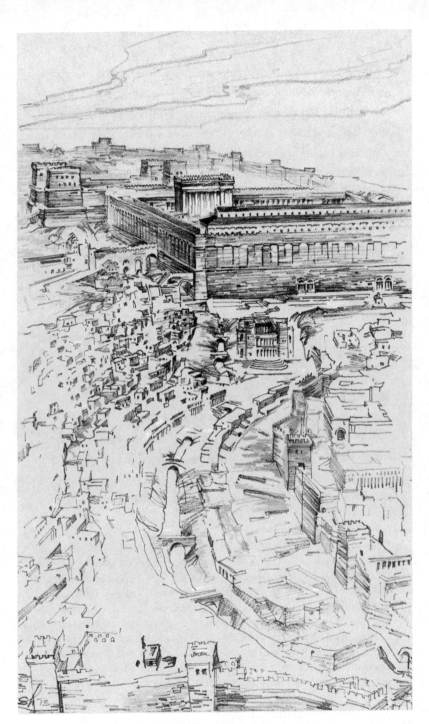

View of the Temple from the south

So as Mary and Joseph make their way through the courts, the sounds and smells of cows and sheep fill the air as priests prepare the animals for their ceremonial death on the altar, strip dead carcasses, and clean up the gallons of blood that flow when an animal is offered up to God. Ritual animal sacrifices are a constant of Temple life. An animal is slaughtered in order that an individual's sins might be forgiven. The rich smell of blood inevitably fills the air.

Finally, outside, on the terrace where the sages and scribes teach the Scriptures to believers during Passover and other feasts, Mary hears Jesus's voice. But the words coming from his mouth sound nothing like those of the son she knows so well. Jesus has never shown any sign of possessing such deep knowledge of Jewish law and tradition. So Mary and Joseph gasp in shock at the ease with which he is discussing God.

Nevertheless, they are also understandably irate. "Son," Mary stammers. "Why have you treated us like this? Your father and I have been anxiously searching for you."

"Why were you searching for me?" he responds. There is innocence to his words. "Didn't you know I had to be in my father's house?"*

If the esteemed Temple rabbis overhear Jesus's response, they

---

*Clearly no one understands the statement at the time, but this passage in Luke 2:49 is the beginning of Jesus unfolding the full meaning of "Son of God." One important note, however, is that the passage includes a Greek literary device written as δεῖ, meaning "it is necessary." Luke uses this linguistic phrase eight times in a strategic fashion with respect to Jesus. He alludes to a "necessary" relationship with the Father, though no reaction or explanation is given. As the Gospels unfold, the title becomes imbued with greater significance as Jesus's personal claims of divinity and acts of divinity become pronounced—but even though references are made, the disciples and the people don't comprehend the magnitude of what he is saying.

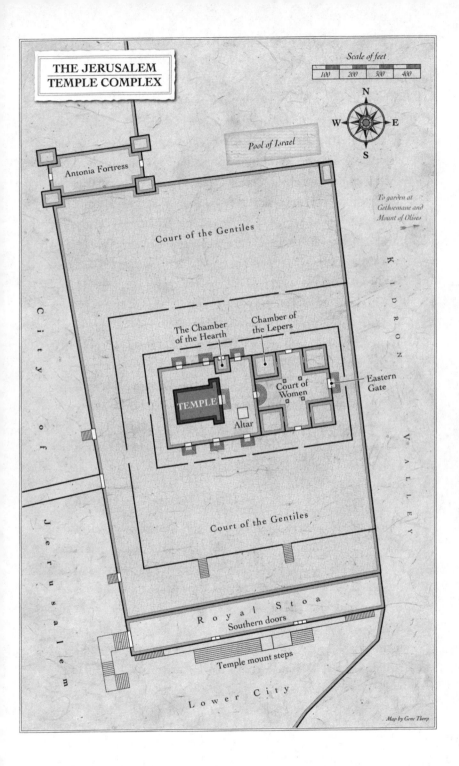

THE JERUSALEM
TEMPLE COMPLEX

Scale of feet
100   200   300   400

N
W — E
S

Pool of Israel

Antonia Fortress

To garden at
Gethsemane and
Mount of Olives

Court of the Gentiles

K
I
D
R
O
N

C
i
t
y

o
f

J
e
r
u
s
a
l
e
m

The Chamber
of the Hearth

Chamber of
the Lepers

TEMPLE

Altar

Court of
Women

Eastern
Gate

V
A
L
L
E
Y

Court of the Gentiles

R o y a l   S t o a
Southern doors

Temple mount steps

L o w e r   C i t y

Map by Gene Thorp

don't let on. For if the boy is inferring that God is his *actual* father—literally, not just figuratively—then it is tantamount to blasphemy, being a claim to divinity, and no different, in their eyes, from the claims of Caesar Augustus. But the Roman emperor is not a Jew and thus not held accountable for his blasphemy under Jewish law. If he were, the punishment handed down through the Jewish patriarch Moses would be death.

But Jesus is a Jew. And Jewish law says that upon commitment of blasphemy, the entire congregation should place their hands upon him, then step back and hurl rocks at his young and defenseless head and body until he collapses and dies.

For Jesus of Nazareth is not claiming Joseph, the carpenter and son of Jacob and the man standing helplessly at Mary's side in the Temple courts, as his father. Jesus is instead claiming that the one true God of the Jewish people is his rightful parent.

But under the law, Jesus cannot be convicted of blasphemy. He has not come of age and is not yet responsible for his words. So perhaps the rabbis do hear his bold statement and breathe a sigh of relief, knowing that this brilliant young scholar is exempt from a most cruel death.

†††

Mary and Joseph lead their son from the Temple and back home. The roads are unpaved, and the village is not protected from invaders by walls or other fortifications. At that time, various families shared dwellings, sometimes separated by small courtyards. Nazareth is situated in a hollow formed by the rolling hills of rural Galilee. An ancient caravan route passes within six miles, but no major highways go through Nazareth. It is a small town that is destined to remain that way, thanks not just to the topography but also to the fact that the only water source is a single freshwater spring.

And yet Nazareth is a wondrous place for a young boy to grow up.* There are hills to climb, caves to explore, and fields through which to run. In the summer, when the air is so hot that Jesus sleeps on the flat dirt roof of the family home, figs and olives grow fat on the trees. Spring is a time for planting the wheat that will provide their daily bread. Nazareth is only twenty miles from the Mediterranean Sea, but it might as well be a thousand, because fish is almost as rare as red meat in young Jesus's diet. So while it is not a life of excess, there is always enough: the trees and fields produce wheat, olives, onions, lentils, the occasional piece of lamb, and eggs that can be poached in that most precious of all staples: olive oil. This is also used for lighting lamps, rubbing into chapped skin, and cooking meals.

Mary and Joseph are devout in their faith and have gone to great lengths to pass this love of God on to Jesus. A small wooden box containing a parchment scroll hangs on their doorpost. On it is written the Shema, that most elemental of Jewish prayers: "Hear, O Israel, the Lord our God, the Lord is One." It is a prayer that the family recites upon rising in the morning and after bringing the animals into the house at bedtime each night. Jesus is circumcised, in keeping with God's covenant with Abraham. His clothing is adorned with tassels, in accordance with the writings in

---

*The Gospels clearly state that Jesus had four brothers: James, Joseph, Judas, and Simon. They also mention that he had sisters, but the number is not specified. The Roman Catholic Church believes that Mary remained a virgin throughout her entire life. This doctrine was first put forth four centuries after Jesus lived, by an early leader in the Church named Simon. The Church considers the siblings mentioned by the Gospels to be Jesus's cousins. Eastern Orthodox Christians believe them to be stepbrothers and stepsisters brought into the marriage by Joseph, a widower before he married Mary. Most other Christian sects believe that Mary did not remain a virgin for her entire life and that these siblings were Jesus's brothers and sisters.

Numbers,* and he attends synagogue every week. There, Jesus wears a prayer shawl while sitting on a bench with his back against the wall of the small square room, reading from the sacred scrolls and singing the Psalms. It is in the synagogue that, as a young boy, he learns to read and write, because during this time of Roman occupation, holding on to their traditions has become an even greater priority to the Jewish people. A group of pious teachers known as the Pharisees has helped to ensure a system of schools in synagogues, teaching the children Hebrew and instructing them in Jewish law.

It is in the Nazareth synagogue that Jesus sits beside Joseph on the Sabbath, surrounded by those who call Joseph a friend. These men of Nazareth have all made the long walk to Jerusalem together as part of the great Passover caravan, and many can even remember the sight of a pregnant and unwed Mary enduring the pilgrimage before Jesus was born. These men remember the shame attached to the early days of that relationship between Mary and Joseph, when it was announced that she was pregnant out of wedlock. They recall Joseph's stubborn loyalty and his refusal to shun her. The village of Nazareth eventually followed his example, accepting the eventual union between Joseph and Mary. In this way, Jesus came of age, growing into a hardworking man of the Jewish faith, intent on living a spiritual life, just like the other men and women of Nazareth.

The history of the Jews is a litany of resisting the oppression brought by foreign invaders who conquered the land now known as Israel. In a way, the Roman occupation links the people of

*Numbers 15:38. Also, Deuteronomy 22:12: "You should make tassels on the four corners of the cloak you wear."

Galilee to a centuries-long tradition. Thus, the worsening situation under Caesar Augustus is quietly accepted, but with a growing bitterness.

There is nothing exceptional about Jesus's upbringing. To the people of Jerusalem, where he returns each year for Passover, his thick Galilean accent is noticeable. He labors six days a week as a carpenter alongside his father, building the roofs and doorposts of Nazareth and laying the foundation stones of sprawling nearby Sepphoris. Jesus seems destined to remain here always, raising his own family and building his own home into the slope of a Nazarene hill.

But the young Jesus is not long for this small town. The holiness and magnificence of Jerusalem call to him. He comes to know the smells and music of the city during his annual visits, even as he becomes comfortable navigating his way through such local landmarks as the Mount of Olives, the garden at Gethsemane, the Kidron Valley, and the Temple itself. With every passing year, as Jesus grows from a small child into a man with a carpenter's square shoulders and callused hands, his wisdom and awareness of his faith increases. He develops the gifts of serenity and powerful personal charisma, and he learns to speak eloquently in public.

Yet Jesus is cautious when he talks to crowds. As a full-fledged member of the Jewish religious community from the age of thirteen on, he knows he is accountable for his behavior and that blasphemous talk about being the Son of God will lead to a very public execution. The Jews would stone Jesus for such language, and the Romans might kill him for suggesting he is their divine emperor's equal. Stoning would seem a tame way to die in comparison with the evils of which the Romans are capable—evils Jesus has seen with his own eyes.

††

It was just a year earlier that Judas of Gamala* was likely crucified in Sepphoris. Jesus and every other Galilean bore witness to
that horror. Judas was a learned man, and also a husband and
father, who longed to raise his children in a better world—a
Galilee ruled by Israelites instead of Roman puppets who crippled
the people with unbearable taxes. Judas traveled through the
farming villages and fishing ports of Galilee preaching a message
of sedition to the impoverished peasants, urging them not to pay
taxes to Rome or to tithe to the Temple in Jerusalem. He even
founded a new sect of the Jewish faith, one that espoused a radical new theology of unwavering devotion to the Israelites' one
true Lord. Bowing down to Caesar Augustus and Rome is sinful,
Judas told all who would listen.

The Romans might have overlooked Judas as an overzealous
religious crank if he had not raised an army of displaced peasants
to attempt a violent overthrow of the Roman-sponsored government in Galilee. That action brought an immediate response:
Judas must die.

It was on the order of Herod Antipas, the fifth-born son of
Herod the Great, who himself had once hunted the baby Jesus.

---

*Judas of Gamala, a Galilean, is not to be confused with Judas of Galilee,
who fomented rebellion after the death of Herod the Great in 4 B.C. They are
two separate individuals, but some historical accounts mistake the two men.
Both died horrible deaths for their uprisings. No one knows for sure how
Judas of Gamala was executed, but crucifixion is a very likely option. And
while Rome practiced this manner of execution almost exclusively during this
time, crucifixion was certainly within the Jewish tradition. Most famously,
Josephus writes that the Jewish ruler Alexander Jannaeus crucified some
eight hundred Pharisees in 88 B.C. (It should be noted that the historical
record confirms that both of Judas of Gamala's sons were crucified.)

Both father and son had done everything in their power to brutalize and fleece the good people of Galilee.

Of course, Caesar Augustus got the first cut of all tax proceeds. He had mellowed since his younger days. Absolute power became him, and the vainglorious heir of Julius Caesar who was jeered for cowardice at Philippi was now a seventy-year-old monarch renowned for erecting opulent buildings and temples throughout his empire. He even had an admiration for the Jews and their reverent adherence to their teachings. Caesar Augustus lived in splendor, though not overt decadence. That fondness for the abundant and perverse was preferred by Tiberius, his adopted son and heir.

But it was Caesar Augustus who had allowed Herod the Great to remain on the throne of Judea for almost four decades, just as it was he who had personally divided the kingdom after that tyrant's death and granted control of Galilee to Herod Antipas.

The soldiers of Antipas quickly captured Judas of Gamala and began the crucifixion process by stripping him naked in the palace courtyard.

A crowd had been let in to watch and could clearly see the agony of Judas. Among them were Judas's sons, Jacob and Simon. Little did the boys know then, but they were destined one day to be crucified themselves for trying to avenge their father's death.

The soldiers of Antipas forced Judas of Gamala to his knees, facing a low post. He was tied to the wooden shaft with his hands above his head. Two soldiers retrieved short-handled whips, whose three leather tendrils were tipped with lead balls and mutton bones. The soldiers stood ready to take turns laying the leather across Judas's back, leaning into each blow with all their might. As each lash was inflicted, the leather thongs tore open the skin and muscles, even as the lead and bone created deep bruising.

This, in turn, led to profuse internal bleeding. As with all aspects of Roman execution, the stripping and lashing had a specific purpose: the public nudity humiliated, while the whip broke Judas's will so that he would offer no resistance when hurled to the ground and nailed to the cross. Crucifixion, Roman-style, was not just a barbarous way to kill, but also a process of mentally and physically destroying the victim—whether it be man, woman, or child. Judas would be nothing but an empty husk by the time he hung from the cross.

Jewish law says that a man can be lashed only thirty-nine times—"forty minus one," as it is written. Not so with the Romans—or, in Herod Antipas's case, Gentile mercenaries behaving like Roman soldiers. These non-Jews could lash a man as long as they liked. The only requirement was that their victim be able to carry his crossbeam to the site of crucifixion. So even as a soldier counted each and every time the *flagrum* was brought down upon Judas's back, upper legs, and head, it was understood he would receive far more than thirty-nine lashes. He was no common criminal. He was a traitor whose crime had been to "exhort the nation to assert their liberty" from Rome, as the great historian Josephus would write. But more important, Judas had sought to free the Judean people from the unfair taxation being inflicted by Rome and Herod. He had compared the taxation to a form of slavery and had encouraged his fellow Jews to rise up against their oppressors.

Judas cried out in agony as a soldier delivered another blast of leather onto his flesh. But he knew better than to curse his executioners because that would only mean more blows. So he endured the torture. In moments, Judas was covered with blood.

The most common modes of killing a condemned man in the Roman Empire were hanging, burning him alive, beheading, placing him inside a bag full of scorpions then drowning him, and crucifixion. As terrible as the four might be, the last is considered the worst by far. So even as crucifixion was now practiced throughout the Roman Empire, even by a tetrarch such as Herod Antipas, it was a death so horrible that it was forbidden to execute Roman citizens in this manner.

Judas of Gamala lay limp and bleeding after his lashes were administered. Soldiers then brought out a rough-hewn piece of lumber and hurled it to the ground. Despite the blood pouring down his back, Judas was forced to stand. His executioners lifted this splinter-filled *patibulum*, as it was known, onto his shoulders. This would become the crossbeam of his crucifix, and, like all condemned men, Judas was to carry it outside the city walls of Sepphoris to a spot where a vertical pole in the ground would form the second part of his crucifix. He would be nailed to that cross and left to die. His legs would be broken to make the torturous process even more ghastly. He would hang in full view of the thousands that called Sepphoris home, helpless to stop the urination and defecation that would stain his cross and compound his humiliation. Judas would be dead by nightfall—if he was lucky.

The story of Judas's execution spread throughout Galilee. But he was not alone in his persecution. There were countless other would-be prophets who thought violence could bring an end to Roman occupation. They all paid for this conceit with their lives. And then they were forgotten, so that, generations later, few remember the story of Judas of Gamala.

††↑

Galilee is the northernmost province in what was called Canaan by the patriarch Abraham. One of Abraham's grandsons was a man named Jacob, who also went by the name Israel and fathered the people who would come to be known as the Israelites. In time, the Roman-controlled territory now known as Judea will come to bear that name.

A pair of "seas" anchor Galilee's borders: the Mediterranean and the large inland lake often called the Sea of Galilee, dotted by fishing villages such as Capernaum. Syria lies to the north and west and Samaria to the south. It is an uncrowded landscape defined by rolling hills, wide fields, small villages, and farmers tending plots of land that were passed on to them as part of their inheritance.

Since returning to Galilee a decade ago, Herod Antipas has devoted himself to rebuilding the city of Sepphoris. Antipas has made the revitalized city his home and is determined to make it even more regal than Jerusalem. The partition of his father's empire between him and his siblings means not only that Judea is a divided nation, ruled by three separate individuals—Antipas in Galilee, his brother Philip in what is now Jordan, and his brother Archelaus to the south, in Jerusalem—but that, for the first time in history, the ruler of Galilee actually lives in Galilee. So it is that Sepphoris becomes the cosmopolitan hub of the region, juxtaposed with the agrarian lifestyle and landscape of rural Galilee. This is the city where Joseph of Nazareth finds steady employment in Antipas's never-ending stream of building projects. Whether constructing one of the city's elaborate new mansions or plastering walls or laying the mosaic floors of the basilica, a builder has plenty to do in this vast and shining limestone metropolis perched atop a hill.

Sepphoris is so large that it has two markets, an upper and a lower. Anything a man could ever want is for sale: glass, pottery, dried fish, onions, herbs, cattle, and even sex, if one furtively strays away from the hustle and bustle and into the quiet of an alley.

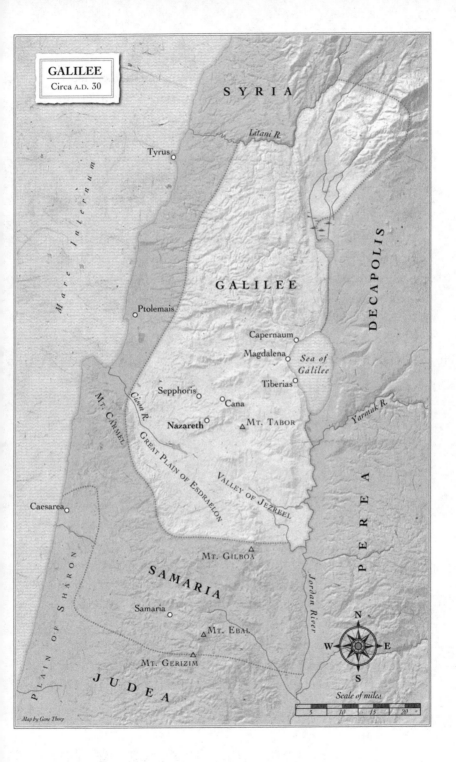

GALILEE
Circa A.D. 30

SYRIA

Litani R.

Tyrus

Mare Internum

GALILEE

Ptolemais

Capernaum

Magdalena
Sea of Galilee

Tiberias

Sepphoris
Cana

Nazareth
△ Mt. Tabor

Kison R.

Mt. Carmel

Great Plain of Esdraelon

Valley of Jezreel

Yarmuk R.

Decapolis

Perea

Caesarea

Plain of Sharon

Mt. Gilboa △

Samaria

Samaria

△ Mt. Ebal

△ Mt. Gerizim

Judea

Jordan River

N
W   E
S

Scale of miles
5   10   15   20

Map by Gene Thorp

Sepphoris is walled, just like Jerusalem, and donkey caravans appear at the city gates each week begging for entry so they might sell their wares. It is a city unlike any other in Galilee. Since its repopulation and rebirth, it is home to doctors, lawyers, craftsmen, tax collectors, and entertainers who perform mime and comedic plays at the theater. But the building of this wondrous metropolis has come at a great cost. Thanks to Antipas, Sepphoris is also home to many people who have lost their farms to excessive taxation. With no fields to till or homes to call their own, they crowd into the poorest sections of the city, making a life by stealing, selling their bodies, or begging. So beneath the veneer of progress and sophistication, there is decadence and decay to this self-styled "ornament of Galilee."

For while Sepphoris is the very picture of prosperity, many in Galilee are starving.

†††

Joseph and Mary, as do most other Jews, live in fear of Herod Antipas. With a dark beard covering the tip of his chin and a thin mustache wreathing his mouth, Antipas resembles a true villain. While his father, Herod the Great, had grave faults, he also performed many constructive acts. Not so Antipas, a callow man who has never known want and who always expected to be given a kingdom.

Antipas was born in Judea but educated in Rome, a city he adores. He pays homage to Caesar Augustus and Rome not only by taxing the Jews blind but also by ordering a Roman-style form of execution for any who would dare defy him.

Galilean outrage against Rome has been building for decades. The people have been levied with tax after tax after tax. Antipas is nothing if not "a lover of luxury," and he uses these taxes both

Herod Antipas

to rebuild Sepphoris and to finance his own lavish lifestyle. And the more luxury he needs, the higher the taxes climb.

Actual money is scarce. Every adult male Jew has to pay his annual half-shekel tax to the Temple in coin. Farmers can pay the rest of their obligation in figs, olive oil, or grain. They have no way of skirting the taxes because they must travel to Sepphoris to sell their harvest. The hated taxman is always on hand when they arrive at their destination. Fishermen have it no better. They are levied special rights fees, in addition to a portion of their daily catch, for permission to drop their nets or to dock in a port.

No men are more despised than the tax collectors, who not only extort funds from people with very little but also publicly abuse and even torture those who fall behind on their payments. There is no leeway. Those who can't pay must borrow grain or oil from the storage silos manned by Antipas's men. The interest rates are exorbitant—100 percent on oil and 25 percent on grain. And falling behind on these debts means ruin. Peasants are often forced to sell their children to creditors as debt slaves or to sell their farms and work the land as sharecroppers. Some lose their homes and inheritance and become beggars, the dignity of life as a Jewish landowner replaced by a degraded existence outside normal society.

There is, however, a booming city of some forty thousand residents to which many of these people have migrated and are accepted, despite their lowly status. This place is called Magdala— "Magdalena" to the Romans and "Magdalene" in the Greek language of the Gospels—and even as Jesus of Nazareth walks the streets of Sepphoris, a vibrant young girl named Mary walks the streets of Magdala. Her parents have nothing. Mary's innocence will inevitably be shattered in the shabby confines of that outlaw village. She will grow up to be a prostitute, doing what she must do to survive, though she longs for something better in this world.

†††

Because Joseph is a skilled carpenter, he is able to pay his taxes. And, indeed, most people in Galilee can do the same—but just barely. Many Galileans suffer malnutrition because they have no food left with which to feed themselves. And in the throes of that hunger, as hair falls out and both muscles and hope wither, they quietly seethe. But rather than point the finger of blame at Rome or Caesar Augustus, the people of Galilee begin to vent their rage at one another. They stop loaning grain or oil to friends and relations, fearing that their own supply will run out. They ignore the Jewish tradition of forgiving debts. The tight-knit peasant community that has sustained itself for so many generations, through rule by the Greeks and Persians and Assyrians, begins to unravel under the reigns of Augustus and Antipas.

The great legends of the Jewish people tell of heroes of their faith rising up to defeat foreign invaders. The people long for the glory days of King David, so many hundreds of years ago, when the Jews were their own masters and God was the undisputed and most powerful force in all the cosmos. The residents of Galilee are independent thinkers. Their persistent belief that they will ultimately control their destiny is one reason Judas of Gamala's demand that they rise up against Rome had such a profound effect.

In that belief, there is hope. The hardships of the land and the cruelty of Rome have bred a resurgent faith in the power of the Jewish God, to whom they pray for rescue, power, and relief. This is the world a young Jesus of Nazareth inhabits. These are the prayers he hears poured forth every day. The promise of God's deliverance is the one shaft of daylight that comforts the oppressed people of Galilee. Someday, in some way, if they just hold on, God will send someone to make things right, just as he did with Abraham, Moses, Daniel, Samson, and David.

Ten years after the death of Herod the Great, the populace of Jesus of Nazareth's village and his land eagerly await a new king of the Jews.

✝✝✝

How much Jesus is affected by all the turbulence in his town is unknown. He grows into a strong man, respectful of his parents. Joseph dies sometime between Jesus's thirteenth and thirtieth birthdays, leaving Jesus the family business. Jesus remains devoted to his mother, and she to him. But as he passes his thirtieth birthday, Jesus of Nazareth knows that silence is no longer an option.

The time has come to fulfill his destiny.

It is a decision that will change the world.

It will also lead to his agonizing death.

BOOK

II

Behold the Man

CHAPTER SIX

JORDAN RIVER, PEREA
A.D. 26
MIDDAY

JOHN THE BAPTIZER STANDS WAIST DEEP IN THE COLD, BROWN river, waiting patiently as the next pilgrim wades out to stand at his side. He looks to the shore, where scores of believers line up on the Jordan's muddy bank, oblivious to the heat as they wait to experience the full immersion ritual that will cleanse them of their sins.

The believers are mostly poor working people. They are electrified by John and his radical teachings. The long-haired young man with the sunburned skin and unkempt beard has disciplined himself by living alone in the desert, existing on a diet of locusts for protein and honey for energy. His clothes are not the elaborate robes of the haughty Pharisees, now spying on him from the shore, but a coarse tunic stitched from the skin of a camel and cinched tightly around his waist with a simple leather belt. John is celibate, with a passion for God and God alone. Some think him eccentric, others consider him a rebel, and many find his direct manner of speaking to be caustic, but all agree that he has boldly promised them something that neither Rome nor the high priests can offer: hope. Thus, the believers have come to redeem that promise.

The end of the known world is coming, John preaches. A new king will come to stand in judgment. Wade into the water and be cleansed of your sins, or this newly anointed ruler—this "Christ"—will punish you in the most horrible manner possible. It is a message both religious and political, one that directly challenges the Roman Empire and the hierarchy of the Jewish Temple.

John extends an arm as the next pilgrim draws near. But before he can baptize the man, a tax collector cries out from the shore, "Teacher, what should *we* do?" He speaks for his profession, well aware that he is despised for diverting Jewish money to a pagan king in Rome.

"Don't collect any more than you are required," John answers.

There is little shade along the Jordan, and the believers have waited in line patiently for the chance to be immersed in these cool waters. But despite their discomfort, one and all listen closely to what John has to say.

"And what should *we* do?" calls out a soldier. Many soldiers have been known to engage in unethical practices in the name of that perverted and despised new Roman emperor Tiberius.

John's answer is nonjudgmental. "Don't extort money and don't accuse people falsely. Be content with your pay."

The Baptist turns his attention back to the man who stands at his side in the river. He listens intently as the man confesses his many sins. Then John prays for him: "After me will come one more powerful than I, the thongs of whose sandals I am not worthy to stoop down and untie. I baptize you with water, but he will baptize you with the Holy Spirit."

Only a slave would be tasked with loosening a man's sandals, so John's words are powerful, a tremendous show of respect. As the pilgrim nods in understanding, John places one hand in the center of the man's back and slowly guides him down into the water, holds him under for a few seconds, and then lifts him back to his feet. The relieved pilgrim, his transgressions now forgiven, battles the lazy current back to shore. Before he has even reached the bank, another believer is wading out to experience the same sensation.

"Who *are* you?" demands a voice from the shore. John has been waiting for this question. It is the condescending request of a priest, sent from Jerusalem to judge whether John is committing heresy. The holy man is not alone, having made the journey in the company of other Pharisees, Sadducees, and Levites.*

"I am *not* the Christ," John shouts back. The high priests know that he is referring to the new Jewish king, a man like Saul and David, the great rulers of generations past who were handpicked by God to lead the Israelites.

"Then who are you?" demands a Pharisee. "Are you Elijah?"

John has heard this comparison before. Like him, Elijah was a prophet who preached that the world would soon end.

---

*These were the top religious voices of their day. The Pharisees were sticklers about religious law; the Sadducees were equally pious but were wealthy and more liberal in their thinking; and the Levites were a tribe of priests and Temple guards directly descended from Levi, a son of the patriarch Jacob.

"No," John replies firmly.

"Who *are* you?" the priests ask once again. "Give us an answer to take back to those who sent us."

John prefers to invoke the prophet Isaiah, a man whose name meant "the Lord saves." He lived eight hundred years ago and was said to have been martyred by being sawed in half for uttering his many bold prophecies. In one particular prediction, Isaiah foretold that a man would come to tell the people about the day the world would end and God would appear on earth. This man would be "a voice of one, calling in the desert, preparing the way for the Lord, making straight paths for him."*

John has prayed and fasted for many days. He truly believes that he is the man of whom Isaiah wrote. Even if he dies a most horrible death, he feels obligated to travel from city to city, telling one and all that the end of the world is near and that they must prepare by being baptized.

"Who *are* you?" the priests demand once again, their voices angrier and more insistent.

"I am the voice of one," John responds, "calling in the desert."

✝✝✝

The Temple priests are not the only officials keeping a close eye on John the Baptist. From his stunning new capital city of Tiberias, which he has built on an even grander scale than Sepphoris, Herod Antipas has sent spies to the Jordan River to track John's every movement. The Baptist is the talk of Galilee, and Antipas

---

*This is in reference to the common practice of improving roads before a king journeys from one country to another. Valleys are filled in and crooked paths are made straight so that the king's travels might be as smooth as possible.

Turndown Bedtime Facts

Bermuda Pink Sand

Bermuda sand boasts the vivid red colour of a multitude of skeletons from a tiny single-celled animal called a Foram. Growing on the underside of reefs these skeletons fall to the sea floor when the animal dies. These skeletons and the sand particles with which they mix are quite large and coarse out by the reefs but by the time they reach our shores they have been tossed around by all the wave action and are much smaller, thus making our sand so soft and fine. The tiny particles of broken up Foram skeletons are what give our sand its pink hue.

fears that this charismatic evangelist will persuade the people to rise up against him.

Antipas is prepared to deal with John in the same manner as Judas of Gamala nearly twenty years ago. But there is something about John's nonviolent message that makes him a much greater threat. Life in Galilee has become even more difficult since Judas was executed. Antipas's decision to build Tiberias on the sunny shores of the Sea of Galilee a decade after rebuilding Sepphoris has increased the financial burden borne by the people of Galilee. As with all of Antipas's building projects, no expense was spared. Once again, the peasants of Galilee are being taxed to cover these costs.

Antipas has named the new city in honor of the Roman emperor who succeeded the late Caesar Augustus twelve years ago. Tiberius was once a great general, defending Rome from Germanic barbarians. But a lifetime of personal sadness has turned him into a horrible man. Tiberius knows no boundaries. One of his amusements is swimming with handpicked "tiddlers," naked young boys whose job is to chase him around the imperial pool and nibble between Tiberius's legs.

The swimming sessions are the least of the emperor's considerable depravities, but Antipas knows better than to pass moral judgment. Even after more than two decades on the throne, he rules solely at the pleasure of Rome. And indeed Antipas has his own depraved résumé. He has divorced his own wife and married that of his brother, an act of abomination to the Jewish people.

So it is that even as he began making plans to kill John the Baptist—a man whose only crime is an outspoken passion for the coming of the Lord—Antipas named the capital city of a devout

Jewish province after a sixty-eight-year-old pagan who hosts orgies in his private villa and dispatches his enemies by throwing them off a thousand-foot cliff.

And while Antipas refuses to pass moral judgment on Tiberius, the vile man who controls his destiny, the Baptist will have no such qualms.

✝✝✝

In Jerusalem, there now exists an uneasy alliance between faith and state. That unholy collaboration is also tracking the Baptist.

Since Augustus declared Herod the Great's son Archelaus unfit to rule twenty years ago, four other Roman governors have been in charge of Judea.

The fifth has just arrived. His name is Pontius Pilate.

✝✝✝

As John the Baptist is preaching on the banks of the Jordan River and Jesus of Nazareth is about to end years of self-imposed silence about his true identity, Pontius Pilate steps ashore in the seaside fortress town of Caesarea to fill the role recently vacated by Valerius Gratus.

Thickly built and prone to arrogance, Pilate is a member of the equestrian class and a former soldier from central Italy. He is married to Claudia Procula, who accompanies him to Judea. It is a dismal appointment, for Judea is known to be a very difficult place to govern. But if her husband excels in this remote diplomatic posting, the powers in Rome might make sure that Pilate's next assignment will be somewhere more prestigious.

Pilate is no friend of the Jews. One of his first official acts is to order Roman troops in Jerusalem to decorate standards* with busts of Emperor Tiberius. When the people rise up in protest of these graven images, which are forbidden by Jewish law, Pilate responds by having his soldiers surround the protesters and draw their swords as if to attack. The Jews refuse to back down. Instead, they bend forth and extend their necks, making it clear that they are prepared to die for their beliefs.

For the first time, Pilate sees with his own eyes the power of the Jewish faith. He orders his men to stand down. The standards are removed.

Pilate now finds a new strategy for dealing with the Jews. He forms an uneasy bond with Caiaphas, the most powerful high priest in the Jerusalem Temple. Caiaphas is from a family of priests and lives in a lavish home in the upper city. He has complete power over religious life in Jerusalem, including the enforcement of Jewish law—even if that means condemning a man or woman to death.

Of course, while Caiaphas may be able to pass sentence, it is the Roman governor who decides if it should be carried out.

Pilate is a Roman pagan. Caiaphas is a Jew. They worship different gods, eat different foods, have different hopes for their

---

*The Roman standard was a statue of an eagle, or *aquila*, situated atop a metal post. In the case of the dispute with Pilate, an emblem bearing a likeness to Tiberius was affixed just below the eagle. The standard was the symbol of a legion and was carried at all times by a standard-bearer (from which we get the modern term for someone who represents an ideal or a value). To lose in battle was considered an enormous form of disgrace. When the dying legionaries at the Battle of Teutoburg Forest in A.D. 9 surrendered three standards (legions XVII, XVIII, and XIX), the Roman Empire scoured the Germanic regions in an attempt to get them back. They ultimately succeeded. Worth noting is that an image of Jesus would adorn Roman standards beginning in the fourth century.

future, and speak in different tongues. Pilate serves at the behest of a divine emperor, while Caiaphas serves at the behest of God. But they share a command of the Greek language and a belief that they are entitled to do anything in order to stay in power.

In this way, state and faith keep a stranglehold on Judea. And now it is Caiaphas who plays his role in their partnership, sending a team of religious authorities out into the wilderness to cast a critical eye on the ministry of John the Baptist.

†††

"You brood of vipers," John screams at the Temple priests who have come to the river to question him. "The axe is already at the root of the tree, and every tree that does not produce good fruit will be cut down and thrown into the fire."

All eyes turn to the shocked religious authorities and then back to John, eager to hear what he will say next. For although it is known that some of these learned men are enormously hypocritical, no one dares criticize them in public. But John defiantly commands the Pharisees and Sadducees either to be baptized or to burn in an eternal fire.

The clerics are stunned by John's words. They say nothing.

John returns his focus to the throngs who have come to be baptized. Farmers, craftsmen, tax collectors, and soldiers—they all respect John's monastic lifestyle and his outspokenness and energy. There is a fearless independence to his behavior that many long to mimic. He seems immune to the threats of Rome. Some in the crowd are curious whether John pays his taxes—and, if not, what will happen to him.

Most of all, each and every one of these people, deep in his heart, wonders if John himself is the coming Messiah of whom he preaches.

††††

The answer comes the following day.

Once again John stands in the Jordan. The village of Bethany is behind him, on the far bank. As usual the day is hot, and long lines of believers wait their turn to be baptized.

In the distance, John spies a man walking down to the river. Like the Baptist, Jesus of Nazareth has long hair and a beard. He wears sandals and a simple robe. His eyes are clear and his shoulders broad, as if he is a workingman. He looks younger than John, but not by much.

Suddenly a dove lands on Jesus's shoulder. When Jesus makes no move to shoo it away, the bird is quite content to remain there.

The dove changes everything.* In that instant, the rage that so often fuels the Baptist's words disappears. In its place is wonder, brought on by the awareness that his vision has now become a reality. As the crowd of pilgrims looks on, an awestruck John motions toward Jesus. "Look, the Lamb of God. I saw the Spirit

---

*The appearance of the dove is recounted in each of the four Gospels of the New Testament and might be seen as an attempt to insert overt spiritual symbolism into the Gospel narrative. But, in fact, each time the word *dove* is used in the canonical Gospels and the Old Testament, each of them is an allusion to actual doves—not divinity. The Gospels of Matthew, Mark, and Luke (known as the Synoptic Gospels) recount that the dove appeared *after* Jesus's baptism. John has the bird landing on Jesus beforehand. The Gospels are a combination of oral tradition, written fragments from the life of Christ, and the testimony of eyewitnesses. This would explain the discrepancy. The appearance of the dove may have been coincidental with Jesus's baptism. However, the Gospels were written as many as seventy years after Jesus's death (Mark in the early 50s, Luke between 59 and 63, Matthew in the 70s, and John between 50 and 85). For the dove to remain a part of Jesus's oral tradition for that long indicates that the bird's appearance must have been remembered quite vividly by all who were there.

come down from heaven as a dove and remain on him. I would not have known him, except that the one who sent me to baptize with water told me, 'The man on whom the Spirit will come down and remain is he who will baptize with the Holy Spirit. I have seen and I testify that this is the Son of God.'"

The believers drop to their knees and press their faces into the earth. Jesus does not react to this sign of worship. He does nothing to discourage it, either. The Nazarene simply wades down into the water and takes his place alongside John, waiting to be baptized.

John is dumbstruck. "I need to be baptized by *you*, and yet you come to me?"

Jesus does not clarify his identity. He is a simple carpenter, a builder who has labored his whole life. He has memorized the Psalms and Scripture. He pays his taxes and takes care of his mother. To a casual observer, he is just one of many hardworking Jews. There is no obvious sign of his divinity.

In the Jewish culture, to proclaim you are God is a capital offense. So now, speaking softly with John the Baptist, Jesus does declare who he is. Bowing his head to accept the water, Jesus tells John, "Let it be so. It is proper for us to do this to fulfill all righteousness."

John places one hand on Jesus's back and slowly lowers him into the water. "I baptize you with water for repentance," John says as he submerges Jesus in the current.

He then lifts Jesus to his feet.

"I have seen and I testify that this is the Son of God," John cries out.

"Son of God" is a regal title indicative of one's being a Messiah, a title attributed to King David. It is believed that when the

Messiah returns, he will be king of the Jews, in keeping with David, the perfect king. The people looking on understand "Son of God" as a Davidic title, the anointed one, who is coming as ruler and king.*

The crowd remains on its knees as Jesus steps onto the shore and keeps on walking. He is headed alone into the desert to fast for forty days and nights. It is a journey he makes willingly, knowing that he must confront and defeat any and all temptation in order to make his mind and body pure before publicly preaching his message of faith and hope.

John the Baptist's work is now done. But along with that, his fate has been sealed.

✝✝✝

John is that rarest of all prophets: a man who lives to see his predictions come true. The people still desire to be cleansed of their sins through baptism, and huge crowds continue to follow John wherever he goes. If anything, his following is growing even larger. And while there is no longer a need to prophesize the coming of a new Christ, John has a powerful gift for speaking. He is not the sort to remain silent about immorality and injustice. So when he learns that Herod Antipas has divorced his wife and

---

*This is a seminal moment in Jesus's ministry for two reasons. First, the allusions are back to Psalm 2:7 and Isaiah 42:1, and possibly Isaiah 41:8. Psalm 2 is a regal psalm, with 2:7 referring essentially to the Messiah, validated by John the Baptist's comments in Luke 3:16. The Isaiah references, particularly 42:1, are the references to the servant, who has both prophetic and deliverance attributes. Thus the baptism blends two portraits into the figure of the Messiah/servant. Second, the baptism itself marks the beginning of Jesus's ministry with divine endorsement. The endorsement is through both the divine word from heaven and the anointing by the Spirit.

then violated Jewish religious law by taking his brother's former spouse for his new bride, he cannot remain silent. Walking the countryside, John the Baptist loudly decries Antipas wherever he goes, turning the people against their ruler.

Antipas orders the spies who have been keeping an eye on John to arrest him. John is chained and then marched fifteen miles over hot desert terrain. Finally, he sees a vision in front of him. It is Antipas's mountaintop fortress at Machaerus. John is then forced to walk three thousand feet up to the citadel, which is surrounded on all sides by rocky ravines. Antipas has sought to make this castle impenetrable. He fears attack from Arabia, which lies to the east, so he has enhanced these natural fortifications by erecting sixty-foot-thick walls and corner towers ninety feet high. "Moreover," the historian Josephus will one day write of Antipas's designs for Machaerus, "he has put a large quantity of dart-throwers and other machines of war into it, and contrived to get everything thither that might any way contribute to its inhabitants' security under the longest siege possible."

The view from the palace, which lies at the center of the forti-fied structure, is stunning. If John were allowed to enjoy it, he might be able to see the slender brown curves of his beloved Jordan River snaking through the valley so far below. And per-haps John does pause for a final glimpse as he is marched through the great wooden doors that allow entrance to the citadel. But those doors close behind him all too quickly. Still in chains, he is marched into Antipas's throne room, where he stands defiant and fearless before this man who says he is king of the Jews. And even when given a chance to recant his charges, John does not. "It is not lawful," he tells the ruler, "for you to have your brother's wife."

The woman in question, Herodias,* sits at Antipas's side. With his charges, John is not only condemning her husband but her as well. Still, Herodias sees that Antipas is actually fearful of John and is afraid to order his death. Herodias, however, is a patient woman and knows that she will find a way to exact her revenge. How dare this unkempt savage insult her?

And so it is that John is hurled into the dungeons of Machaerus, there to rot until Antipas sets him free—or Herodias has him killed.

Meanwhile, a far greater threat to Antipas is beginning to emerge. Jesus of Nazareth has now embarked on a spiritual journey, a mission that will challenge the world's most powerful men.

---

*For Antipas, the issue is moral as well as political. Josephus shows that the woman Antipas planned to divorce in order to marry Herodias was daughter of King Aretas IV of Nabatea. This arrangement aroused severe tension between the kingdoms. Many of Antipas's subjects in Perea were ethnically Nabatean, thus more loyal to Aretas than to Antipas. The arrest of John would of course make matters worse—when Aretas later defeated Antipas in battle, people said it was God's judgment on Antipas for what he'd done to John the Baptist.

CHAPTER SEVEN

VILLA JOVIS, CAPRI

A.D. 26

NIGHT

FAR AWAY FROM GALILEE, THE ROMAN WHO CONSIDERS HIM-
self to be the stepson of god is on the move. Life in Rome has
been hard on Tiberius Julius Caesar Augustus—or so he thinks.
So he has exiled himself to this mountaintop island fortress on
Capri to live out his days in pleasure and privacy. Now he reclines
in his bedroom as nude handmaidens and young boys copulate in
front of him. They were handpicked for their beauty and brought
from the far-flung reaches of the Roman Empire against their
will to perform erotic sexual acts for "the old goat," as the sixty-
eight-year-old Tiberius is called behind his back. Some days the
children might be asked to dress as Pans and nymphs, then flit
about the royal garden, offering themselves to one another and to
the emperor's invited guests.

Tonight the orgiasts remain inside this sprawling palace with its marble floors, erotic statues, works of art, and stunning views of the Mediterranean Sea far below. In case the performances of the young girls and boys ordered to submit to the jaded, pockmarked emperor lack imagination, explicit sex manuals from Egypt are on hand for instruction.

The young performers can't help but sneak a glance at Tiberius. If all goes well, he will join in, perhaps selecting one of the teen-aged boys or girls for himself. But if they fail, and if Tiberius doesn't find their contortions stimulating, the emperor will not simply leave the room. He will do something far worse. There is a good chance he will hurl their bodies off "Tiberius's Leap," the thousand-foot cliff alongside the palace. From that height, it doesn't matter if a person lands in the sea or on the rocks jutting out into the Gulf of Naples. There is no surviving the fall.

Which is just as Tiberius designed it. Perversely, just as he enjoys sex and watching others have sex, he also finds delight in watching his victims scream for their lives.

The truth is, almost all of tonight's players will suffer the terrifying fate of being thrown off the cliff. Tiberius cannot abide the thought of rumors about his debauchery making their way back to Rome. The best way to keep these children silent is to kill them after he uses them.

But the young players don't know this. They actually believe they will one day make it out of Villa Jovis alive and return home to their villages. So they perform as if their lives depend upon it, succumbing to any whim or want of the vile Tiberius.

Meanwhile, the aging emperor—a man who once knew true love and happiness—reclines on a pile of pillows, a cup of wine always within reach, his eyes glazed and his skin mottled from eczema and boils. Tiberius is a man without a conscience.

✝✝✝

It could have been the deaths of his two sons that brought Tiberius to Capri. Or perhaps it was the unbearable presence of his mother, the scheming Livia, widow of the great Caesar Augustus. Maybe it was the dreadful crowds of petitioners who besieged him each day in Rome, reeking of desperation as they begged for this favor or that. It might have been the fear of assassination, because court intrigue in the form of angry lieutenants, jilted spouses, and distant nephews with their sights set on his throne seemed to grow more pervasive by the day.

Or it might have been something as simple as Tiberius being tired of people whispering that he drinks too much. He has long worn the mantle that comes with being born into a lifetime of power, with its expectations and judgments. Whatever the reason, he has escaped to a hilltop castle in beautiful Capri, over the sparkling waters of the Mediterranean, an otherworldly turquoise, where he can eat what he wants, sleep with whom he desires, drink as much as he wants, and rule Rome from a distance.

So that he knows what fates the gods will bring, Tiberius has brought along the one man he trusts above all others: Thrasyllus, the royal astrologer. In addition to the baths, cisterns, great hall, private suites, and lighthouse Tiberius built to make life on Capri as comfortable as possible, he also constructed the special observatory that will allow Thrasyllus to make sense of the stars each night.

Of course, should Thrasyllus fail Tiberius, whether through bad information or willful manipulation, his long fall into the sea will be no different from that of the young sex slaves.

For Tiberius learned long ago that no one can be trusted. He

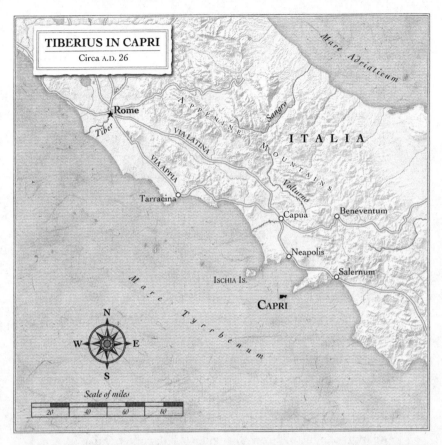

TIBERIUS IN CAPRI
Circa A.D. 26

Mare Adriaticum

Rome

Tiber

ITALIA

APPENNINE

Sangro

VIA LATINA

MOUNTAINS

VIA APPIA

Volturno

Tarracina

Capua

Beneventum

Neapolis

Salernum

ISCHIA IS.

CAPRI

Mare Tyrrhenum

N
W E
S

Scale of miles

20   40   60   80

ISCHIA IS.

MAINLAND ITALIA

VILLA
JOVIS

"TIBERIUS'S
LEAP"

ISLAND OF CAPRI

Mare Tyrrhenum

Map by Gene Thorp

was born two years after the death of Julius Caesar, whose name has been incorporated into his own. When his mother divorced his natural father to marry the man who would one day be known as Augustus, the three-year-old Tiberius actually benefited from the betrayal. The Roman emperor soon adopted him as his own son, and Tiberius rode through the streets of Rome in Augustus's chariot during the public celebration marking the crucial victory over Marc Antony and Cleopatra.

The boy grew up privileged, trained in the classical manner, excelling in oratory and rhetoric. By age twenty, he was commanding armies. A brilliant tactician and fearless fighter, Tiberius was known for his successes on the battlefield—but also for his dark and gloomy behavior and the severe acne covering his face. Upon his return to Rome, he found love and married a young woman of noble birth named Vipsania. They had a child, Drusus Julius Caesar, after which Vipsania was soon pregnant with a second baby. But Augustus cruelly intervened. In an act that would dramatically transform Tiberius, the self-proclaimed son of god ordered Tiberius to divorce Vipsania after eight years of marriage and wed Augustus's recently widowed daughter, Julia. When Tiberius argued against the divorce, he was ordered to be compliant or suffer harsh punishment. Devastated, Vipsania suffered a miscarriage.

Tiberius was distraught but obeyed the emperor. A short time later he accidentally ran into his beloved Vipsania on the streets of Rome and broke down, making a very public display by sobbing and begging for forgiveness. When news of this behavior reached Augustus, he demanded that Tiberius never again speak with Vipsania.

And so died the human part of Tiberius. At that moment, his

Emperor Tiberius

life of cruelty, depravity, and drunkenness began. The man who once studied rhetoric and who loved the mother of his child was emotionally destroyed. Never again would he act in a humane manner. But his behavior didn't bother his new wife, Julia, who herself embraced debauchery. She had a fondness for dwarves, and when Tiberius once again marched off to war—this time in Gaul—she kept such a man nearby at all times for her immediate pleasure. Julia was a great beauty, which made it easier for her to indulge her base instincts. She attended orgies, openly prostituted herself, and publicly flaunted her disregard for Tiberius. Most grievous of all, when Tiberius returned from Gaul, he found that she had turned their home into a brothel.

Even Augustus was appalled. He granted Tiberius a divorce. But the man who would one day be emperor would never marry again.

Deeply shamed, Tiberius, approaching forty years old, exiled himself to the Greek island of Rhodes. There he began to drink in ever-larger quantities and established a pattern of cruel behavior that he would embrace to the day he died. He routinely committed murder, even ordering the decapitation of a man whose only crime was making a poor mathematical calculation.

In the final years of his reign, Augustus recalled Tiberius from Rhodes, grooming him to become emperor. There was no other suitable prospect. Tiberius accepted the challenge in willing and ruthless fashion. After Augustus died in A.D. 14, Tiberius ordered the execution of any would-be pretender. For twelve long years, Tiberius did battle with the Senate and oversaw the empire in a proficient, workmanlike manner. But upon the sudden and unexplained deaths of his adopted son Germanicus* and natural-

---

*Germanicus died of a mysterious illness. He was a popular general, particularly among the legions. He was responsible for avenging the defeat at the Battle of Teutoburg Forest and for retrieving the fallen eagle standards of legions XVII, XVIII, and XIX. Many thought he would attempt to claim the throne upon the death of Augustus, but he deferred to Tiberius. There were whispers that Tiberius had him killed because he was too great a threat to the eventual ascension of Drusus to the throne. This rumor gained more credibility when Gnaeus Calpurnius Piso, the governor of Syria who was to go on trial for Germanicus's death, committed suicide rather than testify. And while Germanicus would never serve as emperor, his son Caligula would succeed Tiberius on the throne and become infamous for a level of debauchery transcending even that of Tiberius.

born son Drusus,* ages thirty-three and thirty-four, respectively, Tiberius could take no more.

Fed up with the intrigues of Rome, Tiberius ordered that renovations and enhancements be made to Augustus's villas on the island of Capri. This included the construction of "lechery nooks" and the special pools in which he now swims naked with young boys. His servants are authorized to kidnap children, and Tiberius even employs a man known as "Master of the Imperial Pleasures," whose sole job is providing the emperor with new bodies.

In the midst of all this, Tiberius continues to hold control of the vast Roman Empire. From high on a mountain, safe from assassination plots, and surrounded only by those he can murder on a whim, Tiberius Julius Caesar Augustus issues the moral and legal decrees that will determine the fate of millions. Those mandates especially affect Roman administrators.

Pontius Pilate, newly installed as Roman governor of Judea, knows that his personal and professional future depends on making the degenerate Tiberius happy. Despite his own pagan lifestyle,

---

*Drusus was poisoned by his wife, Livilla, and her lover, Lucius Aelius Sejanus. This was done so skillfully that it would be eight years before their plot was uncovered. When it was, Livilla was forced to commit the slow death of suicide by starvation. Sejanus's death was far more gruesome. He had assumed great power in Rome, thanks to Tiberius's self-imposed exile to Capri. On October 18 of A.D. 31, upon learning that Sejanus had murdered Drusus by poisoning his wine, Tiberius ordered his arrest. Sejanus was strangled that night in Rome and his body was thrown to a crowd of onlookers, who tore his corpse to pieces. After this, they conducted a manhunt for all his friends and relatives and killed them, too. Sejanus's son and daughter were arrested in December of that year and killed by strangulation. When Tiberius was informed that the girl was a virgin, and thus not able under the law to be killed for a capital offense, he ordered the executioner to place the rope around her neck, rape young Junilla, and then, only after the young girl had been deflowered, pull the rope tight.

Tiberius admires the Jews' religious ways. He considers the Jews the most devout subjects in the empire when it comes to keeping the Sabbath holy. Tiberius sends an order to Pontius Pilate on how to treat the Jewish population: "Change nothing already sanctioned by custom, but to regard as a sacred trust both the Jews themselves, and their laws, which are conducive to public order."

So it is that Pontius Pilate honors that "sacred trust" by strengthening his bond with the high priest Caiaphas, the figurehead of the Jewish faith and the most powerful man in Jerusalem. According to Tiberius's orders, Pilate is not to meddle in matters of Jewish law.

It is an order that Pilate will remember all too well.

†††

Herod Antipas, now approaching fifty, understands that allegiance to Tiberius is vital. He has spent a great deal of time in Rome, educating himself in Roman ways and customs and absorbing Romans' fondness for literature, poetry, and music. The Jew Antipas even dresses like Roman aristocracy, wearing the semicircular piece of cloth known as a toga rather than the simple robes of the Jewish people.

During his time in Rome, Antipas learned to douse his food with fermented fish sauce, a pickled condiment favored by Romans with a strong taste that masked spoilage from lack of refrigeration. He attended chariot races at the Circus Maximus. He might even have taken a slave for a lover. In Rome, prostitution is legal and even taxed. The only shame was for a male citizen of Rome to be the submissive partner in a homosexual relationship, which was why Julius Caesar's long-rumored affair with the king of Bithynia was never forgotten by his enemies.

Antipas has great power over the Jewish peasants, but he must do as Rome tells him to do. He can never comment negatively on anything Tiberius does—even though the Jews are every day becoming more disenchanted with Roman rule. His fear of Tiberius also prevents Antipas from making any reforms that would help the Jewish people. Caught in the middle, Antipas keeps his mouth shut and accumulates as much wealth as he can.

†††

The Roman Empire may be vast, but all those roads built by the legions, and all those shipping lanes plied daily between Rome and her many outposts, mean that rumors travel fast. Household servants gossip, and word has spread about Tiberius's aberrant and violent behavior. He murders at will, killing entire families for any perceived slight. He defiles even the youngest child. He retaliates against any woman who will not have him—even a woman of noble birth and marriage—by letting his servants violate her.

But Antipas is not Tiberius. The ruler of Galilee has many faults, among them vanity and personal weakness, but his behavior is nothing like that of the emperor of Rome. Yet the moral depravity of Tiberius cannot help but seep into the fiber of even the most far-flung province, causing an erosion of discipline and justice. While the emperor will never make his way to Judea and never come face-to-face with Jesus of Nazareth or with the Passover pilgrims who flock to Jerusalem each year, every decision ordered by the new Roman governor Pontius Pilate is made to gain Tiberius's approval. It is the same with Antipas, as evidenced by his naming his dazzling new city on the Sea of Galilee after the all-powerful emperor.

Such is life in the Roman Empire, which has begun its slow

decline into ruin. There is little justice or nobility among the ruling class. And so the Jewish peasants look for a savior, a man promised to them by the prophets. For a time, some thought the savior might be John the Baptist. But he languishes in prison.

Now there is cautious conversation about a new man, one far more powerful than John. Jesus of Nazareth is about to arrive.

CHAPTER EIGHT

JERUSALEM
APRIL, A.D. 27
DAY

J ESUS CLENCHES A COILED WHIP IN HIS FIST AS HE MAKES HIS way up the steps to the Temple courts. Passover pilgrims surround him. Hundreds of thousands of Jewish believers have once again traveled a great distance—from Galilee, Syria, Egypt, and even Rome—to celebrate the climax to the Jewish year. Not that they have a choice: failure to visit the Temple during Passover is one of thirty-six transgressions that will result in the holy punishment of *karet*, being spiritually "cut off" from God. Those who transgress will suffer a premature death or other punishment known only to the deity.* So, as he has done every spring since childhood, Jesus of Nazareth has made the trek to Jerusalem.

---

*Scholars debate the exact nature of *karet*. Josephus wrote that it was a physical punishment, perpetrated by man. Some thought it meant dying well before one's time, likely between the ages of fifty and sixty, "by the hand of heaven." There is, however, a provision for repentance, which annuls the *karet*.

The spiritual emotion that flows through the city is wondrous, as these many Jews come together to openly celebrate their faith and sing praises to God. Agents of the Temple have repaired the dirt roads coming into town to make them smooth after the hard winter rains. Grave sites are clearly marked, so that no pilgrim will inadvertently suffer impurity by touching one. Special wells are dug so that every man and woman can immerse him- or herself in the ritual bath, in order to be pure upon entering the Holy City. *Mikvot* (purification pools) are carved into the bedrock and lined in plaster, into which an observant pilgrim steps down for cleansing.

Jesus himself submerges himself in a *mikvah* as a last stop before Jerusalem. Inside the city walls, he sees the hundreds of temporary clay ovens that have been constructed in order that each pilgrim will have a place to roast his Passover sacrifice before sitting down to the evening Seder feast. He hears the bleat of sheep as shepherds and their flocks clog the narrow streets, just down from the hills after lambing season. And Jesus can well imagine the peal of the silver trumpets and the harmonious voices of the Levite choir that will echo in the inner courts of the Temple just moments before an innocent lamb is slaughtered for the Passover sacrifice. A priest will catch its blood in a golden bowl, then sprinkle it on the altar as the lamb is hung on a hook and skinned. The Hallel* prayers of thanksgiving will

---

*A recitation of the six Psalms, 113–18. While the complete verses are too lengthy to be included in this brief space, their themes, in order, are: a celebration of God's majesty and mercy; a reminder that Judea is God's sanctuary; praise to the Lord as the one true God; thanks to God for deliverance from death; a reminder of God's enduring faithfulness; and a thanksgiving for deliverance from enemies. The term *psalm* is Greek. The traditional Hebrew words are *tehillim* ("praises") or *tephillot* ("prayers"). There are 150 Psalms in all, of which Psalm 117 is the shortest, at just three sentences.

soon follow, and the Temple courts will echo with songs of hallelujah.

This is Passover in Jerusalem. It has been this way since the rebuilding of the Temple. Each Passover is unique in its glory and personal stories, but the rituals remain the same.

Now, as he steps into the Court of the Gentiles, Jesus is about to undertake a bold and outrageous moment of revolution.

For this Passover will not be like those that have come before. It will be remembered throughout history for words of anger. Unfurling his whip, Jesus prepares to launch his ministry.

✝✝✝

The partially enclosed Temple courts reek of blood and live-stock. Tables piled with coins line one wall, in the shade of the Temple awnings, lorded over by scheming men known as *shul-hanim*, "money changers." In long lines, out-of-towners await their chance to exchange their meager wealth in the form of coins minted by agents of Rome. The Roman coins are adorned with images of living things such as gods or with portraits of the emperor. But this coinage must be converted into shekels,* the standard currency of Jerusalem. In keeping with the Jewish law forbidding graven images, these special coins are decorated with images of plants and other nonhuman likenesses. Also

---

*To this day, the Israeli unit of currency is known as the shekel. It was thought to be more metallically pure than the common currency in the Roman Empire, the denarius. One denarius was worth between ten and sixteen *assarions* ("asses"), the smallest coin in regular circulation at that time. A denarius was usually silver and stamped with the image of the reigning emperor. The rate of exchange for denarii into shekels was typically four to one.

known as the "Temple tax coin," the shekel is disparaged by many pilgrims because it is the only form of money acceptable for paying the annual tax or for purchasing animals for ritual slaughter.

The money changers demand unfair exchange rates for the privilege of turning local money into shekels. The Temple high priests also profit from this scam. Within the Temple's inner courts are massive vaults filled with shekels and the foreign coins exchanged each year by pilgrims. When the Temple loans that money—as it so often does, to peasants who need help paying their taxes—the interest rates are exorbitant. Ledger sheets within the Temple's grand vaults keep tally of all debts, and those who cannot repay suffer severe indignities: the loss of a home, loss of land and livestock, and eventually life as a debt slave or membership in the "unclean" class. The slums of lower Jerusalem are packed with families who were driven from their land because they could not repay money they borrowed from the Temple.

So while Passover might be a holiday about faith and piety, it is also about money. As many as four million Jews make their way to Jerusalem each year. This means more income for the local shop owners and innkeepers, but the Temple priests and their Roman masters get most of the profit through taxation and money changing. Even more money is made when the poor must buy a lamb or dove for the mandatory Passover sacrifice. If a priest should inspect the animal or bird and find even a single blemish, the sacrifice will be deemed unclean and the peasant will be forced to buy another. It is no wonder that the people quietly seethe when doing business with the Temple priests. Many wish they could burn the ledger books and loot the Temple vaults.

And in four decades, the sons and daughters of Israel will do just that.

But that event is far away during this Passover week. Today Jesus climbs to the Court of the Gentiles and makes his way into the broad open-air plaza. Since his baptism and time spent fasting in the desert, his ministry has been a quiet one. Jesus of Nazareth has no army. He has no wealth. He has no sword. He has no headquarters and none of the infrastructure needed to support a movement. Nothing in his behavior so far has been rebellious or confrontational. His greatest social outing since being baptized by John has been attending a wedding in the Galilean village of Cana with his mother. If Jesus means to start a revolution by revealing himself as God, the planning is taking place only within his head. He has not preached a single message before a crowd. He has not challenged Rome or the Temple's high priests—nor does he seem interested in doing so.

But now, as Jesus walks past the tables piled high with coins and sees the people of Galilee standing helpless before these greedy money changers and the haughty high priests overseeing them, something in him snaps. This Passover ritual of money changing has not altered one bit since he was a child, but on this day Jesus feels empowered to do something about this obvious wrong.

The Nazarene is not normally prone to anger, and certainly not rage. In fact, Jesus usually exudes a powerful serenity. So when he boldly storms toward the money changers' tables, those who know him become alarmed. There is a power to Jesus's gait and a steely determination to his gaze.

The tables are made of wood. Their surfaces are scarred and dented from the thousands of coins that have been pushed back and forth across them. The coins are uneven in size and shape, so they do not stack well. Instead, the money changers sit before enormous piles of currency. The money gleams in the strong Jerusalem sun.

Heavy as the tables might be, their weight does not bother Jesus—not after twenty years of hauling lumber and stone alongside his father. He places two hands beneath the nearest table and flips it over. A small fortune in coins flies in every direction. And even as the stunned *shulhanim* cry out in a rage, and coins cascade down onto the stone courtyard, Jesus is already at the next table, and then on to the next.

Nobody has ever seen anything like this. Jesus's behavior is an act of madness and the sort of thing that could get a man killed. As the crowd gasps in shock, Jesus brandishes the whip he has made from cords of rope. He moves from the money changers' tables to where goats and sheep are being sold. He cracks his whip, sending the animals running. He marches over to the cages of doves, also being sold for slaughter, and opens the doors to set them free.

And nobody tries to stop him.

Jesus is such a force that not even the strongest man dares step in his path. Men, women, and children scatter before Jesus and his whip. "Get out of here," he screams to the money changers and the men selling livestock. "How dare you turn my Father's house into a market!"

These men who enjoyed absolute power over the pilgrims just moments ago now cower, terrified that Jesus will turn his whip on them. The money changers see their fortunes littering the ground but make no move to pick the coins up. Livestock run loose across the Court of the Gentiles—cows, goats, and sheep galloping aimlessly through the throngs, their rendezvous with the slaughtering knife temporarily put on hold.

The Temple courts are so vast that Jesus's outburst goes unheard by the priests and worshippers within the Temple itself. And many believers who have not seen him scatter the animals are now surprised by the sight of these small herds in their midst. But those poor and oppressed who have witnessed Jesus's act of defiance know they have seen something very special. They stand rooted to the ground, eagerly watching this powerful and unexpected moment of theater.

Suddenly, a circle of pilgrims and Temple officials forms a ring around Jesus, who holds his whip firmly in one hand, as if daring them to challenge him. "What miracles can you show us to prove your authority to do all this?" demands a money changer. Despite the commotion, soldiers do not run in to quell the disturbance. Better to let this madman explain himself.

"Destroy this Temple," Jesus vows, "and I will raise it up in three days."

Now they know he's insane. "It has taken forty-six years to build this Temple and you are going to raise it in three days?" scoffs a money changer. Among the onlookers is Nicodemus, a devout Pharisee and a member of the Jewish ruling council, who watches Jesus with interest and waits for his answer to that question.

But Jesus says nothing. He knows his words will not change hearts and minds in the Temple.

No one blocks Jesus's path as he leaves the Court of the Gentiles and walks toward the Temple itself. Behind him comes the clink of silver and bronze as the money changers scurry to sweep up every last coin. The men selling livestock race to rein in their beasts. It is the pilgrims who continue to marvel at what they have just witnessed. Many of them have long dreamed of committing such a bold act of social unrest. From his Galilean accent and simple robes to his workingman's physique, it is clear that Jesus is one of them. For some, this man is a hero. And his actions will be discussed everywhere.*

✝✝✝

Night in Jerusalem is a time of quiet celebration, as pilgrims pack into local courtyards and inns to bed down. It is customary to open one's home for the visitors, and to do so with a glad heart. But there is only so much room for all these hundreds of thousands of travelers, so campfires dot the steep hillsides and valleys outside the city walls. From the thick groves of trees on the Mount of Olives, across the Kidron Valley, and down toward the old city of David, which lies just south of the Temple, families and friends spread out their blankets and bedrolls to spend the night under the stars.

Among them is Jesus. He has returned to the Temple time and again during his Passover stay, teaching from that Temple cloister known as Solomon's Porch. This is his favorite place in the Temple, and even when he is not listening to the scholars or joining in to offer his own teachings about the kingdom of God, he often lingers in that area, walking and soaking in the atmosphere. Wherever he goes, crowds now flock to him, asking questions about God's kingdom and listening reverently to his answers.

---

*Before being written down, the Gospels were oral histories. This might explain some discrepancies among them. The story of Jesus and the money changers is placed at the beginning of Jesus's ministry in John (2:14–22), while Matthew (21:12–17), Mark (11:15), and Luke (19:45) all place it at the end. This has led some to speculate that Jesus performed this cleansing twice, as specific details of the various Gospel accounts differ.

Jesus has made a deep impression in a short amount of time. His dramatic assault against the money changers seems to have paid off.

The Nazarene is comfortable in public. He enjoys people and speaks eloquently, often using stories to illuminate his teachings. Sharing his message is a great liberation after so many years of self-imposed silence, and his natural charisma and gentleness only make his listeners long for more. But it is no surprise, particularly given his outrageous behavior toward the money changers, that Temple officials have begun to watch him closely. The Pharisees, those men who obsess about all aspects of Jewish law, are paying particular attention. They are skeptical about Jesus and would like specific information before passing religious judgment on him.

Now, under cover of darkness, the Pharisee Nicodemus, who enjoys a powerful role as a member of the Jewish ruling council, approaches the Nazarene. He has chosen nighttime because it would be awkward for him to say what is on his mind in the midday Temple courts, where even the lowliest peasant could hear his words. Nicodemus also knows that this quiet hour means that he can have an uninterrupted discussion with Jesus.

"Rabbi," Nicodemus begins deferentially, stepping into the light cast by the flames. If Jesus is surprised to see such an exalted Pharisee stepping from the darkness, he does not let on. "We know you are a teacher who has come from God," Nicodemus continues, speaking for his fellow Pharisees.

"I tell you the truth, no one can see the kingdom of God unless he is born from above," Jesus replies, expressing the predominant theology of his teaching. He has been telling all who will listen that a person must be spiritually reborn if he is to be judged kindly by God.

This is a new concept to the Pharisees. "How can this be?" Nicodemus asks in astonishment. "How can someone be born when he is old? Surely he cannot enter a second time into the mother's womb?"

"Flesh gives birth to flesh," Jesus replies. "Spirit gives birth to spirit. You should not be surprised at my saying you must be born again."

Nicodemus is thoroughly confused. "How can this be?" he asks again.

"You are Israel's teacher, and do you not understand these things?" Jesus asks, assuming the debater's rhetoric he so often uses when speaking with other teachers in the Temple. If he is uncomfortable scolding one of the most powerful religious leaders in Jerusalem, it does not show. "For God so loved the world that he gave his one and only son, that whoever believes in him shall not perish but have eternal life. For God did not send his son into the world to condemn the world, but to save the world through him."

Nicodemus is intrigued but frustrated. He is a man dedicated to stated religious law. Now Jesus is telling him that God is about love, not rules. And that the Son of God has come to save the world, even insinuating that this is *his* true identity. Then the Nazarene adds talk about being reborn, as if such a thing were humanly possible. Rather than answering Nicodemus's questions, Jesus is raising even more.

"Whoever lives by the truth comes into the light," Jesus concludes, "so that it may be seen plainly that what he has done has been done through God."

Nicodemus has heard Jesus teaching in the Temple courts, so he knows that the Nazarene likes to speak in allusions and parables. It's not clear that the reference to stepping into the light has anything to do with his own appearance by the fire tonight, but like the other statements it is giving him a great deal to think about.

As he walks alone back up the hill and into Jerusalem, Nicodemus finds himself fascinated by Jesus and his teachings—impressed enough that he is destined to remember him for as long as he lives.*

✝✝✝

The men of Nazareth pray the Shema, their voices blending together as one: "Hear, O Israel: Jehovah our God is one Jehovah; and thou shalt love Jehovah your God with all your heart and all your soul and all your might."

It is the Sabbath day, and the Shema marks the beginning of the Sabbath worship. Jesus is home from Jerusalem and now sits with his head uncovered in the same Nazareth synagogue where he has worshipped his whole life. The room is small and square, with wooden benches pressed against each wall. The Temple in Jerusalem, with its priests and vaults and animal sacrifices, is the center of Jewish life. The local synagogue, however, is the lifeblood of the faith, an intimate place where believers worship and teach, taking turns reading from the parchment scrolls on which the Scriptures are written. Indeed, the synagogue is so important

---

*Not much is known about Nicodemus, other than that he was a very wealthy Pharisee and a member of the Sanhedrin. The historian Josephus mentions a Nicodemus ben Gurion, who counseled against the Jewish rebellion against Rome in the first century A.D. This is very possibly the same man, for Nicodemus was not a common name. The Talmud mentions a man named Nakdimon ben Gurion, who is thought to be the same man ("Nicodemus" being a Greek version of the name). Nakdimon originally came from Galilee, which might explain his affinity for Jesus. He is said to have lost his fortune late in life and was eventually martyred.

to the Jewish faith that there are more than four hundred synagogues in Jerusalem, allowing believers to gather in a less formal setting than the Temple itself. In the synagogue, there are no high priests or clergy, no standard liturgy, and anyone is allowed to play the part of rabbi, or "teacher." Also, there is no money on the tables.

Jesus joins in as the men of Nazareth lift their voices in song, chanting the words of the Psalms. He has known all these men since he was a child, just as they know him and his family.

But Jesus has changed. No longer content to be a mere builder, he has spent the months since returning from Jerusalem traveling through Galilee, teaching in synagogues. He has become popular, praised everywhere he goes for the depth and insights of his teaching. There are rumors that he commits the "sin" of speaking to Samaritans. Even more confusingly, no one can explain how this man with no medical knowledge healed a dying child in the fishing village of Capernaum. So now the sight of Jesus sitting in the midst of this Nazareth congregation has become an event, and there is anticipation as he stands to read from the scrolls.

An attendant hands Jesus the words of the prophet Isaiah. "The Spirit of the Lord is on me," the Nazarene reads in Hebrew, "because he has anointed me to preach good news to the poor. He has sent me to proclaim freedom for the prisoners and recovery for the sight of the blind, to release the oppressed, to proclaim the year of the Lord's favor."

Jesus remains standing, translating the words he has just read into Aramaic, for the benefit of those not fluent in Hebrew. It is customary to stand while reading and sit while teaching. So now he sits down again and presses his back against the wall, aware that all eyes are upon him. "Today this Scripture was fulfilled in your hearing," Jesus calmly informs them.

The crowd is shocked. This reading is a pivotal moment. The passage that Jesus reads refers to an anointed deliverer, a man both prophetic and messianic. He will set them free. Jesus is saying that it refers to him, right now.

"Isn't this Joseph's son?" they ask rhetorically. For while they know the answer, the words are a reminder that Jesus should remember his place: his family is not the wealthiest in town; nor is he the smartest among them. He is the son of Joseph, and nothing more. In their eyes, Jesus exalting himself as the man sent by God to preach the good news is offensive. Even Jesus's family members do not believe he is such a man.[*]

But Jesus doesn't back down. He has been expecting this response. "I tell you the truth," he predicts. "No prophet is accepted in his town." He then makes a lengthy speech suggesting his belief that the words he has just read refer specifically to him. Jesus then interjects two extremely volatile references to Elijah and Elisha, two prophets who were rejected by the nation of Israel.[†] The audience knows its history and immediately gets the message. In essence, Jesus tells these men he has long known not only that he is the Son of God but that their rejection of this claim will cause God to turn his back on them. Jesus uses words such as *famine*, *widows*, and *leprosy* in a way that enrages the entire synagogue.

Disregarding that they are in a house of worship, some men leap to their feet and prepare to attack Jesus. Moving quickly, he races out the door. But they follow him. Working together, the men who, just moments ago, were praying, now cut off any route of escape. Jesus is forced to the edge of town, where a tall cliff provides a commanding view of Galilee.

---

[*]John 7:5: "For even his own brothers did not believe in him."

[†]For Elijah see 1 Kings 17–18 and for Elisha see 2 Kings 5.

The men's intention is to hurl Jesus to his death. And it appears that might happen, for Jesus seems powerless. But at the last minute he turns to face his detractors. Drawing himself up to his full height, Jesus squares his shoulders and holds his ground. He is not a menacing individual, but he has a commanding presence and displays an utter lack of fear. The words he says next will never be written down, nor will the insults these men continue to hurl at him ever be chronicled. In the end, the mob parts and Jesus walks away unscathed.

And he keeps walking.*

✝✝✝

Jesus has issued three pronouncements about his identity: one to the public in Jerusalem, one to Nicodemus the Pharisee, and the third in the intimate setting of his own town synagogue, to the people he knows best of all. Three times he has declared himself to be the Son of God, a blasphemous statement that could get him killed. It is a statement that cannot be retracted, just as he can never return to the humble and quiet life he knew growing up. There is no turning back. Nazareth is no longer his home, and he is no longer a carpenter.

Jesus will never write a book, compose a song, or put paint on canvas. But two thousand years from now, after his message has spread to billions of people, more books will be written about his life, more songs sung in his honor, and more works of art created in his name than for any other man in the history of the world.

But now the Nazarene is completely alone, cut off from the life he once knew, destined to wander through Galilee preaching words of hope and love.

---

*The confrontation in Nazareth comes from Luke 4:30.

Those words will eventually rally billions of human beings to his spiritual cause. But they will not convert the powerful men who currently hold the life of Jesus in their hands.

To them, the Nazarene is a marked man.

CHAPTER NINE

CAPERNAUM, GALILEE

SUMMER, A.D. 27

AFTERNOON

THE LOCAL FISHING FLEET HAS JUST RETURNED FROM A LONG night and day on the water, and great crowds fill the markets along Capernaum's waterfront promenade. Paved with black volcanic basalt, just like the eight-foot seawall on which it rests, the walkway is a center of activity: fishermen sorting their catch into clean and unclean before making the official count for the taxman;* large freshwater holding tanks filled with live fish; Matthew, the local tax collector, sizing up the day's haul at the marine toll station; and everywhere, customers eager to purchase

---

*According to Jewish law, as set forth in Leviticus 11:9–12, fish with scales and fins are considered clean and are acceptable for eating. Eels and catfish, on the other hand, are considered unclean.

the freshest catch for their evening dinner. What doesn't get sold this day will be shipped to Magdala for drying and salting, whereupon it will be packed tightly into baskets and exported throughout the Roman Empire.

For more than two centuries, the business of fishing has defined the bustling town of Capernaum on the Sea of Galilee, as boats and nets line every inch of the hundred feet between the stone piers and the breakwater. Some are ferries, designed to carry passengers quickly and easily down to Magdala or across the eight miles of sea to Gergesa. But most boats are for fishing. Of the more than one dozen major fishing villages on the shores of Lake of Gennesaret, as the freshwater sea is also known, none is busier than Capernaum—not even Antipas's brand-new creation, Tiberias city. A detachment of one hundred Roman soldiers has even been posted here, to ensure that all taxes are collected according to the law.

So it would seem that Jesus has come to the right place if he is looking for an audience—which, indeed, he is. The problem, however, is that Capernaum is actually too busy. No one will be able to hear him over the clink of sinker leads dropping onto stone and the haggling between shopkeepers and customers. The fishermen themselves are exhausted from hours of throwing out their flax fishing nets and hauling them hand over hand back into their boats, and they are in no mood to listen to a religious sermon.

Jesus is undeterred. He stops to look up and down the long, fingerlike row of piers, carefully studying the various fishing boats. He is looking for one boat and one man in particular.

Each boat features a step mast for sailing and oars for rowing when the wind is calm. The boats are constructed of wood and made stronger by the mortise-and-tenon joints* used in place of nails and the thick handcrafted ribs that run along the interior, just below the deck. The average boat size is thirty feet long, eight feet wide, and four feet high. The bow comes to a point, while the stern is rounded. Local shipwrights use cedar for the hull, oak for the frame, and Aleppo pine, hawthorn, willow, and redbud where needed. These are sturdy craft, designed to withstand the temperamental local winds that can turn the Sea of Galilee from dead calm into tempest in a matter of moments.

The fishermen themselves are even sturdier, with thick hands and forearms heavily callused from a lifetime of working the nets. The sun has made their faces leathery and deeply tanned. It is a tan that extends over the entire body, for those who fish with cast nets (as opposed to the larger dragnets or multilayer trammel nets) must often jump into the water to retrieve their catch, and so prefer to work naked.

Jesus narrows his search to two empty boats. He has met the owners before and now sees them washing and stretching their twenty-foot-wide cast nets in preparation for the next voyage. The two men take care to eliminate knots and tangles, while also replacing any sinker weights that have fallen off. Though he knows next to nothing about fishing, Jesus walks down the pier with confidence and steps into one of the empty craft. No one stops him.

As he gazes back toward the shoreline, Jesus can see the raised central roof of the town synagogue a block from the water. It stands taller than the homes and waterfront administrative offices,

---

*This method of crafting wood into slots and grooves to hold two pieces together was also commonly used to secure the two parts of the crucifix.

reminding him that Capernaum's citizens worship God and hold a teacher like him in great reverence.

A fisherman in his early twenties walks to the boat. Simon, as he is known, is a simple, uneducated, impulsive man. He knows Jesus from their previous meeting during the summer, as he and some others were fishing for the tropical musht fish in the warm mineral springs down the coast, near Tabgha. At the time, Jesus had called upon Simon and his brother Andrew to join him as he preached his message throughout Galilee and to save souls by becoming "fishers of men." While Simon had initially accepted that call to evangelism, he also has a wife and mother-in-law to care for. The task of being one of Jesus's disciples and spreading the word about his message is difficult to balance with his need to make a living. His commitment to Jesus has flagged.

But now Jesus is back, standing before him in his boat.

Simon doesn't tell him to leave. He just asks Jesus what he wants. Jesus tells Simon to push the boat away from the dock and drop anchor a little way offshore. The spoken word carries easily across the lake's surface, and Jesus knows he will be heard by one and all if he teaches from a place upon the water.

Simon is exhausted and dejected. He has been up for twenty-four hours straight, sailing his small boat out onto the lake and dropping his nets again and again. His back aches from his leaning over the side to pull those nets in. He has been in and out of the inland sea countless times, without success. He needs a drink of water and a meal. He needs a soft bed. But most of all, he needs to pay his taxes, and last night did nothing to help this, for he did not catch a single fish.

Perhaps Simon has nothing else to do at this moment, or perhaps he can't face the thought of returning home to his wife and mother-in-law empty-handed. Perhaps he hopes the teacher will say a few words that will lighten his burden. Or maybe he just feels guilty for reneging on his original commitment. Whatever the reason, Simon undoes the knot connecting his boat to its anchorage, pulls the rope toward himself, and pushes away from the pier.

Jesus has been standing this whole while. But when Simon's boat floats just far enough from the shore that Jesus can be clearly heard by one and all, he takes a seat, adopting the traditional pose for teaching.

Thanks to Simon and his boat, Jesus is soon regaling the entire waterfront at Capernaum with his insightful words. As always, people are overcome by his charisma. One by one, they stop what they are doing to listen.

"Put out into deep water," Jesus tells the weary fisherman when he is finished speaking, "and let down your nets for a catch."

"Master," Simon responds, "we've worked hard all night and haven't caught anything."

Sending his boat out into the deep water is the last thing Simon wants to do, yet he also feels powerless to say no.

So with Jesus sitting calmly amidships, Simon hoists the small sail and aims his boat for the deepest waters of the Sea of Galilee.

†††

A short time later, Jesus and Simon are catching so many fish that the nets start to break. The sheer volume of carp, sardines, and musht threatens to capsize Simon's small craft, and he is forced to signal to James and John, the partners in his fishing cooperative, to come help.

Rather than rejoice, Simon is terrified. From the moment

Jesus first stepped into his boat, something deeply spiritual about his presence made Simon uncomfortable. He feels unholy in comparison, even more so after hearing Jesus's teachings about repentance and the need to be cleansed of all sins. Simon wants this man out of his life immediately. He throws himself onto his knees atop a pile of writhing fish and begs Jesus to leave him alone. "Go away from me, Lord. I am a sinful man."

"Don't be afraid," Jesus tells Simon. "From this day on, you will catch men."

✝✝✝

And so it is that Simon—whom Jesus renames Peter, meaning "rock"—becomes Jesus's first disciple. Peter cannot explain why Jesus has selected him—not the local rabbi, not the most pious teachers in Capernaum, not even some of the more devout fishermen—for this honor. Other disciples soon join him, including Matthew, Capernaum's despised local taxman, who oversees all collections for Herod Antipas.

By early in the year 28, Jesus has selected twelve men to follow him and learn his teachings as disciples, so that they may one day go out alone into the world and preach his message.

Four of the apostles—Peter, Andrew, James, and John—are fishermen. Jesus has specifically singled out men from this calling because their job requires them to be conversant in Aramaic, Hebrew, Greek, and a little Latin, which will allow them to speak with a wider group of potential followers.

All of the children are from Galilee, except one. He is from a town called Carioth—or "Iscariot," as it will one day be translated into the Greek of the Gospels. His name is Judas. He speaks with the polished accent of Judea's southern region and is so good with money that Jesus selects him as the group's treasurer instead of Matthew. Jesus chooses Judas as one of his twelve disciples* and refers to him openly as a friend. One day that will change.

Galilee is a small region, measuring roughly thirty by forty miles. Its cities are interconnected by a series of ancient highways and Roman roads† plied daily by traders, pilgrims, and travelers. Capernaum is a savvy choice for a base of operations, as the fishing community is constantly sending out its product to far-flung markets, and those who hear Jesus speak in and around that city spread the news about his ministry when they travel to places such as Tyre and even Jerusalem to sell their baskets loaded with salted fish. Crowds begin to find him on those days when Jesus ventures out from Capernaum to preach. He is not always on the move, for his disciples still have jobs and families to support. But as the months pass and his popularity grows, when Jesus does preach, the crowds that gather to hear him grow in size. The

---

*The words *apostle* and *disciple* are both used to describe the twelve members of Jesus's inner circle. A disciple is a follower, while an apostle (taken from the Greek *apostello*, "to send forth") is someone who puts his faith into action by going out into the world to share those teachings. As it has often been noted, all apostles are disciples, but not all disciples are apostles. The twelve followers of Jesus do not go out into the world on their own until the winter of 28, almost a year after Jesus calls them to be disciples. This transformation from disciple to apostle will be most evident after the death of Jesus, when they will travel far beyond the boundaries of Judea to spread Jesus's message.

†There is a key distinction between "Roman roads" and the dirt highways found elsewhere in Judea. The Romans paved their roads in stones, with a crest in the middle to facilitate drainage. They began by digging a trench three feet deep and as much as twenty feet wide. Upon a bed of large stones, laid together tightly, a layer of gravel and concrete was poured. Gravel was laid on top of that and then leveled before paver stones were added for the actual road surface. Roman roads had gutters and curbs, and each mile was clearly marked, indicating the distance from Rome.

Nazarene teaches in synagogues and in open fields, in private homes and along the lakeshore. Men and women abandon their labors to hear him speak, and vast audiences crowd close together to hear Jesus's simple message of God's love and hope.

Not everyone adores him, however. It would seem that a lone man preaching such a noncombative message would not present a problem for Rome or its henchman Antipas. The Roman governor, Pontius Pilate, has a palace in Caesarea, just a day's ride from Capernaum. Thanks to Roman spies, word has reached Pilate about a potential Jewish rebel. The spies of Herod Antipas are also keeping a close eye on Jesus, whom they perceive to be a consort of and successor to John the Baptist. The Jewish religious authorities in Jerusalem and Galilee, particularly the law-centric Pharisees, are now watching him closely for any violation of religious law, and they seek to debunk his teachings. They mock him for drinking wine with sinners and for selecting a much-despised tax collector, Matthew, as a disciple. And when news of supernatural healings performed by Jesus begin to make the rounds in Galilee, the religious authorities become even more alarmed.

But Jesus does not back down.

Instead, he asserts himself. For the poor and oppressed people of Galilee, the sermon he will soon preach from a mountainside outside Capernaum will define their struggle in a way that will never be forgotten.

✝✝✝

"Blessed are the poor in spirit, for theirs is the kingdom of heaven," Jesus begins. "Blessed are they who mourn, for they will be comforted.

"Blessed are the meek, for they will inherit the earth.

"Blessed are those who hunger and thirst for righteousness, for they will be filled.

"Blessed are the merciful, for they will be shown mercy.

"Blessed are the pure in heart, for they will see God.

"Blessed are the peacemakers, for they will be called sons of God.

"Blessed are those who are persecuted because of righteousness, for theirs is the kingdom of heaven."

Jesus is sitting, letting his powerful speaking voice carry his words out to the massive crowd. There are Pharisees among the people. And no doubt they are stunned as Jesus sets forth his own interpretation of religious law. What begins as a message designed to remind the men and women of Galilee that their current circumstances will not last forever soon becomes a lengthy poetic dissertation on adultery, murder, false oaths, alms to the poor, loving one's enemies, and even, most shockingly, defying the powers that be.

Jesus is telling the crowd that they should defer to God in all matters. And the words he speaks are like an emotional rejuvenation in the hearts of these Galileans, who feel oppressed and hopeless.

"This, then, is how you should pray," Jesus tells them. No one speaks. The crowd leans forward, straining to listen.

"Our Father, who are in heaven, hallowed be your name. Thy kingdom come, thy will be done, on earth as it is in heaven. Give us this day our daily bread, and forgive us our debts, as we also have forgiven our debtors. And lead us not into temptation, but deliver us from the evil one."

It's all there. Everything that a peasant in Galilee can relate to as a part of life under Roman rule: the need to rely on God, the worry about daily nourishment, the constant struggle to stay out of debt, and, finally, a reminder that in the midst of this cruel life, succumbing to the temptation to lie, cheat, steal, or sleep with another man's wife is a false act that will only lead people farther and farther away from God.

The crowd is stunned as Jesus finishes. The speech is less than two thousand words long. Yet there is great power in its brevity. "The Sermon on the Mount," as it will come to be known, may be the most important speech in history.

The crowds follow Jesus down the mountain that day, through the tall spring grass and around small limestone boulders, past the fields of new wheat, trailing him all the way back to Capernaum.

There, soon after entering the city, a most amazing thing happens: the Roman military officer in charge of Capernaum declares himself to be a follower of Jesus.

Jesus is astonished. This admission could end the man's career or even get him killed. But Jesus turns to the centurion. "I tell you the truth," he says with emotion. "I have not found anyone in Israel with such great faith."

✝✝✝

Three months after the Sermon on the Mount, Jesus is in the home of a local Pharisee. He has been invited to dinner to discuss his teachings. The Pharisee, Simon, does not like Jesus. And even though Simon invited Jesus to dinner, he is demonstrating his contempt for him by not playing the role of a good host. Though Jesus walked the four dusty miles from Capernaum to Magdala in sandals to be here, Simon has not provided him with water to wash the dust from his feet, as per custom. Simon did not offer him a respectful kiss of greeting on the cheek or anoint him with olive oil upon his arrival.

The Pharisees number some six thousand members throughout

all of Judea, and their name means "separated ones," in reference to the way they hold themselves apart from other Jews. There is no middle class that falls in between the royalty of the state and the religious teachers. Farmers, artisans, and merchants all constitute the lower class. The Pharisees, who have appointed themselves guardians of Jewish religious law, believe that their interpretations of Scripture are authoritative. Wherever they go to teach in synagogues, this is considered to be true. But now Jesus has chosen to interpret the Scriptures himself. And that is threatening to the establishment, as the people of Galilee are eagerly listening to Jesus. So Simon the Pharisee has invited the Nazarene to a gathering of friends, to see if he can trap him into saying something blasphemous.

A young woman enters the room silently. She is a prostitute who has heard Jesus speak. She has been invited by Simon as part of his elaborate plan to test the Nazarene. The moment is obviously awkward, for rarely does a woman of ill repute enter the home of a holy Pharisee. Nevertheless, Mary of Magdala*—or Mary Magdalene, as she will go down in history—now stands behind Jesus. In her hands, she holds a very expensive alabaster jar of perfume. Where she got the money to buy it is left unasked.

It is well known how Mary makes her living, for there are few secrets in the small villages and towns of Galilee. But Mary has come to believe in the love and acceptance preached by Jesus. Now, overcome with emotion, she bends down to pour the aro-

---

*Though Mary Magdalene is not mentioned by name in this story (Luke 7:36–50), it has long been the tradition of Christian teaching that it was she. Luke most likely veiled her true identity because she was still alive at the time he wrote his Gospel. He did the same with Matthew, the tax collector and Gospel author whom he refers to as Levi (Luke 5:27).

matic perfume on his feet. But she begins to sob before she can open the jar. Mary's tears flow freely and without shame, and her face is pressed close to the feet of the Nazarene, which are still coated in road dust from his walk to the Pharisee's house.

Mary's tears continue, and they mix with the perfume she applies to Jesus. She then dries his feet with her long hair, even as she kisses them as a sign of love and respect.

Jesus does nothing to stop her.

"If this man were a prophet," thinks Simon the Pharisee, "he would know who is touching him and what kind of woman she is: a sinner."

"Simon, I have something to tell you," Jesus says as Mary opens the alabaster jar and pours more perfume on his feet. The smell is enchanting and powerful, filling the room with its flowery sweetness.

"Tell me, teacher," Simon replies smoothly.

"Do you see this woman? I came into your house. You did not give me any water for my feet, but she wet my feet with her tears and wiped them with her hair. You did not give me a kiss, but this woman, from the time I entered, has not stopped kissing my feet," Jesus tells the Pharisee. "You did not put oil on my head, but she has poured perfume on my feet. Therefore I tell you, her many sins have been forgiven—for she loved much. But he who has been forgiven little, loves little."

Jesus looks at Mary. She lifts her eyes to see his face. "Your sins are forgiven," Jesus tells her.

If Simon was looking for a chance to catch Jesus in a theological trap, now is the moment. Sins can be forgiven only through sacrificial offerings. In the eyes of the Pharisees, even the baptisms performed in the Jordan River do not officially forgive

Mary Magdalene

sins. And now Jesus is saying that *he* has the authority to obliterate sin.

The other friends of Simon who have come to dinner this evening are dumbfounded by Jesus's words, particularly since he has spoken them in the presence of such a prominent Pharisee. "Who is this who even forgives sins?" they ask one another.

"Your faith has saved you," Jesus tells Mary of Magdala. "Now go in peace."

She goes, but not for long. Mary isn't selected by Jesus to serve as one of his twelve disciples, but she follows them as they travel and never returns to the life she once knew. In the end, Mary will be a powerful witness to the last days of Jesus of Nazareth.[*]

✝✝✝

The last days have come for John the Baptist. He has been in the dungeons of Machaerus for two long years. The dank cells are carved into the rocky hillside, and, in fact, some are nothing more than caves. The floors, ceilings, and walls are impenetrable rock. There are no windows in his cell; the only light comes through small slits in the thick wooden door. The rectangular doorjamb is framed by haphazardly chiseled stones stacked atop one another and sealed with mortar. It is a place of solitude and silence, damp and chill, where hope is hard to maintain through month after month of sleeping on the ground and where one's skin grows pale from never feeling the warmth of sunlight. Now and again it is possible to smell the aromatic bushes that Antipas planted between the castle and the lower city, but the scent is just as quickly swept away on the desert wind, taking with it the brief sensation of beauty. The living hell of the prison has been preying on John's mind. He is now beginning to doubt his initial faith in Jesus as

---

[*]Women often played pivotal roles in Jewish society, so it would not have been unusual for her to follow Jesus and the disciples. The pages of Jewish history are full of heroic matriarchs such as Rachel, Sarah, Leah, and Rebecca. Miriam worked with her brothers, Moses and Aaron, to lead the exodus from Egypt. And of course the prostitute Rahab helped bring about the Israelite victory over Jericho. Women in Jesus's time were considered equal to men, though separate in their worldly responsibilities. They were allowed to choose their marriage partner, enter into contracts, buy and sell property, and speak at weddings. It was forbidden for men to beat or mistreat women, and in the case of rape, it was understood that such an act occurred against a woman's will and that the man was presumed guilty. In fact, women were treated better in the time of Jesus than they are in a great many places in the modern world.

John the Baptist in prison sends his disciples to Jesus

the Messiah. He desperately wants to get word to Jesus and be reassured by him.

John the Baptist has attracted many disciples of his own, though he has also exhorted men to return to their fields and their farms rather than follow him through the wilderness. But at least two such men have come to see him, and now they listen as John sends them on a mission. "Ask him," the Baptist says, referring to Jesus, "'Are you the one who has come, or should we expect someone else?'"

The months in isolation have given John time to reflect on his ministry. He is still a young man, not yet forty. But the longer he remains in prison, the more it appears that he might eventually be executed. His life's work has been to tell people about the coming of a messiah, and now he wonders if it was all in vain. Perhaps

Jesus is just another great teacher, or another man like him, intent on preaching about the coming of God. John's own disciples have come bringing news of Jesus's great speeches and the large crowds that seek him no matter when or where he preaches. They've told John that Jesus is unafraid to eat and drink with the tax collectors and whores and that some of these sinners change their ways after listening to his words of redemption. These disciples have also told John that Jesus has healed the sick and caused men who were completely deaf their whole lives suddenly to hear.

Still, John is not sure. He has seen firsthand what happens when common people become enthralled with charismatic spiritual men. Their behavior is excited and unreasonable. They attribute all manner of miracles to a leader's presence, focusing on the man himself rather than on God. And whether these phenomena occur or not, John does not care. What matters most to him is the kingdom of heaven and when the Messiah will come to earth.

So John sends his messengers on their way. It is hard to imagine anyplace more remote or desolate than Machaerus, situated as it is in the middle of a desert, high atop a mountain. The isolation is brutal.

Weeks pass. The journey from Machaerus to Galilee is just four days. John prays as he waits patiently for more word about Jesus.

Finally, he hears the shuffle of sandals outside the dungeon door. His disciples have returned, bringing with them some very specific words from Jesus. "He told us to go back and report to John what you hear and see: the blind receive sight, the lame walk, those who have leprosy are cured, the deaf hear, the dead are raised, and the good news is preached to the poor. Blessed is the man who does not fall away on account of me."*

---

*Matthew 11:6.

John is relieved. This is the affirmation he was hoping to hear. Now he can finally find some semblance of peace as he languishes in prison. Jesus is once again claiming that he is who John publicly proclaimed him to be: the Messiah.

But there's more. The eager disciples go on to tell John that Jesus not only alluded to his own virgin birth, as foretold by Scripture, but also extended a warm compliment to John as a reminder to stand strong. The moment came as Jesus was teaching to a crowd within earshot of John's disciples. In fact, they were just about to leave when Jesus made sure they heard these words: "What did you go out into the desert to see?" he asked the crowd in reference to John. "A reed swayed by the winds?* A man dressed in fine clothes? No, those who wear fine clothes are in kings' palaces. Then what did you go out to see? A prophet? Yes, I tell you so, and more than a prophet. This is the one about whom it is written: 'I will send my messenger ahead of you, who will prepare your way before you.'

"I tell you the truth: among those born of women, there has not risen anyone greater than John the Baptist."

†††

Another year passes. One night, through the thick stone walls of his prison cell, John can hear the sounds of music and dancing. Antipas has invited the most powerful men in Galilee—high officials, military commanders, and all his wealthy friends—to join him at Machaerus for a lively dinner banquet to celebrate his birthday. Inside the palace, the men and women dine in separate banquet halls, as per custom. In the chamber where Antipas dines with the men, he calls for entertainment and then watches in rapt

*A reed was Herod Antipas's personal emblem of his rule.

attention as his stepdaughter, Salome, steps into the great hall and performs an exotic solo dance. The beautiful young teenager with the raven-colored hair flits slowly around the room, seductively swaying her hips to the beat of the tambourines and cymbals. The men are entranced and unable to take their eyes off her. They roar with approval as the song ends. Antipas is particularly enchanted.

"Ask me for anything you want, and I'll give it to you," he calls out to Salome.

The request, however, does not end there. Knowing that his guests have become enraptured by the beautiful Salome, Antipas wants to make a grand gesture that will impress them. "I swear an oath, whatever you ask, I will give you, up to half my kingdom."

Salome is young, but she is also clever. She rushes from the room to find her mother for advice. "What shall I ask for?" Salome asks.

This is the moment the vengeful Herodias has been waiting for. She tells her daughter: "The head of John the Baptist."

Salome does not hesitate and immediately races back into the banquet hall. Looking directly at her stepfather, she says in a loud voice, "I want you right now to give me the head of John the Baptist on a silver tray."*

Antipas is shocked. He is a man who understands political intrigue, for he has played this game his whole life. He grew up in a household where a father would kill his sons at the slightest sign of disloyalty. His knowledge of this game spared him from execution. But now he is being outwitted and outfoxed by, of all people, his own wife.

---

*In some versions this is written as "silver platter," which has since become a cliché in the modern world.

Killing a man of the people could bring grave consequences. Though fond of perversion, vice, and other self-indulgences, Antipas is still a Jew—even if just marginally faithful. He has enough faith to wonder if there will be divine consequences to such a lethal action. In fact, ten years after the Baptist is executed, the Jewish historian Josephus will proclaim that Antipas's loss of his kingdom was a direct result of God punishing him for the murder of John the Baptist.

And yet he has sworn an oath. To back down in front of these men would put his good word in doubt. When it came time to make a promise to one of his guests on another occasion, they would never believe him.

So it is that John the Baptist hears the creak of his cell door swinging open. An executioner carrying a broad, sharpened sword enters alone. By the light of the moon, he forces John to his knees. The Baptist is resigned to his fate. The swordsman then raises his weapon high overhead and viciously brings it down.

John does not feel the weight of the heavy steel blade as it slices his head from his body.

The voice of one crying out in the wilderness is now silent.

Grasping John's head by the hair, the executioner places it upon a tray and delivers it to Salome and her mother.

✝✝✝

Herodias has had her revenge against the Baptist. But if she (or Antipas) thinks that killing John will end the religious fervor now sweeping through Galilee, she is very wrong. John may have stirred strong emotions by cleansing believers of their sins, but another presence is challenging authority in ways never before seen or heard.

Jesus of Nazareth has one year to live.

CHAPTER TEN

GALILEE
APRIL, A.D. 29
DAY

JESUS HAS BECOME A VICTIM OF HIS OWN CELEBRITY, AND with every passing day, his life is more and more in danger. Many Galileans believe Jesus is the Christ—the anointed earthly king who will overthrow the Romans and rule his people as the king of the Jews, just as David did a thousand years ago. Because of this, the Roman authorities are paying even closer attention to Jesus. For, under Roman law, a man who claims to be a king is guilty of rebellion against the emperor, a crime punishable by crucifixion. Knowing this, Jesus takes great care no longer to proclaim publicly that he is the Christ.

The chief Galilean administrator of the Jews, Herod Antipas, does not believe the Nazarene is the Christ but, instead, the reincarnation of John the Baptist. It is as if Antipas is being haunted by the dead prophet as punishment for ordering his murder. Antipas is openly fretting about Jesus and the troubles he could cause. And the tetrarch is prepared once again to use extreme measures to solve the Jesus problem.

But Pontius Pilate and Antipas are not acting yet. So far, Jesus has shown himself to be a peaceful man. Other than the lone incident with the Temple money changers, nothing Jesus has done threatens them or their way of life. He has never once suggested that the people of Galilee rise up against Rome. Nor has he told his vast audiences that he is king of the Jews. So the Roman governor of Judea and the Jewish administrator of Galilee are content to watch Jesus from afar.

Not so with the religious authorities. Led by the Temple high priest Caiaphas, the teachers of Jewish law see Jesus as a very clear and present danger. Caiaphas has amassed his wealth and power through Temple taxes, profits from the money changers, and the Temple concession for sacrificial lambs. His family also owns tenant farms outside Jerusalem, so he has a great deal more than just religious teachings at stake.

Just as an armed revolutionary is a military threat to Rome, so Jesus's preaching is a threat to the spiritual authority of the Sadducees, Pharisees, and Temple teachers and scribes. Thus these self-proclaimed men of God have devised a specific plan for handling the Nazarene: a quiet arrest followed by a hasty execution.

But the religious leaders would be rendered impure if they murder the Nazarene in cold blood. They cannot pay someone to run him through with a sword or to wrap their hands around his throat and strangle him in his sleep. No, the Pharisees must play by traditional rules, and this means killing Jesus for a public violation of religious law.

In search of such an offense, a select team of Pharisees and scribes now travels from Jerusalem to Galilee to observe Jesus in person. They are men well versed in Scripture. If anyone can find fault with the Nazarene, it is they.

Or so the religious leaders believe.

†††

Things go wrong from the start. The Pharisees and Sadducees are frustrated at every turn, for Jesus is a spiritual and intellectual rival unlike any they have ever faced. Despite their best efforts to weaken his movement by interrogating him publicly, the Nazarene outwits them at every turn, and his popularity continues to soar. The people of Galilee begin to monitor Jesus's travels so closely that they anticipate where he is going and then race ahead to wait for him. Stories of Jesus turning water into wine and making the lame walk and the blind see have so electrified the region that it is now commonplace for almost anyone with an ailment to seek him out, even if that means being carried for miles to await his appearance. Indeed, the Pharisees themselves witness a puzzling event, as Jesus apparently heals a man's severely withered hand on the Sabbath,* an act that the Pharisees promptly and publicly condemn as a violation of religious law.

Jesus shows himself to be an adroit intellectual foil by using logic and words of Holy Scripture to upend their arguments. "There is nothing unlawful," he reminds the Temple squad, "about doing good." Making matters more difficult for the holy men is Jesus's ability to amaze the peasants of Galilee by seemingly performing supernatural acts. The Pharisees now hear that

---

*The Sabbath was a day of complete rest, beginning at sundown on Friday and continuing until three stars were visible in the sky on Saturday evening. Strenuous work was forbidden, as were many other activities, in an effort to replicate God's day of rest after creating the universe.

he transformed two fish and five loaves of bread into a feast that fed five thousand people in the mountains near Bethsaida early this spring. And even more fantastic is word that Jesus allegedly brought a dead girl in Capernaum back to life. Finally, the most astounding happening of all: Jesus's disciples claim to have seen him walk atop the Sea of Galilee in the midst of a violent storm.

The Pharisees refuse to believe any of this, even though they have witnessed firsthand an unexplainable act of healing. Yet a staggering number of witnesses are attesting to each and every one of these *pela'oth*, *othoth*, and *mophethim*. The Greek of the Gospels will later translate these Hebrew words into *dunameis*, *semeia*, and *terata*—power (or force), signs, and wonders. The simple Aramaic-speaking people of Galilee prefer just one word to describe the acts of Jesus: *nes.**

The Pharisees believe in miracles but not in Jesus. Time and again throughout Jewish oral history—from Moses to Job to Esther—God reveals himself through such actions. When the Pharisees finally put the oral tradition of the Jewish people onto the page two centuries from now, the Talmud will be filled with stories of God's miracles.

But Jesus is not God, of that the Pharisees are sure. He is an agitator, a false teacher, a dangerous charlatan. Rather than a heavenly palace, Jesus takes a room in the simple earthly home of his disciple Peter. Clearly this cannot be the supreme deity whom the Pharisees have spent their lives contemplating.

This troubles the Pharisees deeply. Jesus is undermining their authority. If allowed to flourish, his movement will destroy their way of life, stripping them of wealth and privilege. And that can-

---

*Somewhere in the twelfth century, these supernatural happenings will come to be known as miracles.

not be allowed to happen. For as much as the Pharisees say they love God, most of them are arrogant, self-righteous men who love their exalted class status far more than any religious belief system.

It is a status the Temple priests have enjoyed for almost six centuries. Since the time of the Babylonian captivity, when the last true Jewish king was toppled from the throne, a power vacuum has existed among the Jewish people.* Holy men such as the Pharisees have filled that void by strictly interpreting the laws of Moses. They gained respect from the Jewish people by adding hundreds of new commandments and prohibitions to Moses's original list of ten, then passing them on through an oral history known as the Tradition of the Elders.

Few ever question these laws, especially not the uneducated peasants of Galilee. But now Jesus, through his actions and teaching, has shown many of these mandates to be absurd and the behavior of the Pharisees and Sadducees to be even more so.

The time has come to move against the Nazarene.

---

*Zedekiah was the last king of Israel. The dates are unclear, but his reign was most likely 597–86 B.C. Zedekiah was installed on the throne at the age of twenty-one, by Nebuchadnezzar II, the king of Babylon. When Zedekiah stopped paying tribute some years later, Nebuchadnezzar brought his army to Jerusalem and laid siege to the city. It eventually fell, and the people were taken off to Babylon for a lifetime of slavery. The Temple was destroyed at this time and not rebuilt until Cyrus gave the approval to the Jewish people to return home and rebuild the Temple. Work began around 536 B.C. and finished in 516 B.C. This Second Temple was completely renovated under Herod the Great. Zedekiah, who had ignored the counsel of the prophet Jeremiah to be more diligent in worshipping God, was captured as he tried to flee his fallen capital. At Nebuchadnezzar's orders, the king's young children were put to the sword before his eyes. This would be the last sight Zedekiah would ever see, for he was immediately blinded (the preferred technique was to press thumbs into a man's eye sockets), chained, and marched off to Babylon as a slave.

†††

One spring day, a Pharisee taunts Jesus: "Why don't your disciples live according to the traditions of the elders instead of eating their food with unclean hands?"

Jesus is calm. He begins by answering a question with a question, a technique he often uses. "Why do you break the command of God for the sake of your tradition?"

It is April in Galilee, a time on the Roman Empire's Julian calendar when shepherds and their flocks dot the hillsides and farmers conclude the barley harvest and turn their attention to the great fields of wheat. Jesus and his disciples have just purchased a meal in the marketplace and have retired to enjoy it. Soon a circle of Pharisees gathers around to condemn them for not engaging in the ceremonial washing of the hands. This ritual includes a pre-meal cleansing of cups, plates, and cutlery, and is far more suited to the Temple courts than a Galilean fishing village. Of course, the famished disciples are in no mood to indulge in such a lengthy process.

Jesus says little at first. The Pharisees take this as a sign to move closer. A crowd of curious onlookers gathers just behind them. The two groups form a tight ring around Jesus and his disciples. It is a noose of sorts, within which the Nazarene is trapped. He has nowhere to run—just as the Pharisees planned.

The trap is baited. The Pharisees hope that Jesus will now utter words of blasphemy and heresy. If he does that, he can be condemned. The pronouncement that the Pharisees want to hear more than any other is a claim of divinity, a public proclamation by Jesus that he is the Son of God—not an earthly king, but one exalted above the angels and seated on the throne with God.

That would be enough to have him stoned to death.

The religious leaders are dressed in expensive robes adorned with extra-long blue tassels. Small wooden boxes are fastened to their foreheads by a headband. Inside each is a tiny scroll of Scripture telling about the exodus from Egypt. Both the fringe and the phylactery, as this box is known, are designed to call attention to the Pharisees' holiness and to remind one and all of their religious authority.

But Jesus does not recognize this authority.

He stands to address the Pharisees. The people of Galilee press closer to hear what the Nazarene will say. These simple artisans and fishermen look poor and tattered in comparison with the Pharisees. Jesus, their fellow Galilean, is dressed just like they are, in a simple square robe over a tunic, with small fringes and no phylactery.

The people know that this is not the first time the Pharisees have tried to goad the Nazarene into a public incident, and the drama and wit of Jesus's responses are widely known.

"Isaiah was right when he prophesied about you hypocrites," Jesus says, looking directly at the Pharisees and Sadducees. The Nazarene then quotes from the Scripture: " 'These people honor me with their lips, but their hearts are far from me. They worship me in vain; their teachings are but rules taught by men.' "

Jesus is fearless. The force of his words carries out over the crowd. There is a deep irony to his lecture, for while the Pharisees have come here to judge Jesus, the tone of his voice makes it clear that it is *he* who is judging them. "You have let go of the commands of God and are holding on to the traditions of men," he scolds his accusers.

Before they can reply, Jesus turns to the crowd and says, "Listen to me. Understand this: Nothing outside a man can make him 'unclean' by going into him. Rather, it is what comes out of a man that makes him unclean."

✝✝✝

The Pharisees walk away before Jesus can further undermine their authority. The remaining crowds make it impossible for the disciples to eat in peace, so Jesus leads them into a nearby house to dine without being disturbed.

But the disciples are unsettled. In their year together, they have heard and absorbed so much of what Jesus has said and have been witness to many strange and powerful events they do not understand. They are simple men and do not comprehend why Jesus is so intent on humiliating the all-powerful Pharisees. This escalating religious battle can only end poorly for Jesus.

"Do you know that the Pharisees were offended?" one of them asks Jesus, stating the obvious.

Then Peter speaks up. "Explain the parable to us," he asks, knowing that Jesus never says anything publicly without a reason. Sometimes the Nazarene's words are spiritual, sometimes they contain a subtle political message, and sometimes he means to be uplifting. In the past few months, Jesus has debated the Pharisees about everything from eating barley on the Sabbath to hand washing, today's debate, which seemed pointless to Peter. Perhaps the disciples have overlooked an important subtext to Jesus's teaching.

"Are you still so dull?" answers an exasperated Jesus.

Jesus continues: "Don't you see that whatever enters the mouth enters into the stomach and then out of the body. But the things that come out of the mouth come from the heart, and these make a man unclean. For from within, out of men's hearts come evil thoughts, sexual immorality, theft, murder, adultery, greed, malice, deceit, lewdness, envy, slander, arrogance, and folly. All of these evils come from inside and make a man unclean."

Judas Iscariot is among those listening to the words of Jesus. He is the lone disciple who was not raised in Galilee, making him a conspicuous outsider in the group. There is no denying this. He wears the same robes and sandals, covers his head to keep off the sun, and carries a walking stick to fend off the wild dogs of Galilee, just like the rest of the disciples. But his accent is of the south, not the north. Every time he opens his mouth to speak, Judas reminds the disciples that he is different.

Now Jesus's words push Judas further away from the group. For Judas is also a thief. Taking advantage of his role as treasurer, he steals regularly from the disciples' meager finances.* Rather than allow Jesus to be anointed with precious perfumes by his admirers, Judas has insisted that those vials of perfume be sold and the profits placed in the group's communal moneybag—all so that he might steal the money for his own use. Judas's acts of thievery have remained a secret, and, like all thieves, he carries the private burden of his sin.†

Now Jesus is deepening Judas's shame by reminding him that he is not merely a sinner but also unclean. To be morally unclean in Galilee is not just a spiritual state of mind; it is to enter a different class of people. Such a man becomes an outcast, fit only for backbreaking occupations such as tanning and mining, destined to be landless and poor for all his days.

Judas has seen these people. Many of them fill the crowds that

---

*The source of some of Jesus's income can be found in Luke 8:2–3, where it is specified that there were many who gave of their own money to financially support Jesus and his ministry.

†John 12:6.

follow Jesus, simply because they have nothing better to do with their time, and Jesus's words offer them a measure of hope that their lives will somehow improve. They have no families, no farms, and no roof over their heads. Others turn to a life of crime, becoming brigands and highwaymen, banding together and living in caves. Their lives are hard, and they often die young.

This is not the life Judas Iscariot has planned for himself. If Jesus is the Christ, as Judas believes, then he is destined one day to overthrow the Roman occupation and rule Judea. Judas's role as one of the twelve disciples will ensure him a most coveted and powerful role in the new government when that day comes.

Judas apparently believes in the teachings of Jesus, and he certainly basks in the Nazarene's reflected celebrity. But his desire for material wealth overrides any spirituality. Judas puts his own needs above those of Jesus and the other disciples.

For a price, Judas Iscariot is capable of doing anything.

†††

Frustrated by their inability to trap Jesus but also believing they have enough evidence to arrest him, the Pharisees and Sadducees return to Jerusalem to make their report. And while it may seem as if Jesus is unbothered by their attention, the truth is that the pressure is weighing on him enormously. Even before their visit, Jesus hoped to take refuge in a solitary place for a time of reflection and prayer. Now he leaves Galilee, taking the disciples with him. They walk north, into the kingdom ruled by Antipas's brother Philip, toward the city of Caesarea Philippi. The people there are pagans who worship the god Pan, that deity with the hindquarters and horns of a goat and the torso and face of a man. No one there cares if Jesus says he is the Christ, nor will the authorities question him about Scripture. While Caesarea Philippi is just thirty-four miles north of Capernaum, Jesus might as well be in Rome.

Summer is approaching. The two-day journey follows a well-traveled Roman road on the east side of the Hulah Valley. Jesus and his disciples keep a sharp eye out for the bears and bandits that can do harm, but otherwise their trip is peaceful. Actually, this constitutes a vacation for Jesus and the disciples, and they aren't too many miles up the road before Jesus feels refreshed enough to stop and relax in the sun.

"Who do the people say I am?" Jesus asks the disciples, perhaps inspired by the great temple at Omrit, dedicated to Caesar Augustus, a man who claimed to be god but who was, in the end, just as mortal as any other man.

"Some say John the Baptist, others say Elijah, and still others Jeremiah or one of the prophets," comes the reply.

It is often this way when they travel: Jesus teaching on the go or prompting intellectual debate by throwing out a random question. Rarely does he confide in them.

"But what about you?" Jesus inquires. "Who do you say I am?"

Peter speaks up. "You are the Christ, the son of the living God."

Jesus agrees. "Blessed are you, Simon son of Jonah, for this was not revealed to you by man but by my heavenly father," he says as he praises the impulsive fisherman, using Peter's former name. "Don't tell anyone," Jesus adds as a reminder that a public revelation will lead to his arrest by the Romans. They may be leaving the power of the Jewish authorities behind for a short while, but Caesarea Philippi is just as Roman as Rome itself.

But if the disciples think that Jesus has shared his deepest secret, they are wrong. "The Son of Man must suffer many things and be rejected by the elders, chief priests, and teachers of the law," Jesus goes on to explain.

This doesn't make sense to the disciples. If Jesus is the Christ, then he will one day rule the land. But how can he do so without the backing of the religious authorities?

And if that isn't confusing enough, Jesus adds another statement, one that will be a source of argument down through the ages.

"He must be killed," Jesus promises the disciples, speaking of himself as the Son of God, "and on the third day be raised to life."

The disciples have no idea what this means.

Nor do they know that Jesus of Nazareth has less than a year to live.

CHAPTER ELEVEN

JERUSALEM
OCTOBER, A.D. 29
DAY

PONTIUS PILATE SITS TALL AS HE RIDES TO JERUSALEM. HIS wife, Claudia, travels in a nearby carriage, as Pilate and his escorts lead the caravan through unfriendly terrain. Pilate has three thousand men at his disposal. They are not actual Roman soldiers but the same mix of Arab, Samarian, and Syrian forces who once defended Herod the Great.

Pilate's military caravan has set out from the seaside fortress of Caesarea. The Roman governor makes the trip to Jerusalem three times a year for the Jewish festivals.* The sixty-mile journey takes

---

*The three major Jewish pilgrimage festivals were Passover, Tabernacles, and Weeks—in Hebrew, Pesach, Sukkot, and Shavuot. Jews were required to attend all three, but many preferred to attend only Passover, which was sometimes held in conjunction with the Feast of Unleavened Bread. Since the destruction of the Temple in A.D. 70, it is no longer required that Jews make the pilgrimages to Jerusalem. They instead attend the festivals that take place at their local synagogues. It should be noted that the most holy holiday on the Jewish calendar is Yom Kippur, the Day of Atonement.

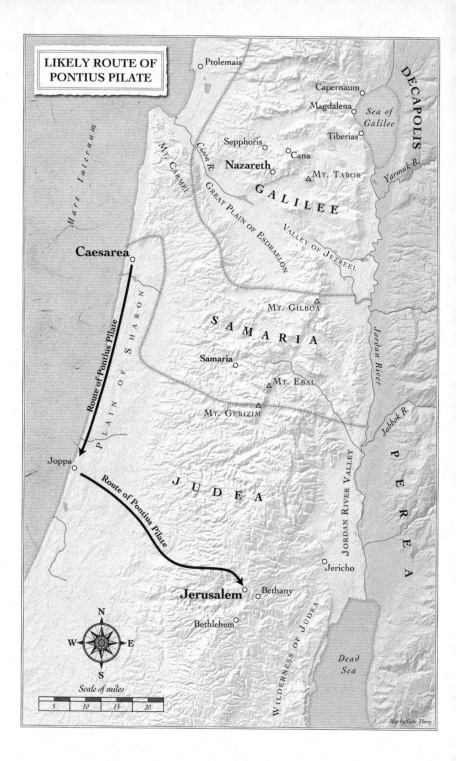

LIKELY ROUTE OF
PONTIUS PILATE

DECAPOLIS

Ptolemais

Capernaum
Magdalena
Sea of
Galilee
Tiberias
Sepphoris
Cana
Nazareth
Mt. Tabor
GALILEE

Mt. Carmel
Cison R.
Great Plain of Esdraelon
Valley of Jezreel
Yarmuk R.

Mare Internum

Caesarea

Route of Pontius Pilate
Plain of Sharon

Mt. Gilboa

SAMARIA

Samaria

Mt. Ebal
Mt. Gerizim

Jordan River

Joppa

Route of Pontius Pilate

JUDEA

Jordan River Valley

Jabbok R.

P
E
R
E
A

Jericho

Jerusalem
Bethany

Bethlehem

Wilderness of Judea

Dead
Sea

N
W E
S

Scale of miles
5   10   15   20

Map by Gene Thorp

them south along the Mediterranean, on a paved Roman road. After an overnight stop, the route turns inward, onto a dirt road across the Plain of Sharon and on up through the mountains to Jerusalem.

Pilate intends to lend a dominant Roman presence to the Feast of Tabernacles,* one of three great celebrations on the Jewish religious calendar. Much like Passover, this holiday involves pilgrims by the hundreds of thousands traveling to Jerusalem to celebrate. The Jews commemorate forty years of wandering in the desert and enjoy a feast to celebrate the completion of the bountiful harvest. Pilate has little patience for Jewish ways. Nor does he think the Jews are loyal to Rome. The governor walks a fine line during these festivals: if the Jews revolt—which they are wont to do when they gather in such large numbers—he will take the blame, but if he cracks down too hard, he could be recalled to Rome for disobeying Tiberius's order that these people be treated as a "sacred trust."

Thus Pilate endures the festival weeks. He and Claudia lodge themselves in the opulence of Herod the Great's palace and venture out only when absolutely necessary.

Pontius Pilate has been prefect of Judea for three years. His job as governor should be as simple as mediating local disputes and keeping the peace, but in fact the role of the occupier is always fraught with peril. The Jewish philosopher Philo will one day write that Pilate is "a man of inflexible, stubborn and cruel disposition," and yet the Jews have already managed to outsmart him and damage his career. On the occasion that Pilate ordered Roman standards to adorn the Temple, not only did the residents

---

*Sukkot, as the festival is known in Hebrew, commemorates the years of nomadic dwelling while Moses searched for the Promised Land.

of Jerusalem succeed in having them removed, but they also wrote a letter to Emperor Tiberius detailing Pilate's indiscretion.

Tiberius was furious. As the historian Philo will report, "Immediately, without even waiting for the next day, he wrote to Pilate, reproaching and rebuking him a thousand times for his new-fangled audacity."

This year, tensions are running even higher, and the finger of blame can be pointed only at Pilate. He had the ingenious idea of building a new aqueduct to bring water to Jerusalem, but he faltered in this act of goodwill by forcing the Temple treasury to pay for it. The Jewish people were outraged about this use of "sacred funds," and during one recent festival, a small army of Jews rose up to demand that Pilate stop the aqueduct's construction. They cursed Pilate when he appeared in the streets of Jerusalem, taking courage from the size of the crowd, thinking that their words would be rendered anonymous.

But Pilate anticipated the protest and disguised hundreds of his soldiers in the peasant robes of Jewish pilgrims, with orders that they conceal a dagger or club beneath the folds of their robes. When the crowd marched on the palace to jeer more violently at Pilate, these men surrounded the mob and attacked them, beating and stabbing the unarmed pilgrims. "There were a great number of them slain by this means," the historian Josephus would later write, "and others of them ran away wounded. An end was put to this sedition."

To the Jewish people, Pilate is a villain. They think him "spiteful and angry" and speak of "his venality, his violence, his thefts, his assaults, his abusive behavior, his frequent executions of untried prisoners, and his endless savage ferocity."*

Yet one of their own is just as guilty.

---

*The description is from the philosopher Philo, a Jew living in Egypt.

†††

Pontius Pilate cannot rule the Jewish people without the help of Joseph Caiaphas, the high priest and leader of the Jewish judicial court known as the Sanhedrin.

Caiaphas is a master politician and knows that the emperor Tiberius not only believes it important to uphold the Jewish traditions but is also keeping the hot-tempered Pilate on a very short leash. Pilate may be in charge of Judea, but it is Caiaphas who oversees the day-to-day running of Jerusalem, disguising his own cruel agenda in religiosity and piety. Few people in Jerusalem realize that the same man who leads the rite for the atonement of sins, appearing in the Temple courts on Passover and Yom Kippur wearing the most dazzling ceremonial robes,* is a dear friend of Rome and of the decadent emperor Tiberius.

The glamour of his position is most spectacularly evident during the annual Yom Kippur atonement ceremony, when Caiaphas enters alone a Temple sanctuary known as the Holy of Holies, where it is believed that God dwells. To Jewish believers, this places him closer to God than any mortal man. He then walks back out to stand before the believers who pack the Temple courts. A goat is placed on either side of Caiaphas. As part of the ritual atonement, this high priest must decide which goat will go free and which will be sacrificed for the sins of the Jewish people.

This same man who stands in the presence of God and sees that sins are forgiven is also the high priest who does not object

---

*"Dazzling" does not begin to describe the Temple robes. Caiaphas's was a long blue tunic decorated with bells and long tassels. He cinched it tight at the waist with a sash, then slipped on a boldly colored waistcoat embroidered in gold, with the twelve tribes of Israel listed upon its shoulders and a breastplate coated in precious stones that reflected the sun. His head was covered in a turban upon which rested a three-tiered gold crown bearing the name of God.

when Pilate loots the Temple funds. Caiaphas also says nothing when Jews are massacred in the streets of the Holy City. He doesn't complain when Pilate forces him to return those jewel-encrusted ceremonial robes at the end of each festival. The Romans prefer to keep the expensive garments in their custody as a reminder of their power, returning them seven days prior to each festival so that they can be purified.

Prior to Caiaphas, high priests were puppets of Rome, easily replaced for acts of insubordination. But Caiaphas, a member of the Sadducee sect, has developed a simple and brilliant technique to remain in power: stay out of Rome's business.

Rome, in turn, usually stays out of the Temple's business.

The former helps Pilate keep his job. The latter increases Caiaphas's power.

Both men know this and are comfortable with the arrangement. So while Caiaphas's four predecessors served just one year as high priest before being deposed, Caiaphas has now been in office for a dozen years—and shows no sign of going anywhere soon. And every year he is in power, the connection between Rome and the Temple grows stronger, even as the chasm between the high priest and the working-class Jews grows wider.

It helps that Pilate and Caiaphas are more alike than they are different. Pilate was born into the wealthy equestrian class of Romans,[*]

---

[*]The equestrians were a significant step below the aristocratic senatorial class in Roman culture. For a man to move upward, he needed to show brilliance in politics and on the battlefield and also to accrue tremendous wealth. Being a prefect was an ideal way to become wealthy, mostly through taking a cut of all mining licenses, monopolies, and taxes. Pilate does not appear to have had any previous diplomatic experience before his posting to Judea, so it is likely that he had the assistance of a high-ranking friend to get the job. Some believe that he was close to Lucius Aelius Sejanus, the ill-fated administrator who oversaw much of the Roman Empire while Tiberius was off in Capri.

and Caiaphas was born into a centuries-long lineage of wealthy Temple priests. Both men are middle-aged and married. Each likely enjoys a glass of imported wine at the end of the day. When Pilate is in Jerusalem, the two men live just a few hundred yards apart, in the posh Upper City, in palaces staffed by male and female slaves. And they consider themselves devout men, though they worship far different deities.

The last thing Pilate or Caiaphas needs is a messianic figure to upset this careful balance of power—which is precisely why Caiaphas and the religious authorities plan to arrest Jesus the minute he sets foot inside the Holy City.

The Pharisees have done their due diligence and have reported back a litany of transgressions against religious law by the Nazarene. The plot to kill Jesus is about to unfold.

✝✝✝

But Jesus has other plans.

He has returned from his brief time in Caesarea Philippi and now remains in Galilee, even as the disciples travel to Jerusalem for the festival. The disciples are so eager for Jesus to come with them and publicly announce that he is the Christ that they try to give him a piece of advice, something they've never done before.

"Go to Jerusalem," they beg before setting out. "No one who wants to become a public figure acts in secret. Since you are doing these things, show yourself to the world."*

"The right time for me has not yet come," Jesus answers. "For you any time is right. The world cannot hate you, but it hates me because I testify that what it does is evil. You go to the feast. I am not going, because for me the right time has not yet come."

---

*John 7:4.

The religious leaders in Jerusalem remember the disciples' faces from their mission to Galilee in the spring. So when they see the disciples enter the city without Jesus, they are immediately frustrated. Once again, Jesus appears to be getting the best of them.

"Where is that man?" the Pharisees ask one another, studying faces in the crowds filling the Temple courts. "Where is that man?"

Rumors about Jesus swirl as the feast begins. The people in the villages and towns surrounding Jerusalem know little about him, other than from rumor. Many believe the innuendo is being spread by the religious authorities in an attempt to portray Jesus as a demon and a charlatan. Pilgrims from Galilee, however, rave about Jesus's goodness. Others, meanwhile, gossip that Jesus is now being hunted.

For days, speculation spreads through the city. No one has an answer about where Jesus is, not even his own disciples.

The Feast of the Tabernacles is eight days long, and it is halfway through the celebration that Jesus slips quietly into the Temple courts. He has traveled in secret to Jerusalem. Jesus fearlessly begins to teach. There has been an aura of sadness about him in recent months, a greater need to be alone. He speaks more and more in parables when he teaches, knowing that such stories are far more memorable and provide more context than merely quoting Scripture. Above all, he seems to be coming to terms with the imminent death of which he told his disciples.

But that time has not yet come, so now, within earshot of the sanctuary, easily heard and seen by any passing Pharisee or Sadducee, Jesus boldly preaches about truth and justice. Within moments, a circle of pilgrims stands before him, listening in amazement as Jesus shares his insights about God.

"Isn't this the man they are trying to kill?" ask some in the crowd.

"Have the authorities really concluded that he is the Christ?" ask others.

This idea is met with skepticism. For it is hard to imagine that the Christ would come from a backwater province such as Galilee. Instead, he would be from Bethlehem, the city of David, as told by the prophets. "We know where this one is from."

"Yes, you know me," Jesus answers, hearing their words. "And you know where I am from. I am not here on my own, but he who sent me is true. You do not know him, but I know him, because I am from him and he sent me."

Jesus is on the verge of admitting that he is the Christ. The Pharisees and high priests send the Temple guards to arrest him for blasphemy. But the guards return empty-handed and then stand before Caiaphas and the Pharisees, unable to explain their failure to do so. Standing among these chief priests is Nicodemus, the Pharisee from Galilee who questioned Jesus about being born again. "Why didn't you bring him in?" the high priests demand to know.

"No one ever spoke the way this man does," a guard explains.

"You mean he has deceived you also?" demand the Pharisees. Their rage is so profound that they forget their place, for only the high priests are allowed to ask questions within the Temple.

Nicodemus steps forward. "Does our law condemn anyone without first hearing him to find out what he is doing?"

The other religious leaders quickly turn on Nicodemus, insulting him even though he is one of their own.

"You are from Galilee?" they say with scorn. "A prophet does not come out of Galilee."

†††

Jesus continues to teach in the Temple courts for the rest of the festival. "I am the light of the world," he tells the crowds. "Whoever follows me will never walk in darkness but will have the light of life."

"I am going away," he adds. "Where I go you cannot come." And soon after, he disappears. As pilgrims travel back to their homes—whether they be in Egypt, Syria, Galilee, Greece, Gaul, or Rome—they talk about Jesus. Many now believe that Jesus is indeed the Christ. Others are not sure, but they heard his pronouncements that he was sent by God and desperately want to put their faith in the Nazarene.

Whether or not they believe Jesus is the Christ, Jews everywhere long for the coming of a messiah. When that moment arrives, Rome will be defeated and their lives will be free of taxation and want. No longer will soldiers loyal to Rome be allowed to corral Jews like cattle, then stab and beat them until the gutters of their Holy City are choked with Jewish blood, as Pilate so infamously arranged. For these people, this hope is like a lifeline, giving them courage in the face of Rome's unrelenting cruelty.

Only the Christ can lead them. The prophets have promised that such a man will come. And to be sure, Jesus has made several allusions to being the Jewish Messiah. He talks about his father and that he came from above. But he hasn't come out and publicly said the words "I am the Christ."

Jesus has appeared in the Temple courts many times, defying the priests and Pharisees whenever given the chance. He is powerful and confident, as a leader should be. If Jesus is the Messiah who will come to save the Jewish people, then let him reveal himself. Some are growing impatient.

The less literate among the pilgrims are waiting for a verbal pronouncement from Jesus. The more enlightened don't need to hear the words; they are simply waiting for the moment when Jesus rides into Jerusalem on a donkey. Then and only then will they be sure that he is the one true Christ.

"See your king comes to you, righteous and having salvation," the prophet Zechariah predicted five hundred years ago, "gentle and riding on a donkey."

✝✝✝

Each and every member of the Sanhedrin knows the words of Zechariah. Months have passed since the end of the Feast of Tabernacles, and they gather now, seventy-one religious authorities strong, in a special meeting chamber known as the Hall of Hewn Stones. Opulent and regal, the place of legal judgment rests near the north wall of the Temple Mount. Half of it is inside the sanctuary and half outside. Doors lead into the room from either direction. As its name suggests, iron implements were used in its construction, making the hall unsuitable for ritual worship.*

The Sanhedrin is the ultimate Jewish religious court, a body of men even more powerful than the tetrarch Antipas. And within this chamber, Caiaphas holds the ultimate authority.

Pontius Pilate is now safely back at his seaside palace in Caesarea,† destined not to return to Jerusalem until April and the Passover celebration. Jesus is reported to have left Galilee, destined for parts unknown. Witnesses say he is performing miracles

---

*God instructed Moses to construct an altar of uncut stone, thus making it sacred. "And if you make for me an altar of stones, do not build it of hewn stones; for by wielding your tool upon them you have profaned them" (Exodus 20:25). An entire room made in a similar fashion would have been a most sacred place.

†Not to be confused with the distant inland city of Caesarea Philippi.

once again. In one startling account out of the town of Bethany, a man named Lazarus came back from the dead. And Lazarus was not recently deceased. He was four days dead and already laid in the tomb when Jesus is said to have healed him before a great crowd.

Lazarus's body already reeked of decomposition when Jesus ordered that the stone covering the tomb entrance be rolled away. This was not just an act of healing but a display of powers far beyond those of a normal human being.

"Here is this man performing many miraculous signs," a Pharisee says. "If we let him go on like this, everyone will believe in him, and then the Romans will come and take away both our place and our nation."

Caiaphas agrees. "You do not realize that it is better for you that one man die for the people than that the whole nation perish."

Nothing more needs to be said.

✝✝✝

Whether knowingly or unknowingly, Jesus has led a life that is a continual fulfillment of Jewish prophecy. He was born a Jew. His lineage is that of David. A great star rose in the morning sky as he was being born in Bethlehem. It could be argued that as he grew and learned Scripture, he intentionally began contriving his actions and words to mimic the prophets' predictions. And now comes the ultimate symbol: if Jesus chooses to ride into Jerusalem at Passover astride a donkey, he will be sending a powerful message. As the prophet Zechariah wrote, "Rejoice greatly, O Daughter of Zion! Shout, Daughter of Jerusalem! See, your king comes to you, righteous and having salvation, gentle and riding on a donkey, on a colt, the foal of a donkey. He will proclaim peace to the nations. His rule will extend from sea to sea and from the River to the ends of the earth."

Fulfilling Zechariah's prediction would be easy. Donkeys are everywhere in Judea. Jesus would simply have to tell a disciple to bring one to him.

At the age of thirty-six, Jesus is clever enough to act out any prophecy. His understanding of faith is profound and his knowledge of Scripture encyclopedic.

But Jesus would be a fool to ride a donkey into Jerusalem. That would be a death sentence. For while the prophets have been very specific about the way the king of the Jews would be born and live his life, they are just as clear about how he will die.

He will be falsely accused of crimes he did not commit.

He will be beaten.

He will be spat upon.

He will be stripped, and soldiers will throw dice to bid for his clothing.

He will be crucified, with nails driven through his hands and feet—yet not a single one of his bones will be broken.

And those who love him will look on in mourning, unable to do anything to stop the agony.*

✝✝✝

It is Sunday, April 2, A.D. 30. Pontius Pilate has just returned to Jerusalem and taken up residence in Herod the Great's palace. Herod Antipas, the tetrarch, arrives in the city and stays just a

---

*In order, these prophecies are: Psalms 27:12 and 35:11; Micah 5:1; Isaiah 50:6; Psalms 22:18; Psalms 22:16, Zechariah 12:10, and Deuteronomy 21:23; Numbers 9:12, Psalms 34:20, and Exodus 12:46; and Zechariah 12:10.

block away, at the Hasmonean Palace. At the same time, Caiaphas prepares for the biggest festival of the year at his palace home in the Upper City.

Passover week is now about to begin.

The disciples begin the search for a donkey.

Jesus of Nazareth has six days to live.

If You Are the Son of God, Take Yourself off This Cross

CHAPTER TWELVE

THE DUSTY DIRT ROAD FROM GALILEE IS ONCE AGAIN CLOGGED with Passover pilgrims eager to enter the walls of Jerusalem and put their journey behind them. The day is sunny, as it is so often this time of year. The travelers push past date palm plantations and the former winter palaces of Herod the Great in the lush oasis of Jericho. Small farming villages soon follow, where fruit orchards, vineyards, and olive trees grow alongside irrigated fields of vegetables. Many of the travelers stop here for their ritual *mikvah*, purifying themselves for the final three miles of the journey.

The purification process is vital to properly celebrating Passover. It creates a physical and emotional state of mind that prepares a worshipper to embrace God's holiness—thus the need to arrive in Jerusalem almost a week before the holy day. Men will immerse in the *mikvah*, then cease having sex with their wives until after Passover, believing the act of ejaculation makes the body impure. Similarly, menstruating women will be unable to immerse in the *mikvah* and will also be forbidden from entering the Temple grounds. Touching a reptile also makes a body impure,[*] and anyone coming in contact with a dead body or even having their shadow touch a dead body is immediately rendered impure and unable to celebrate Passover. This, of course, also applies to anyone who kills a person.

So even before the pilgrims see Jerusalem, they are mentally preparing for the week to come. They think of the need for a *mikvah* and they refrain from any intimate contact that might stir physical longings. Anticipating the smell of roast lamb that will hang over Jerusalem as the Passover feasts are being cooked in ovens, the pilgrims count their money, worrying about how they will pay for that feast and the inevitable taxes they will incur in the city. Despite their sore feet and aching legs from walking mile after rugged mile through the wilderness, the travelers feel themselves transformed by the magnetic pull of Jerusalem. Their thoughts are no longer set on their farms back home and the barley crop that must be harvested immediately upon their return, but on holiness and purity.

Soon they will ascend the hill known as the Mount of Olives and look down upon the heart-stopping sight of Jerusalem in all its glory. The Temple will gleam white and gold, and the mighty walls of the Temple Mount will astound them, as always. The sheer magnificence of the Temple will remind them that they have arrived at the center of Jewish life.

---

*Leviticus 22:4–7.

It has been nearly fifty years since the Temple was refurbished and expanded and the first modern Passover celebrated within its courts. But even for those old enough to have been there that day, this Passover promises to be the most memorable in history. And today's arrival in Jerusalem will be unlike any before—or to come.

†††

"We are going up to Jerusalem," Jesus tells his disciples as they prepare to depart for the Passover. "The Son of Man will be betrayed to the chief priests and the teachers of the law. They will condemn him to death and will turn him over to the Gentiles to be mocked and flogged and crucified. On the third day he will be raised to life."

But if those words disturb the disciples, they don't show it. For theirs has been a journey of many months, rather than the mere days of most pilgrims. After the Feast of Tabernacles six months ago, Jesus and the disciples did not return to Galilee. Instead, they began a roundabout trip. First stop, the village of Ephraim, only fifteen miles north of Jerusalem. From there they traveled as a group due north and away from Jerusalem, to the border of Samaria and Galilee. And then, when it came time for Passover, they turned in the opposite direction and marched due south along the Jordan River, joining the long caravans of pilgrims en route to the Holy City.

The disciples now jockey for position during the walk to Jerusalem. James and John ask the Nazarene if they can be his principal assistants in the new regime, requesting that "one of us sit on your right and the other on your left in your glory." Upon hearing this, the other ten are furious. They have followed Jesus as a collective group for more than two years, giving up their jobs and wives and whatever semblance of a normal life they might have once had. All the disciples hope they will reap the glory that will come after the new Messiah overthrows the Romans. Peter is so sure that Jesus is going to use military might that he is making plans to purchase a sword.

But Jesus has no plans to wage war and no plans to form a new government. Rather than upbraid James and John, he calmly deflects their request. He then calls the disciples together, imploring them to focus on serving others rather than fighting for position. "For even the Son of Man did not come to be served, but to serve, and to give his life as a ransom for many," he tells them.

Once again, Jesus is predicting his death. And yet the disciples are so focused on the glorious moment when Jesus will reveal that he is the Christ that they ignore the fact that he is telling them he will soon die. There will be no overthrow of the Romans. There will be no new government.

But the disciples' willful ignorance is understandable. Jesus often speaks in parables, and the mania surrounding the Nazarene is now phenomenal. The adoration being bestowed upon Jesus makes any talk of death incomprehensible. The thick crowds of pilgrims treat Jesus like royalty, hanging on his every word and greeting him with enthusiastic awe. In the village of Jericho, two blind men call out to Jesus, referring to him as "Lord, Son of David," a designation that could be applied only to the Christ. The disciples are encouraged when Jesus does nothing to rebuke the blind men.

Jerusalem is just a forty-minute walk from the village of Bethany, where they stop for the night. They stay at the home of Lazarus and his sisters Mary and Martha, rather than risk traveling after sundown and on the start of the Sabbath. This will be their base throughout Passover week, and Jesus and the disciples plan to return here most nights for the promise of a hot meal and easy rest.

The Sabbath is the holiest day of the week. The Jews call it Shabbat, but the Romans name it for the planet Saturn.* It is a day of mandatory rest in the Jewish religion, commemorating God's rest after creating the universe. Jesus and the apostles spend that time quietly, preparing for the week to come.

The next morning, Jesus selects two disciples and gives them a most special task. "Go to the village ahead of you," he orders them, "and at once you will find a donkey tied there, with her colt by her. Untie them and bring them to me. If anyone says anything to you, tell him that the Lord needs them, and he will send them right away."

Then Jesus and the other ten disciples set out. Knowing that they will return to Lazarus's home this evening, they travel light, with no need for the satchel of supplies or the walking sticks most pilgrims carry.

Crowds of pilgrims press in around Jesus as he walks. Their voices carry the familiar drawl of their regions. The pilgrims are excited that their journey is almost over, and many are rejoicing that the famous Jesus of Nazareth is in their presence.

Just on the other side of Bethpage, the two disciples stand waiting. One holds the bridle of a donkey that has never been ridden. The animal is bareback. A disciple removes his square cloak and lays it across the animal's back as an improvised saddle. The other disciples remove their cloaks and lay them on the ground in an act of submission, forming a carpet on which the donkey can

---

*The days of the week take their names from the Roman fixation on the heavens. In order, they are named for the Sun, Moon, Mars, Mercury, Jupiter, Venus, and Saturn.

walk. Following this example, many of the pilgrims remove their own cloaks and lay them on the ground. Others gather palm fronds or snap branches off olive and cypress trees and wave them with delight.

This is the sign everyone has been waiting for. This is the fulfillment of Zechariah's prophecy.

"Blessed is the king!" shouts a disciple.

The people join in, exalting Jesus and crying out to him. "Hosanna," they chant. "Hosanna in the highest."

Jesus rides forth on the donkey, and the people bow down.

"O Lord, save us," they implore, thankful that the Christ has finally come to rescue them. "O Lord, grant us success. Blessed is he who comes in the name of the Lord." The words of thanksgiving are from Psalm 118, a psalm sung at Passover. This is the moment for which these simple peasants have waited so long. Of all the thousands of pilgrims who set out from Galilee, these are the lucky few who can tell their children and their children's children that they witnessed the grand moment when Jesus the Christ rode triumphantly into Jerusalem.

But not everyone bows down. A group of Pharisees has been waiting for Jesus and now look on with disgust. They call out to him, giving the Nazarene one last chance to avoid a charge of blasphemy. "Teacher," they yell, "rebuke your disciples!"

But Jesus refuses. "I tell you," he informs the Pharisees, "if they keep quiet, even the stones will cry out."

Others who have heard that Jesus is near have run out from Jerusalem, spreading palm branches across the path of the Nazarene. This is a traditional sign of triumph and glory.

The donkey stops atop the Mount of Olives. Jesus takes it all in. Tents cover the hillside, for this is where the poor Galileans camp during Passover. Jerusalem calls out to Jesus from just across the small Kidron Valley, and the Temple gleams in the midday sun. Throngs of pilgrims line the path winding down into the valley. The mud-and-limestone trail is remarkably steep, and Jesus will have to use great caution to guide the donkey downhill without getting thrown.

This is his day. Jesus's whole life has pointed to this moment, when he will ride forth to stake his claim to the title "king of the Jews."

Suddenly Jesus begins to weep. Perhaps it's the thought of spending a last week with his good friends Lazarus, Mary, and Martha. Maybe he foresees the eventual destruction of this great city. Or perhaps he looks on Jerusalem knowing that his own pageantry will be short-lived. For the Nazarene has powerful enemies within the city walls.

For the past three years, Jesus has been adored, but he has also been subject to attack and suspicion. Even his disciples, despite their deep belief in Jesus and his teachings, sometimes care more about jockeying for power than about understanding his true nature and his message for the world.

He has been very specific with the disciples that he is more than just an earthly Christ.

They don't understand.

He has told them again and again that he is a divine being, the Son of God.

They cannot comprehend that concept.

Jesus has made it clear that he is the Christ but that his kingdom is not of this world.

They don't understand what he's talking about.

Three times, Jesus has told his disciples that he will die this week.

But his followers refuse even to contemplate that.

Most frustrating of all is the fear that his disciples cannot understand the true message of Jesus. These men know him better than any other. They have walked countless miles at his side, listened to his teaching for hours on end, and sat with him in quiet reverence to pray. Yet the disciples still do not understand who he truly claims to be.

† † †

In his moment of triumph, Jesus is experiencing agony. He has long strategized about the words he will say at Passover and the effect they will have on his followers, both old and new. He knows that his claims of being a king will lead to his crucifixion. He will be sacrificed, just as surely as those countless Passover lambs. It is just a matter of when.

The Nazarene stares down at the path coursing through the olive trees. In the distance, he sees the garden at Gethsemane and then the flat depression of the narrow Kidron Valley. Looking across the valley, he sees this same well-trod path rising up to Jerusalem's city walls. The city gates are clearly visible, as are the Roman soldiers who man the entrances. Jesus sees the people rushing out to worship him, eagerly ripping palm branches off nearby trees and waving them. The green flutter of respect impresses Jesus, for it is a reminder that many believe he is the anointed one—Moses and David in the flesh, come to save them and lead them out of bondage.

But Jesus knows that while Moses and David are remembered for their great achievements, they were also cast out by society. Jesus is not a prince like Moses or a warrior like David. He is an intellectual. He deals in logic. The book of Deuteronomy predicted: "The Lord your God will raise up for you a prophet like me from among you, from your fellow Israelites. You must listen to him."

But that prophecy is dangerous. To claim he is the Son of God would make Jesus one of three things: a lunatic, a liar, or a divinity who fulfills Scripture. Few in the crowd believe that Jesus is deranged or a charlatan. But will they make that incredible leap to believe that Jesus is God in the flesh?

✝✝✝

Time to go. As the hosannas rain down on all sides, and the Pharisees look on from a place nearby with their usual veiled contempt, Jesus coaxes the donkey forward. Step by careful step, the two descend the Mount of Olives, cross the Kidron Valley, and travel through a tunnel of worshippers, with Jesus riding majestically up the hill and into the great and golden city of Jerusalem.

CHAPTER THIRTEEN

JERUSALEM
MONDAY, APRIL 3, A.D. 30
MORNING

IT IS DAWN. JESUS AND THE DISCIPLES ARE ALREADY ON THE move, walking purposefully from Bethany back into Jerusalem. The pandemonium of yesterday's jubilant entry into that city still rings in the Nazarene's ear. He was adored by the people as "Jesus, the prophet from Nazareth in Galilee" when he dismounted at the city gates. It was a coronation of sorts, a celebration. But to the authorities, the exhibition is cause for great concern. Jerusalem hasn't seen such a moment since Jewish rebels tried to capture the city in 4 B.C. and again in A.D. 6. Those rebels, of course, paid for the action with their lives.

Jesus knows this, just as he knows that the Roman governor and the Jewish high priest are constantly on the lookout for rebels and subversives. He is well aware that Pilate and Caiaphas received at least some word that the Nazarene had ridden into the city on a donkey, stirring up the Passover crowds. During the event, Jesus was calm, stepping down off the animal and walking straight up the great steps into the Temple courts. He did not go there to teach but to be a pilgrim just like any man from Galilee, observing the sights and smells and sounds of the Temple during Passover week.

Roman soldiers are posted throughout the Court of the Gentiles, and the Temple guards no doubt took note of Jesus and the people who crowded around him. But none of them made a move to arrest the Nazarene. Apprehending such a beloved public figure might cause a riot. With Jews pouring into Jerusalem by the hundreds of thousands, even the smallest confrontation could quickly get out of hand. The soldiers and guards are armed, but their numbers are minuscule in comparison with the number of pilgrims. Anyone trying to take Jesus into custody could be overwhelmed by the peasant hordes. Anger about the injustice of arresting such a peaceful man as Jesus would blend with the people's simmering rage about heavy taxation.

It was late afternoon when Jesus departed the Temple courts in order to get back to Bethany before nightfall. He and the disciples retraced their steps back out of Jerusalem, past the tent camps on the Mount of Olives, where trampled palm leaves and olive branches still littered the dirt road. Even though the crowds made it clear that they wanted him to be their king and treated his arrival as a prelude to his coronation, Jesus neither said nor did anything to lead Caiaphas or Pilate to believe he was plotting a rebellion.

But this day, a Monday, will be very different.

†††

Jesus spots a fig tree. He and the twelve are just outside Bethany, and Jesus has had little to eat this morning. He walks alone to the tree, hoping to pluck a piece of fruit, even though he knows that figs are out of season. Jesus scours the twisted branches but sees only leaves. He is annoyed at the tree. "May no one ever eat fruit from you again," he says.

The outburst is uncharacteristic, and the disciples take note.

But Jesus is just getting started. Once again the group walks into Jerusalem and straight to the Temple. It has been three years since Jesus turned over the money changers' tables, but now he plans to do it again. Only this time he has no whip, and he is no longer an unknown figure. The first incident was not quite forgotten, but it was minor enough that Jesus was able to resume his teaching in the courts almost immediately.

Things are different now. The stakes are higher. Jesus of Nazareth is famous. People follow him wherever he goes. His every movement is watched, as the Pharisees wait for him to make the vital slipup that will allow them to turn public opinion against him. The smart move would be for Jesus to avoid controversy, to remain peaceful, and to let the status quo hum along as smoothly as during every other Passover. A jarring public display of temper would be most unwise.

Jesus doesn't care. Without warning, he flips over a table and sends coins flying. Then another. And another. There are no vendors selling sheep and cattle today, so Jesus makes his statement by releasing the caged sacrificial doves and overturning the benches of the men who sell them. He then confronts those standing in line before the tables, driving away anyone in the act of buying or selling. He is angry but not out of control. His actions are methodical, and his every movement shows that he fears no soldier or guard.

When the confrontation is done, Jesus stands in the middle of the carnage. Coins litter the ground. Doves circle and land. "Hosanna," comes the cry of a spectator.

"It is written," Jesus calls out to the crowd now ringing him. The onlookers include irate money changers and the sellers of doves. Also present are parents with their children in tow, just like Mary and Joseph were with the young Jesus so many years ago. A substantial number of people in the crowd are followers of the Nazarene.

"My house will be called a house of prayer," Jesus says, quoting Isaiah, the prophet who foresaw so much of the Nazarene's life. "But you are making it a 'den of robbers.'"

The "robbers" quote comes from Jeremiah, the prophet who was threatened with death for daring to predict the fall of the Temple.

The Temple guards are tense. They know that arresting Jesus is now completely justifiable. He has interfered with the flow of commerce and called the Temple his home—as if he were God.

But a quick scan of the crowd shows that this would be unwise. The people aren't afraid of Jesus; they're empowered by him. He's just done something they've wanted to do every time they stood in that long line to change their money, watching corrupt men siphon off a significant piece of their earnings.

Even the little children are cheering for Jesus. "Hosanna to the Son of David," a child calls out.

And then, as if it were a game, another child calls out the same thing. Soon, some in the crowd beg to be healed, right there in the Temple. The Pharisees, as always, are watching. "Do you hear what these children are saying?" the chief priests and scribes call out indignantly to Jesus. The chief priests have now joined the crowd and observe Jesus with great concern. They will report his every move back to Caiaphas and perhaps even to Annas, the powerful former high priest who is also Caiaphas's father-in-law. The aging Annas is just as wily as Caiaphas and still wields a great deal of influence.

More Hosannas ring throughout the Temple courts, shouted again and again by children.

"Do you hear what these people are saying?" the chief priests repeat.

"From the lips of children and infants, you have ordained praise," Jesus tells them, quoting from David.

The religious leaders know the psalm well. It is a call for God to bask in the adoration of the children, then to rise up and strike hard at the powers of darkness that stand against him.

If the Pharisees' interpretation is correct, Jesus is actually comparing them with forces of evil.

Still, they don't motion for Jesus to be arrested. Nor do they try to stop him as he leaves the Temple, trailed by his disciples.

The sun is now setting, and the first cooking fires are being lit on the Mount of Olives. Jesus and the disciples once again make the long walk back to Bethany. For now, he is a free man.

For now.

†††

Six hundred years ago, when Jeremiah prophesied that the Temple would be destroyed, he was punished by being lowered into an empty well. He sank up to his waist in mud and was left to die.

Thirty-two years from now, a peasant named Jesus ben Ananias will also predict the Temple's destruction. He will be declared a madman at first, but his life will be spared by order of the

Roman governor—but only after he is flogged until his bones show.*

But the time of Jesus is different. He is not a lone man but a revolutionary with a band of disciples and a growing legion of followers. His outbursts in the Temple are an aggressive act against the religious leaders rather than a passive prediction that the Temple will one day fall. Jesus is now openly antagonistic toward Temple authorities.

Caiaphas has seen what happens when political revolt breaks out in the Temple courts and remembers the burning of the Temple porticoes after the death of Herod. He believes Jesus to be a false prophet. Today's display truly shows how dangerous Jesus has become.

The threat must be squelched. As the Temple's high priest and the most powerful Jewish authority in the world, Caiaphas is bound by religious law to take extreme measures against Jesus immediately. "If a prophet, or one who foretells by dreams, appears among you and announces to you a sign or wonder," the book of Deuteronomy reads, "that prophet or dreamer must be put to death for inciting rebellion against the Lord your God."

Caiaphas knows that Jesus is playing a very clever game by using the crowds as a tool to prevent his arrest. This is a game that Caiaphas plans to win. But to avoid the risk of becoming impure, he must move before sundown on Friday and the start of Passover.

This is the biggest week of the year for Caiaphas. He has an extraordinary number of obligations and administrative tasks to

---

*When Jesus ben Ananias continued for seven more years to proclaim loudly and publicly that the Temple would be destroyed, a Roman soldier permanently silenced him by catapulting a rock at his head. Four months later, the Romans destroyed the Temple as punishment for a Jewish revolt.

tend to if the Passover celebration is to come off smoothly. Rome is watching him closely, through the eyes of Pontius Pilate, and any failure on the part of Caiaphas during this most vital festival might lead to his dismissal.

But nothing matters more than silencing Jesus.

Time is running out. Passover starts in four short days.

CHAPTER FOURTEEN

THE SERENITY OF LAZARUS'S HOME PROVIDES JESUS AND THE disciples instant relief. After the day in the Temple and the two-mile walk from Jerusalem back to Bethany, the men are spent. Hospitality is a vital aspect of Jewish society, dating back to the days when the patriarch Abraham treated all guests as if they were angels in disguise, offering them lavish meals of veal, butter, bread, and milk. So it is that the spacious home of Lazarus, with its large courtyard and thick door to keep out intruders at night, is not just a refuge for Jesus and his disciples but also a vibrant link to the roots of their Jewish faith.

Lazarus's sisters, Martha and Mary,* dote on Jesus, though in

---

*Not to be confused with Jesus's mother or with Mary Magdalene. Mary and Martha were both extremely common names at the time—as was Jesus.

opposite ways. Martha is the older of the two, and hypervigilant, constantly fussing over the Nazarene. Mary, meanwhile, is enthralled with Jesus. She sits at his feet and sometimes shows her respect by anointing them with perfumed oil. In their own way, each woman gives him comfort. They also see to it that Jesus and the disciples remove their sandals and wash their feet upon returning each evening, so that any impurities or infections might be cleansed. A stepped pool in the basement offers Jesus a place to remove his robe and sleeveless knee-length tunic so that Martha and Mary can wash those, too.* He will then bathe and change into his other set of clothes. And of course Jesus and the others will wash their hands before sitting down to eat.

This week, Martha and Mary are serving two meals a day. Dinner consists of fresh bread, olive oil, soup, and sometimes beef or salted fish washed down with homemade wine. Breakfast features bread and fruit—though dried instead of fresh because melons and pomegranates are out of season. As Jesus learned on the road yesterday morning, fruit from the local fig and date orchards will not ripen for months to come.

There is no record about how Lazarus earned money, but

---

*They take care when cleaning the tunic because it is a most unique and expensive garment. Every man, woman, and child wears one as the undergarment closest to their skin. The Pharisees and other people of means wear tunics that extend down to their ankles, while the poor can afford only a knee-length version. Whether made of linen or wool, most tunics are constructed by stitching together rectangles of cloth, leaving seams that chafe and bind in three different places. But Jesus's tunic was woven on an upright loom, which allowed the weaver to construct a fine cylinder of fabric. The tunic is therefore completely seamless. A medieval legend will say it was given to Jesus by his mother, Mary. Others say it was a gift from one of the many benefactors who supported his ministry. Either way, it is unique to Judea, thus making it desirable to any robbers or highwaymen who might waylay Jesus and the disciples.

because Bethany is the breadbasket of Jerusalem, he most likely was a landowning farmer. Lazarus has a reputation for being charitable and can afford to offer his guests gracious hospitality. It is customary to take in passing strangers who need a place to sleep overnight. This becomes an issue during Passover, when entire families require shelter for a week. A man needs to be a shrewd judge of character in times like these, balancing hospitality with the possibility that he might unwittingly invite thieves or ne'er-do-wells into his home.

Even though Lazarus truly enjoys being with Jesus, the Nazarene's presence means much more than that. This is a man whom Lazarus trusts, reveres, and, indeed, says he owes his very life to.* The fact that Jesus travels with a dozen grown men, each with a man-size appetite and requiring a place to sleep, is a small price to pay for the Nazarene's company. Besides, the fussy Martha can easily handle the needs of all the men.

✝✝✝

Dawn breaks. The countdown to Passover continues as the citizens of Bethany stir. Some prepare for a day's work in the nearby fields, and others plan a walk into Jerusalem. Like people everywhere, they start the morning with their daily ablutions. There are no indoor toilets, so men and women alike venture outside to a concealed private spot. A hole in the ground—into which a spade of dirt from a nearby pile of earth is promptly thrown—meets this need. Teeth are cleaned with a short, soft branch pulled straight off a tree and chewed. Inside Lazarus's home, Jesus and his disciples wash their hands and eat their daily bread before setting out for another day in the Temple courts.

---

*The legend of Jesus's raising of Lazarus from the dead became so widespread that it was a main component in the Temple priests' plotting against Jesus.

The group soon falls in alongside a line of travelers. Today will be the last time Jesus ever teaches in the Temple courts, and he has prepared a number of parables that will explain difficult theological issues in ways that even the most unread listener can understand.

"Rabbi, look," exclaims a disciple as they walk past the fig tree Jesus confronted yesterday. Its roots are shriveled. "How did the fig tree wither so quickly?" the disciple asks.

"Truly I tell you, if you have faith and do not doubt, not only can you do what was done to the fig tree, but also you can say to this mountain, 'Go, throw yourself into the sea,' and it will be done. If you believe, you will receive whatever you ask for in prayer," Jesus responds.

For years to come, the disciples will marvel at what happened to that simple tree. They will write about it with awe, even decades from now, and quote Jesus's two-sentence response. Even though Jesus has performed wonders in front of them, this one seems to amaze them almost more than any other.

But the fig tree is just the start. The disciples will remember the events that take place today for as long as they live. They will quote Jesus again and again—not in sentences but in paragraphs and pages. The next twelve hours will be so exhausting that Jesus will make tomorrow a day of complete rest. But it will also be a time of challenge and triumph unlike any they have ever known.

The morning is beautiful. The sun shines. The cool April air is verdant with the fresh smells of new spring growth from the fields and orchards lining the road.

New life is everywhere, even as death approaches.

†††

As the group draws close to Jerusalem, Jesus knows that a drama will unfold. He sensed it yesterday, as the religious leaders hovered at the fringe of every crowd, watching him intently as he interacted with his followers.

This week, these priests and Pharisees are wearing robes that are even more resplendent than normal, choosing their most colorful and expensive garments as a way of setting themselves apart from the drably dressed pilgrims. The priestly robes are a reminder that the priests are vital members of the Temple, not mere visitors.

Jesus, meanwhile, still clothes himself like an average Galilean. He wears his seamless tunic and over it a simple robe. Sandals protect his feet from sharp pebbles and sticks as he walks but do little to keep off the dust. So the walk from Bethany down into Jerusalem often gives him an unwashed appearance by comparison to that of the Pharisees, many of whom have bathing facilities and ritual pools in their nearby homes. And while his accent might sound provincial within the confines of cosmopolitan Jerusalem, Jesus does nothing to hide his native tongue. If anything, it works to his advantage, for it so often leads the religious leaders to underestimate the Nazarene as just another pilgrim from Galilee.

††††

Jesus and the disciples pass through the city gates. Their movements are now being closely tracked by the religious authorities, so their arrival is noted immediately. Jerusalem has grown louder and more festive with every passing day, as pilgrims continue to travel there from throughout the world. Voices in Greek, Aramaic, Latin, Egyptian, and Hebrew fill the air. The bleating of lambs is another constant, as shepherds bring tens of thousands of the small animals into the city to have their throats slit on Friday.

That grisly duty will be performed by high priests, who stand for hours in the hot sun as the blood of the lambs soaks into their white ceremonial robes.

Jesus enters the Temple courts. Today he ignores the money changers and the men selling doves. He selects a spot in the shaded awnings of Solomon's Porch and begins to teach. The religious leaders arrive almost immediately, interrupting him.

"By what authority are you doing these things?" a chief priest demands, referring to reported acts of healing that Jesus performed yesterday. The interrogators who stand before the Nazarene are not just common Pharisees or scribes but the most elite of the religious leaders. Their presence is meant to awe those pilgrims who might otherwise be transfixed by Jesus. Their goal is to use their intellectual prowess to make the Nazarene appear stupid.

"And who gave you this authority?" asks a second priest.

"I will ask you one question," Jesus replies calmly. "If you answer, I will tell you by what authority I am doing these things." He has thought deeply and anticipated their questions.

The religious leaders have spoken with the Pharisees, who traveled to Galilee last year and are well aware that Jesus is clever. But they think him to be uneducated and unread and hope to lure him into a theological trap. The priests await Jesus's question.

"John's baptism," Jesus asks. "Where did it come from? Was it from heaven or from men?"

The religious leaders do not answer immediately. The crowd looks on apprehensively. On one side stands Jesus, on the other side, the self-proclaimed holy men. Finally the chief priests talk among themselves, debating Jesus's question from all angles: "If we say, 'From heaven,' you will ask, 'Then why did we not believe him?'"

Jesus says nothing. The religious leaders continue with their private conversation.

"But if we say that John's baptism came from men, we are afraid of the people, for they all hold that John was a prophet."

Jesus remains silent. The men haven't given him an answer yet, and the crowd knows it. It is becoming clear that the chief priests and elders are no different than those Pharisees who tried but failed to trap Jesus in Galilee. Once again the leaders are on the defensive. Their trap for Jesus has failed.

"We don't know," a chief priest finally says.

"I'll tell you the truth," Jesus replies in full view of his audience. "Tax collectors and prostitutes are entering the kingdom of God ahead of you. For John came to you to show the way of righteousness, and you did not believe him. But the tax collectors and prostitutes did. And even after you saw this, you did not repent and believe him."

The crowd is awed. The high priests are stunned into silence.

✝✝✝

Word of Jesus's intellectual victory spreads through the Temple courts. The pilgrims now love Jesus even more. They are speaking of him as a true prophet and hope he will live up to the promise of his celebratory entry into Jerusalem just two short days ago.

The sun climbs higher and higher in the sky, and business in the Temple courts goes on as Jesus holds the crowd in thrall. Rather than back down after their earlier embarrassment, the chief priests and elders continue to look on.

The Nazarene tells a parable about a wealthy landowner and his troublesome tenants. The summation is a line stating that the religious leaders will lose their authority and be replaced by others whose belief is more genuine.

Then Jesus tells a second parable, about heaven, comparing it to a wedding, with God as the father of the groom, preparing a luxurious banquet for his son's guests. Again the religious leaders are the subject of the final line, a barb about a guest who shows up poorly dressed and is then bound hand and foot and thrown from the ceremony. "For many are invited," Jesus says of heaven, "but few are chosen."

This stings badly. The authority of the religious leaders is that *they* are the chosen ones. For Jesus to state publicly that they are not is an enormous defamation of their character. So they finally leave the Temple courts and switch tactics, sending their own disciples out to wage theological battle. These disciples are smart. Rather than attacking Jesus, they try to soften him up with flattery. "Teacher, we know you are a man of integrity and that you teach the way of God in accordance with the truth. You aren't swayed by men because you pay no attention to who they are."

Then the flattery ends. Aware that they're unlikely to catch Jesus in a theological misstatement, the Pharisees' disciples now try to frame Jesus by using Rome. "What is your opinion?" they ask. "Is it right to pay taxes to Caesar or not?"

"Why are you trying to trap me?" Jesus seethes. He asks for someone to hand him a denarius. "Whose portrait is this?" he asks, holding up the coin. "And whose inscription?"

"Caesar's," they answer.

"Render unto Caesar what is Caesar's," Jesus tells them. "And to God what is God's."

Again the crowd is awed. Although Caesar is a feared name, the Nazarene has marginalized Rome without directly offending it. The brilliance of Jesus's words will last throughout the ages.

✝✝✝

Having failed in their mission, those disciples leave. They are soon replaced by the Sadducees, a wealthy and more liberal Temple sect who count Caiaphas among their number. Once again, they try to pierce the aura of Jesus's vulnerability with a religious riddle, and once again they fail.

Soon the Pharisees step forward to take their turn. "Teacher," asks their leader, a man known for being an expert in the law, "what is the greatest commandment in the law?"

Under the teachings of the Pharisees, there are 613 religious statutes. Even though each carries a designation marking it as either great or little, the fact remains that each must be followed. Asking Jesus to select one is a clever way of pushing him into a corner, making him defend his choice.

But Jesus does not choose from one of the established laws. Instead, he articulates a new one: "Love the Lord your God with all your heart and with all your soul and with all your mind. This is the first and greatest commandment."*

The Pharisees stand silent. How could anyone argue with that? Only, Jesus goes on to add a second law: "Love your neighbor as yourself. All the law and the prophets hang on these two commandments."

Jesus has now defeated the sharpest minds in the Temple. But he does not settle for victory and walk away. Instead, the Nazarene turns and excoriates the priests in front of the pilgrims. "Everything they do is for men to see," he tells the crowd. "They make their phylacteries wide and the tassels on their garments long. They love the place of honor at banquets and the most important seats in the synagogues. They love to be greeted in the marketplace and to have men call them 'Rabbi.'"

Six times, Jesus denounces the Pharisees as hypocrites. He

---

*Taken from Deuteronomy 6:5, which immediately follows Deuteronomy 6:4, the Shema and cornerstone of Judaism.

calls them a brood of vipers.* He tells them they are unclean. He denounces them for focusing on such trivial details of religious life as whether to tithe their allotment of herbs and spices, in the process completely missing the true heart of God's law.

Worst of all, Jesus predicts that these holy men will be condemned to hell.

"O Jerusalem, Jerusalem," Jesus laments, knowing his time of teaching is done. The Nazarene departs the Temple and will not be seen in public until the time of his condemnation. In fact, he seals his death sentence by predicting the destruction of the Temple. "Do you see all these great stones?" he asks. "Not one stone will be left on another; every one will be thrown down."

Jesus says these words to his disciples, but a Pharisee overhears. That statement will become a capital crime.

†††

A short time later, Jesus sits atop the Mount of Olives. A week that began in this very spot with him weeping while astride a donkey now finds him reflective. With the disciples sitting at his side, Jesus summarizes his short life. Darkness is falling as he tells his followers to live their lives to the fullest, speaking in parables so that they will comprehend the magnitude of his words. The disciples listen in rapt fascination but grow concerned as Jesus predicts that after his death they, too, will be persecuted and killed. Perhaps to lessen the impact of this, Jesus shares his thoughts on

---

*It was a widespread belief at the time that vipers were hatched inside their mother, then ate their way through her skin to get out, killing her in the process. Calling the Pharisees a "brood of vipers" was akin to calling them parent murderers, which is a loathsome distinction in any culture, but particularly so in a faith such as Judaism, which reverences family.

heaven and promises the disciples that God will reveal himself to them and the world.

"As you know," Jesus concludes, "the Passover is two days away—and the Son of Man will be handed over to be crucified."

✝✝✝

Even as Jesus speaks, the chief priests and the elders gather at Caiaphas's palace. They are now in a frenzy. Killing the Nazarene is the only answer. But time is short. First, Jesus must be arrested. After his arrest, there must be a trial. But the religious laws state that no trials can be held during Passover, and none can be held at night. If they are to kill Jesus, he must be arrested either tomorrow or Thursday and tried before sundown. Making matters even more pressing is the religious stipulation that if a death penalty is ordered, a full night must pass before the sentence can be carried out.

All of these details, Caiaphas knows, can be massaged. The most important thing right now is to take Jesus into custody. The other problems can be addressed once that occurs. None of the people who have listened to Jesus in the Temple courts can be alerted, or there could be a riot. Such a confrontation would mean Pontius Pilate's getting involved and Caiaphas's being blamed.

So the arrest must be an act of stealth.

For that, Caiaphas will need some help. Little does he know that one of Jesus's own disciples is making plans to provide it.

All he wants in return is money.

CHAPTER FIFTEEN

JUDAS ISCARIOT TRAVELS ALONE. JESUS HAS CHOSEN TO SPEND this day in rest, and now he and the other disciples remain behind at the home of Lazarus as Judas walks into Jerusalem by himself. It has been five days since the disciples arrived in Bethany and three since Jesus rode into Jerusalem on the donkey. But Jesus has yet to announce publicly that he is the Christ; nor has he done anything to lead an uprising against Rome. But he has enraged the religious leaders, which has put targets on his back and those of his disciples. "You will be handed over to be persecuted, and put to death, and you will be hated by all the nations because of me," Jesus predicted yesterday, when they were all sitting atop the Mount of Olives.

Judas did not sign on to be hated or executed. If Jesus just admits that he is the Christ, then he would triumph over the Romans. Surely the religious authorities would then be eager to align themselves with Jesus. All this talk of death and execution might come to an end.

So Judas has decided to force Jesus's hand.

Judas made his decision moments ago, during dinner, when Jesus and the disciples were eating at the home of a man named Simon the leper. The group lounged on pillows around the banquet table, plucking food from the small plates in the center with their right hand. As had happened so many times before, a woman approached Jesus to anoint him with perfume. It was Mary, sister of Lazarus, who broke off the thick neck of the flask and poured nard, an exotic scent imported from India, on Jesus's head in a show of devotion.

Judas expressed revulsion at such a waste of money. Passover, in particular, is a time when it is customary to give money to the poor. This time he was not alone in his disgust. Several other disciples joined in before Jesus put an end to the discussion.

"Leave her alone," Jesus ordered the disciples. "Why are you bothering her? She has done a beautiful thing to me. The poor you will always have with you, and you can help them anytime you want. But you will not always have me. She did what she could. She poured perfume on my body beforehand to prepare for my burial."

Once again, Jesus's words were bewildering. He allowed himself to be anointed like the Christ, and yet he was predicting his death.

Now, Judas boldly walks back into Jerusalem. The night air smells of wood smoke from the many campfires. Passover starts on the night of the first full moon after the spring equinox, which will be Friday evening.

Judas picks his way carefully down the bumpy dirt road. His march could be an act of stupidity—he knows this—for he is intent on going directly to the palace of Caiaphas, the most powerful man in the Jewish world. Judas believes that he has an offer of great value that will interest the leader of the Sanhedrin.

Judas is a known disciple of Jesus, however, and this strategy could very well lead to his arrest. Even if nothing like that happens, Judas is uncertain if an exalted religious leader such as Caiaphas will meet with an unwashed follower of Jesus.

Making his way from the valley and through Jerusalem's gates, Judas navigates the crowded streets to the expensive neighborhoods of the Upper City. He finds the home of Caiaphas and tells the guards his business. Much to his relief, Judas is not arrested. Instead, he is warmly welcomed into the spacious palace and led to a lavish room where the high priest is meeting with the other priests and elders.

The conversation immediately turns to Jesus.

"What are you willing to give me if I hand him over to you?" Judas asks.

If the high priests are surprised by Judas's behavior, they don't show it. They have set aside their normal arrogance. Their goal is to manipulate Judas into doing whatever it takes to arrange Jesus's arrest.

"Thirty silver coins," comes the reply.

This is 120 denarii, the equivalent of four months' wages.

Judas has lived the hand-to-mouth existence of Jesus's disciples for two long years, rarely having more than a few extra coins in his purse, and very little in the way of luxury. Now the chief priest is offering him a lucrative bounty to select a time and place, far from the Temple courts, to arrest Jesus.

Judas is a schemer. He has plotted the odds so that they are in his favor. He knows that if he takes the money, one of two things will happen: Jesus will be arrested and then declare himself to be the Christ. If the Nazarene truly is the Messiah, then he will have no problem saving himself from Caiaphas and the high priests.

However, if Jesus is not the Christ, he will die.

Either way, Judas's life will be spared.

Judas and Caiaphas make the deal. The traitorous disciple promises to begin searching immediately for a place to hand over Jesus. This will mean working closely with the Temple guards to arrange the arrest. He will have to slip away from Jesus and the other disciples to alert his new allies of Jesus's whereabouts. That may be difficult.

Thirty silver coins are counted out before Judas's eyes. They clang off one another as they fall into his purse. The traitor is paid in advance.

Judas walks alone back to Bethany. Robbers may be lurking on the roads. Judas wonders how he will explain his absence to Jesus and the others—and where he will hide such a large and noisy bounty.

But it will all work out. For Judas truly believes that he is smarter than his compatriots and deserving of reward in this life.

If Jesus is God, that will soon be known.

The next few hours will tell the tale.

CHAPTER SIXTEEN

JESUS HAS SO MUCH TO DO IN A VERY SHORT PERIOD OF TIME. He must at last define his life to the disciples. As the final hours to Passover approach, Jesus plans to organize a last meal with his followers before saying good-bye, for they have been eye-witnesses to his legacy. And he must trust them to pass it on.

But although these things are vitally important, there is something holding him back: the terrifying prospect of his coming death.

So Jesus is having trouble focusing on his final message to the disciples. Like every Jew, the Nazarene knows the painful horror and humiliation that await those condemned to the cross. He firmly believes he must fulfill what has been written in Scripture, but panic is overtaking him.

It doesn't help that the entire city of Jerusalem is in an anxious frenzy of last-minute Passover preparation. Everything must be made perfect for the holiday. A lamb must be purchased for the feast—and not just any lamb but an unblemished one-year-old male. And each home must be cleansed of leavened bread. Everywhere throughout Jerusalem, women frantically sweep floors and wipe down counters because even so much as a single crumb can bring forth impurity. At Lazarus's home, Martha and Mary are fastidious in their scrubbing and sweeping. After sundown Lazarus will walk through the house with a candle, in a symbolic search for any traces of leavened products. Finding none, it is hoped, he will declare his household ready for Passover.

At the palace home of the high priest Caiaphas, slaves and servants comb the grounds of the enormous estate in search of any barley, wheat, rye, oats, or spelt. They scrub sinks, ovens, and stoves of any trace of leaven. They sterilize pots and pans inside and out by bringing water to a boil in them, then adding a brick to allow that scalding water to flow over the sides. Silverware is being heated to a glow, then placed one at a time into boiling water. There is no need, however, to purchase the sacrificial lamb, as Caiaphas's family owns the entire Temple lamb concession.

At the former palace of Herod the Great, where Pontius Pilate and his wife, Claudia, once again are enduring Passover, there are no such preparations. The Roman governor begins his day with a shave, for he is clean-shaven and short-haired in the imperial fashion of the day. He cares little for Jewish tradition. He is not interested in the traditional belief that Moses and the Israelites were forced to flee Egypt without giving their bread time to rise, which led to leavened products being forbidden on Passover. For him there is *ientaculum*, *prandium*, and *cena* (breakfast, lunch, and dinner), including plenty of bread, most often leavened with salt (instead of yeast), in the Roman tradition. Back at his palace in Caesarea, Pilate might also be able to enjoy oysters and a slice of roast pork with his evening meal, but no such delicacies exist (or are permitted) within observant Jerusalem—particularly not on the eve of Passover. In fact, Caiaphas and the high priests will even refrain from entering Herod's palace as the feast draws near, for fear of becoming impure in the presence of the Romans and their pagan ways. This is actually a blessing for Pilate, ensuring him a short holiday from dealing with the Jews and their never-ending problems.

Or so he thinks.

✝✝✝

Judas Iscariot watches Jesus with a quiet intensity, waiting for the Nazarene to reveal his Passover plans so that he can slip away and inform Caiaphas. It would be easy enough to ask the high priest to send Temple guards to the home of Lazarus, but arresting Jesus so far from Jerusalem could be a disaster. Too many pilgrims would see the Nazarene marched back to the city in chains, thus possibly provoking the very riot scenario that so terrifies the religious leaders.

Judas is sure that none of the other disciples knows he has betrayed Jesus. So he bides his time, listening and waiting for that moment when Jesus summons his followers and tells them it is time to walk back into Jerusalem. It seems incomprehensible that Jesus would not return to the Holy City at least one more time during their stay. Perhaps Jesus is waiting for Passover to begin to reveal that he is the Christ. If that is so, then Scripture says this must happen in Jerusalem. Sooner or later, the Nazarene will go back to the Holy City.

✝✝✝

Next to the Temple, in the Antonia Fortress, the enormous cita-del where Roman troops are garrisoned, hundreds of soldiers file into the dining hall for their evening meal. These barracks are connected to the Temple at the northwest corner, and most men have stood guard today, walking through the military-only gate and onto the forty-five-foot-wide platform atop the colonnades that line the Temple walls. From there, it is easy enough to look down on the Jewish pilgrims as they fuss over last-minute Passover prep-arations. The entire week has been demanding and chaotic for the soldiers, who have spent hours standing in the hot sun. But tomor-row will be their most demanding day of all. Lambs and pilgrims will be everywhere, and the stench of drying blood and animal defecation will waft up to them from the innermost Temple courts. The slaughter will go on for hours, as will the sight of men clutch-ing the bloody carcasses of lambs to their chests as they rush from the Temple courts to cook their evening Seder.

Normally, the garrison comprises little more than five hun-dred soldiers and an equivalent number of support staff. But with Tiberius Caesar's troops having arrived from Caesarea for Pass-over, the number of legionaries has swollen into the thousands—and accompanying them is a full complement of support units and personal servants to shoe horses, tend to baggage, and carry water. Thus the dining hall is loud and boisterous as the men sit down to a first course of vegetables flavored with *garum*, the fer-mented sauce made of fish intestines that is a staple of Roman meals. The second course is porridge, made more flavorful with spices and herbs. Sometimes there is meat, but it's been hard to procure this week. Bread is the staple of the soldiers' diet, as is the sour wine made by combining vinegar, sugar, table wine, and grape juice. Like everything else set before these famished men, these are consumed quickly, and in large quantities.

Twelve soldiers hunch over their meals with the knowledge that they will witness the slaughter of much more than sheep tomorrow. For these are the men of the crucifixion death squads, soldiers of impressive strength and utter brutality assigned to the backbreaking task of hanging men on the cross, Roman-style.

Each crucifixion death squad consists of four men known as a *quaternio*. A fifth man, a centurion known as the *exactor mortis*, oversees their actions. Tomorrow three teams of killers will be needed, for three men have been condemned to die. The initial floggings will take place within the Jerusalem city walls, but the hard work of hoisting the men up onto the cross will take place outside, on a hill known as Calvaria or, as the Jews say in Aramaic, Gulgalta—or, as it will go down in history, Golgotha. Each word means the same thing: "skull," the shape of the low rise that is a place of execution. Even as the *quaternio* gulp down their dinner, the vertical pole onto which each man will be nailed already rests in the ground. These *staticula* remain in position at all times, awaiting the arrival of the *patibulum*, the crossbar that is carried by the con-demned.

In truth, a crucifixion can be accomplished with fewer than five men. But Roman standards are high, and it is part of each execu-tioner's job to keep an eye on his fellow members of the *quaternio*, ensuring that there is no sign of lenience toward the prisoner. A smaller death squad might not be as diligent. So it is that these well-trained soldiers approach tomorrow's crucifixions with total commitment. Anything less might result in their own punishment.

One of the men they will crucify is a common murderer named Barabbas. The other two are suspected of being his accomplices. In the morning, the death squads will begin the ritual crucifixion process. It is intensely physical work, and by day's end their uni-forms and bodies will be drenched in blood.

East view of the Temple showing the Antonia Fortress

But the soldiers of the death squads don't mind. In fact, many of them enjoy this work. They are thugs, tough men from Samaria and Caesarea whose job it is to send a message: Rome is all-powerful. Violate its law and you will die a grisly death.

✝✝✝

It is evening as Jesus leads the disciples back to Jerusalem for their final meal together. A benefactor has kindly rented a room for Jesus in the Lower City. It is on the second floor of a building near the Pool of Siloam. A long rectangular table just eighteen inches tall is the centerpiece of the room. It is surrounded by pillows on which Jesus and his disciples can lounge in the traditional fashion as they eat. The room is large enough for all to recline comfortably but small enough so that their overlapping conversations will soon fill the room with high-volume festive sounds.

Jesus sends John and Peter ahead to find the room and assemble the meal.*

This is most likely a tense time for Judas Iscariot, for he finally knows that Jesus plans to return to Jerusalem, but he does not know the hour or the exact location—and even when he obtains

---

*The Gospels of Matthew, Mark, and Luke make it clear that Jesus was celebrating the Passover meal a day early. This has prompted some to speculate as to whether Jesus served the traditional Passover menu of roast lamb. Pope Benedict XVI sought to solve this two-thousand-year-old argument by suggesting that Jesus celebrated Passover early by using the solar calendar date found in the Dead Sea Scrolls instead of the lunar calendar, and thus did not celebrate with lamb. Other scholars resolve the issue by arguing that the Synoptics base their calendar days on the Galilean Method (used by Jesus, his disciples, and Pharisees), from sunrise to sunrise; while John bases his calendar days on the Judean Method (used by the Sadducees), from sunset to sunset. This resolves the discrepancy, as the different calendars will place Passover meals at different times.

The Last Supper in the Upper Room

this information, he must still find a way to sneak off and alert Caiaphas.

Once in the room, Jesus begins the evening by humbling himself and washing each man's feet with water. This is a task normally reserved for slaves and servants, and certainly not for a venerated teacher of the faith. The disciples are touched by this show of servility and the humility it implies. Jesus knows them and their personalities so well and accepts them without judgment: Simon the zealot, with his passion for politics; the impulsive Peter; James and John, the boisterous "sons of thunder," as Jesus describes them;[*] the intense and often gloomy Thomas; the

---

*Mark 3:16–17.

upbeat Andrew; the downtrodden Philip; and the rest. Their time together has changed the lives of every man in this room. And as Jesus carefully and lovingly rinses the road dust from their feet, the depth of his affection is clear.

During dinner, Jesus turns all that good feeling into despair. "I tell you the truth," he says, "one of you will betray me."

The disciples haven't been paying close attention to their leader. The meal has been served and they are reclined, chatting with one another as they pick food from the small plates. But now shock and sadness fill the room. The disciples each take mental inventory, search for some sign of doubt or weakness that would cause any of them to hand over Jesus. "Surely, not I, Lord," they say, one by one. The comment goes around the table.

"It is one of the twelve," Jesus assures them. "One who dips bread into the bowl with me. The Son of Man will go, just as it is written. But woe to that man who betrays the Son of Man! It would be better for him if he had not been born."

As the conversation roars back into life, with each man wondering to his neighbor about the identity of the betrayer, Peter, in particular, is agitated. He signals to John, who rests on the pillow next to Jesus.

"Ask him which one he means," Peter says.

"Lord, who is it?" John asks, leaning closer to the Nazarene. He sits to Jesus's right, while Judas sits on Jesus's immediate left.

"Surely not I, Rabbi?" Judas blurts out.

"Yes, it is you," Jesus quietly answers. "What you are about to do, do quickly."

The room is noisy as the men talk among themselves, and most miss the final exchange between Judas and Jesus because the two men are sitting so close together. As Judas hastily stands and leaves, some assume that he is off to get more food or drink.

The traitor steps out into the night. Both he and the Nazarene know exactly where he's going. Jesus once trusted Judas, appointing him treasurer of the disciples, and openly called him friend. But as so often happens when money is involved, years of friendship can quickly evaporate.

Clutching his money bag, Judas walks through the streets and narrow alleys of the Lower City and up the steep hill to give Caiaphas the good news.

†††

The hour is late, and Jesus is on the move. He and his disciples walk across the Kidron Valley to an olive garden at the base of the Mount of Olives. Even though he knows they must be weary from the wine and food, he asks the disciples to stand guard while he climbs the hillside to find a private place to be alone.

"Sit here while I pray," he orders the men before ascending the steep slope. "My soul is overwhelmed with sorrow to the point of death," he tells the disciples. "Stay here and keep watch."

The moon is nearly full and provides ample light. Jesus finds a place in the darkness and prays. "Father, everything is possible for you. Take this cup from me. Yet not what I will, but what you will."

It is a moment of anguish and despair. Jesus is convinced that he will die. It will be a bloody death, on a Roman cross, with all the pain and public ridicule that implies. The people who have heard his marvelous words in the Temple courts will see him humiliated, and they will not understand how a man who claims to be the Son of God can allow himself to be crucified.

It would be so much easier if Jesus could just escape. He could keep on climbing the hill and walk straight back to Bethany. In the morning, he might journey home to Galilee, there to grow old quietly and raise a family. His words have accomplished just enough to give the people hope, but he never planned to lead them in rebellion. Jesus does not believe that is his earthly purpose. So he accepts his coming fate and makes no effort to flee.

After about an hour of prayer, Jesus returns to the garden at Gethsemane. But the disciples are sound asleep. "Could you not keep watch for one hour?" the Nazarene demands to know.

The disciples don't have an answer. But Jesus once again asks that they stay awake while he returns to his private spot for more prayer.

In the solitude of the night, Jesus asks God for relief. He is a man for whom faith comes easily, and making this request should be simple. But it is not. So now he prays a different prayer—one that asks for the strength to endure all that is to come. "My Father, if it is not possible for this cup to be taken away unless I drink it, may your will be done,"* Jesus pleads.

The Nazarene walks back down the slope to check on the disciples. All are again asleep, seemingly untroubled by worry or anguish. They seem to have ignored every single word Jesus has spoken to them about his suffering and impending death. It is as if they are willing to believe parts of his teaching and to wonder at his accomplishments, but they cannot accept the dark side of his message.

Jesus walks back up the hill to pray one last time. In his chronicling of the Nazarene's final days, the physician Luke put forth that Jesus began literally sweating blood. This condition is known as hematidrosis, and it is brought on by intense anxiety. Though

---

*Although none of the Gospel writers was present during Jesus's prayer, it is believed that he shared his words and emotions with those present in the garden that night.

rare, it is most often seen in condemned men as they begin walking toward their execution site.

His prayers finished, Jesus returns to his disciples, exhausted. The hour is past midnight, the air growing colder. Jesus wears just his cloak and sheer tunic, which allow his lean body little defense against the elements. The panic he experienced has not subsided—Jesus knows the end could come at any moment—but now, as he once again enters the garden at Gethsemane, he knows it is time to accept his fate.

"Rise," he tells his disciples. His voice is steady, and he can clearly see the torches and line of men approaching from across the Kidron Valley. Instead of fleeing, Jesus of Nazareth waits.

†††

The traitor Judas leads a pack of Temple guards into the garden. Each man carries either a club or a sword, and some also wield the torches and lanterns that cut through the darkness. Yet the flames are not bright enough to ensure that the guards can see which of the bearded men before them is Jesus. Judas has anticipated this and walks innocently to the Nazarene.

"Greetings, Rabbi," he says coldly, kissing Jesus on the cheek. This is the agreed-upon signal between Judas and the Temple guards.

"Friend," Jesus replies, "do what you came for."

He then turns and looks at the guards. "Who is it you want?"

"Jesus of Nazareth," comes the reply.

"I am he," Jesus answers.

The Temple guards are not Gentile Roman soldiers but Jewish employees of the Temple courts. Nonetheless, they are physical men, well acquainted with the force needed to make an arrest. Before Jesus's wrists can be tied, however, Peter draws his new sword and cuts off the ear of Malchus, the servant of Caiaphas.*

"Put your sword away," Jesus commands the ever-impulsive Peter. "For those who draw the sword must also die by the sword."

Then Jesus submits to being bound and led away. For Judas, all has gone according to plan. At this late hour, few have seen the commotion.

So it is that Jesus, his captors, and Judas march to the home of the high priest on the eve of Passover. The disciples lag behind, frightened for their lives. Since it is the middle of the night, a trial is not possible. If religious law is to be obeyed, Jesus must wait until morning to face his accusers. And based on those same laws, if a death sentence is passed the next morning, the mandatory full day of reprieve before execution would mean that Jesus has at least one or two days to live.

Jesus is not counting on the disciples to come to his rescue. Indeed, if he were, that hope would now be proven futile, for his terrified followers have turned and are now in full flight.

The night air is crisp and cool. Most of Jerusalem is asleep as the prisoner is led to the house of the high priest. The route takes them past the room where, just a few hours ago, Jesus and his disciples celebrated their last supper.

The Nazarene knows he will die alone. Though he is surrounded by men, Jesus has no allies right now. His disciples have disappeared into the night. And those who arrested him would happily beat him into unconsciousness if he tried to flee.

Yet, despite his hopeless situation, Jesus of Nazareth keeps his composure. He will be questioned extensively, and what he says

---

*That scene was witnessed by John, who made it a focal point of his Gospel.

will be written for the ages. His interrogators will be the same men whom he verbally humiliated two days ago in the Temple courts. He saw the hatred in their eyes then.

They pass the houses of the Upper City, which are larger and more regal than dwellings anywhere else in Jerusalem. Jesus is soon led into the palace of the high priest. Only he is not greeted by Joseph Caiaphas but by the true religious power in Jerusalem. Jesus now stands before the aging and regal leader of a priestly dynasty dating back a thousand years. The man before him has great wealth and is so skilled a politician that his sons and the husbands of his daughters are continuing the family lineage of priesthood and power. The man's name is Ananus, son of Sethi—or, as this elderly religious titan is known throughout Jerusalem, Annas.

The courtyard is still. Inside, the interrogation of Jesus commences. Moments later, he is surprised by a sudden and hard blow to the face.

The end has begun.

CHAPTER SEVENTEEN

THE ASSAULT COMES OUT OF NOWHERE, A HARD PUNCH TO the head delivered by a short-fused Temple guard. "Is this the way you answer the high priest?"

Jesus staggers, unable to answer. The opulent palace room reels. His hands are still bound, and he can neither protect himself nor fight back. But even as the Nazarene absorbs the blow, he speaks without fear. "If I said something wrong, testify as to what is wrong," he finally tells the guard. "But if I spoke the truth, why did you strike me?"

A bleary-eyed Annas stands before Jesus. It is closer to dawn than midnight. The high priest is in his midfifties, a man whose entire life has revolved around procuring wealth and power. Normally, men such as Jesus bow to him, pleading for mercy rather than trying to bend his mind with logic at this awful hour. "I have spoken openly to the world," Jesus said just moments ago. "I always taught in synagogues or at the Temple, where all the Jews come together. I said nothing in secret. Why question me? Ask those who heard me. Surely they know what I said."

Those were the fearless and articulate words that spurred the guard to strike Jesus. They now echo in Annas's skull as he tries to figure out his next move.

The patriarch is a Zadokite, descended from a line of priests dating back to King David. Like his sons and son-in-law Caiaphas, he is also a Sadducee, a member of a wealthy Jewish sect that believes only in the Pentateuch, as the five books of Moses are known. Annas has made many compromises with Rome in order to maneuver his way into power. The job of high priest was passed down through the Zadokite lineage for centuries, but Alexander the Great's conquest of the Jewish homeland three centuries ago led to an attempt to Hellenize the region. This is why Annas is fluent in Greek as well as Hebrew, for his family long ago learned the importance of pleasing its conquerors. A group of Jews known as the Hasmoneans put an end to overt Hellenization in 142 B.C. but also stripped the Zadokites of the high priesthood. This became a blessing of sorts when the Romans conquered Jerusalem eighty years later. Non-Zadokite priests were singled out for massacre when Pompey and his troops looted the city after a three-month siege. It was Herod the Great who finally restored the Zadokites to the high priesthood.

But with that power came compromise, for Herod made sure that these new priests served at his favor—and that meant bowing down to Rome. No longer are the high priests autonomous. It is a lesson Annas learned when he was removed from his position by Pontius Pilate's predecessor, Gratus, for imposing and executing capital sentences, which had been forbidden by the imperial government. Making the same mistake twice—or allowing Caiaphas to make this mistake—could be catastrophic. As patriarch, Annas sees that the future of the family dynasty might just rest on how he handles the Jesus situation.

But the title of high priest is one that a man carries for life. Rome likes it that way because it ensures that the money pipeline flows uninterrupted. Annas; his son Eleazar; his son-in-law Caiaphas; and his other sons, Jonathan, Theophilus, Matthias, and Ananus, will all take turns serving as high priest. They will control the sale of Temple lambs at Passover and receive a cut of every exchange made by the money changers. Outside Jerusalem, the high priests own vast farms and estates. The profits from these ventures, in addition to the taxes extorted from the people of Judea, are all shared with Pilate and eventually with the debauched Roman emperor Tiberius, who gets a substantial amount of money in the form of "tribute."

So it is that the lineage of Jesus and Annas has been intertwined for centuries and will be for decades to come. Annas's forefathers served as high priests under Jesus's forebears David and Solomon. And just as Annas now stands in judgment of Jesus, so the younger Ananus will sentence another devout man to death three decades from now.

That man's name is James. He is a sibling of Jesus, and he will be publicly stoned to death.

Indeed, so fierce is Annas and his descendants' loyalty to Rome that the final link in their claim to the priesthood will come to an end thirty years from now, when the younger Ananus is killed in a Jewish uprising for advocating a continuation of Roman rule.*

✝✝✝

Everything about Jesus's interrogation is illegal: it takes place at night, Jesus is asked to incriminate himself without a lawyer, and Annas has no authority to pass sentence. It is also highly unusual for a prisoner to be brought to the high priest's personal residence, rather than to the prison cells at the Roman barracks.

But Jesus has committed a grave offense: he interrupted the flow of funds from the Temple to Rome when he flipped over the money changers' tables. The pipeline is the personal responsibility of Annas. Anyone interfering with the profit taking must be punished. That, of course, includes Jesus and every single one of his disciples. Annas is determined that this will be a cautionary tale for anyone who considers challenging the authority of the Temple courts.

A man like Annas is used to people bowing and scraping in his presence, but it is clear that Jesus will not genuflect to any man. And despite Jesus's weakened condition, he is still capable of great feats of intellect.

Perhaps some time alone with the Temple guards will change Jesus's attitude.

As a former high priest, Annas has no jurisdictional powers. He cannot pass sentence, particularly in matters concerning sedition or insurrection, for that power belongs solely to Rome. Thus

---

*Ananus was killed by poor Jewish rebels who were engaging in an act of class warfare against the wealthy high priests. The historian Josephus wrote that Ananus was "butchered in the heart of Jerusalem." He goes on to claim that this was one of the key events that eventually led to the Temple's destruction by the Romans.

Annas secretly orders a gang of Temple guards to escort Jesus to a quiet place on the palace grounds where they might spend some time together.*

Jesus, still bound, is led away. An urgent call goes out through Jerusalem. The high religious court of the Sanhedrin must assemble immediately.

✝✝✝

Jesus cannot see. The night is dark, and the blindfold covering his eyes shuts out even the minimal light of the small fires.

But he can hear extremely well, and the words directed at him are clearly meant to break his spirit. "Prophesy," a Temple guard calls out scornfully. Jesus is staggered by another hard punch. "Who hit you?" the guard mocks.

Fists and kicks come from all sides. There is no escape and no respite.

"Who hit you?" the guards call out again and again, landing more blows. "Who hit you?"

The beating goes on for hours, until the Temple guards become too tired to continue their savage game.

By the time Jesus is led back into Annas's home to confront the Sanhedrin in yet another illegal trial, he is bloodied and

---

*The guards on duty this night were the Levites who served as the Temple's police force. Under normal circumstances they served as gatekeepers to the Temple entrances, patrolled the Temple grounds day and night, and stood watch at one of the twenty-one posts in the Court of the Gentiles. They also served at the disposal of the Sanhedrin, making arrests and meting out punishments, and were quite used to providing muscle for the chief priests. These actions were carried out so commonly that many Jewish groups complained about the constant abuse of power by aristocratic priests and their Temple guards. The Dead Sea Scrolls, Josephus, and later rabbinic texts chronicle these abuses.

bruised. His face is swollen. Exhaustion and weakness caused by a loss of plasma make it difficult for him to stand, let alone form the coherent arguments that might save him.

Yet once again, the bound and beaten Jesus must rise before his accusers and argue for his life.

✝✝✝

Jesus appears before the Sanhedrin, no longer blindfolded. It is impossible to tell whether all seventy-one members of the religious court are crowded into the room, but he has not been taken to the Temple courts, as law requires. Instead, the clerics surround him in the residential warmth of Annas's palace home, where Jesus can clearly see the mosaic floors and the fashionable paintings hanging from the walls.

Bruises cover Jesus's body and face, and he has not eaten since the Last Supper. Yet the beating and the mocking have not broken his spirit. Despite the late hour, news of Jesus's arrest has made its way around Jerusalem. A small crowd now gathers in the courtyard, warming themselves by the fire pits. A second group stands outside the palace's gates, waiting for any news. Two of the disciples* have had second thoughts about abandoning Jesus and have braved arrest to be here. They stand among a number of men loyal to Caiaphas.

Jesus watches as, one by one, Caiaphas's sycophants come in out of the cold to falsely testify against him. They stand before the Sanhedrin and brazenly lie about Jesus, spinning stories about things he has said and done. The members of the Sanhedrin listen closely, waiting for the one accusation that might allow them

---

*Peter is mentioned by name in John 18:15. The passage references "another disciple," though not by name. Based on his vivid depiction of that night's events, it is widely believed that John was this individual.

to pass the death sentence. They tolerate the litany of lies, trusting that an accusation worthy of a death sentence will eventually be revealed in these proceedings—even if it takes all night. Technically, bearing false witness is a crime punishable by death, but the Sanhedrin is willing to conveniently sidestep that legality for tonight.

Throughout the process, Jesus says nothing.

Then comes the accusation for which the Sanhedrin is waiting. "This fellow," swear two men loyal to Caiaphas, "said, 'I am able to destroy the Temple of God and rebuild it in three days.'"

Caiaphas has been sitting, but now he suddenly rises and advances toward Jesus. To Caiaphas's utter fury, Jesus does not contest this allegation. One look at the Nazarene and it is clear that his will should have been broken hours ago—the dried blood, the residue of spittle, the hematomas, and the swelling. Yet Jesus is placid and ever defiant.

"Are you not going to answer?" Caiaphas demands with indignation. "What is this testimony that these men are bringing against you?"

Jesus remains silent. He can see the question forming on Caiaphas's lips. It is the query to which everyone in the room wants an answer. Indeed, it is the one question that hundreds of thousands here in Jerusalem also want answered. But even as Jesus anticipates what Caiaphas is about to ask next, he also realizes that there is no proper response. His death is imminent, no matter what he says.

"I charge you under oath," fumes Caiaphas, "by the living God: tell us if you are the Christ, the Son of God."

Silence. Outside, the first birds of morning are stirring. Conversations can be heard from beyond the courtroom. But in this public room where Caiaphas usually socializes and privately conducts official Temple business, no one utters so much as a syllable as they anxiously await Jesus's decision: Will he finally speak?

Jesus *does* answer: "If I tell you, you will not believe me. And if I asked you, you would not answer. But from now on, the Son of Man will be seated at the right hand of the mighty God."

"Are *you* the Son of God?" the priests demand.

"Yes," he tells them. "It is as you say."

Then Jesus looks straight at Caiaphas: "*You* will see the Son of Man seated at the right hand of the Power, and coming with the clouds of heaven."*

Caiaphas grabs the front of his own tunic and wrenches the expensive fabric, tearing it down from his chest. Under normal circumstances, high priests are forbidden to display anger in such a manner. But these are not normal circumstances, for Jesus is implying nothing less than that Caiaphas is an enemy of God.

"He has spoken blasphemy," the high priest tells the Sanhedrin. "Why do we need any more witnesses? Look, now you have heard the blasphemy. What do you think?"

Religious law says that each member of the Sanhedrin must cast a vote when passing sentence. But now there is no vote. The verdict is passed by simple consensus. The only voices of dissent come from Nicodemus and a wealthy Sadducee named Joseph of Arimathea.

The sun is rising. Jesus has been convicted of blasphemy and sentenced to death. The next step is as easy, or as difficult, as convincing Pontius Pilate to order his Roman executioners to do the deed.

---

*A combination of Daniel 7:13 and Psalms 110:1.

†††

Across Jerusalem, in the Antonia Fortress, the dozen men who comprise the Roman death squads sit down to *ientaculum*, their big meal of the day. They will most likely not be able to get back to the barracks for the light midday *prandium*, so they enjoy their large portion of porridge. It is often served with cheese and honey to make it ever more filling and to provide more energy for the hard labor to come. Bread, weak beer, and red wine are spread out on the long communal table.

Barabbas and his cohorts, already condemned to death, are being held not far away, in the fortress's stone dungeons. In time, they will be taken into the courtyard for a scourging—or *verberatio*, as it is known by the Romans. Low scourging posts are permanently positioned there for this task. Affixed to the top of each post is a metal ring. Each condemned man will be brought forth with his hands tied. The executioners will strip him of his clothing and then force him to his knees, before binding his hands over his head to the metal ring. The wrists will then also be shackled to the ring. This locks the body in position, preventing any squirming or other attempts to dodge the blows of the *flagellum*. Even before the first lash is laid against a man's back, it is common for the victim to tense every muscle in his body and grit his teeth against the horrible pain that will soon be inflicted.

The key to the executioners' art is not how hard they whip a man but the effort with which they yank the whip's metal- and bone-flecked tendrils away from the flesh after each blow. For this is when the primary damage to the body is done.

To prove themselves superior, the professional killers—now casually eating their morning meal—strive to grip the wooden handle of the flagellum a little harder than their peers and lean into a lash with just a bit more strength. If they do their jobs exceptionally well, they might expose the victim's internal organs. As the historian Eusebius will write of the spectacle, "Bystanders were struck with amazement when they saw them lacerated with scourges even to the innermost veins and arteries, so that the hidden inward parts of the body, both their bowels and their members, were exposed to view."

Yet as horrific as the process of lashing might be, it is just the start of the agony. For *verberatio* is a mere prelude to crucifixion.

The soldiers finish their porridge and push back from the table. Time to go to work.

✝✝✝

The condemned Jesus is marched to the palace of Pontius Pilate. The sound of his sandals, and those of the high priests and Temple guards who surround him on all sides, echo off the cobblestones. It is not yet 7:00 A.M. and Jerusalem is just waking up. The path takes Jesus past the small *stratopedon* ("barracks"), where a garrison of palace soldiers grimly watches the procession, and then winds past the lavish formal garden Herod the Great constructed so long ago, with its ponds, groves of trees, and quiet walkways from which doves can be seen alongside small streams. Palace walls form the northern boundary of the garden, and now Jesus is marched along those walls to the front gate, where soldiers take their four-hour guard shift.

Caiaphas demands an immediate audience with Pilate. He stands outside the gates with Jesus, the Temple guard, and the entire Sanhedrin. But since the high priest cannot enter a Gentile residence so close to Passover, or risk becoming unclean and unable to eat the sacred meal, he requests that Pilate come down to the gate. It is a gross violation of their formal relationship, but surely Pilate will understand.

The palace is enormous, a fortified square measuring 140 meters from south to north. It consists of two lavish wings, one named the Caesareum and the other Agrippium. Towers rise at intervals along its walls, and columned courtyards provide open space. At the south end, just on the other side of the palace walls, is a special courtyard known as the *praetorium*, where pronouncements, trials, and other public gatherings can take place. So it takes a while to get word to Pilate and for the prefect to dress and make his way down to the gate. He could not have been pleased to be faced with the sight of Temple guards, lavishly dressed priests, and a prisoner who was clearly in an advanced state of physical suffering.

"What charges are you bringing against this man?" Pilate asks gruffly.

Caiaphas has been dreading this moment. For, while he wants the Romans to kill Jesus, the charge of blasphemy is a Jewish offense. Rome could not care less about it. And Pilate, with his intolerance for the Jews, is not the sort to risk his career by allowing Jewish law to dictate whom he executes.

"If he were not a criminal, would we have handed him over to you?" Caiaphas replies, avoiding the question.

Pilate is not easily swayed. "Take him yourselves, and judge him by your own law."

"But we have no right to execute anyone," Caiaphas responds.

"I find no basis for a charge against this man," Pilate replies.

Another of the priests speaks up. "He stirs up people all over Judea by his teaching. He started in Galilee and has come all the way here."

"He's a Galilean?" Pilate demands. In this simple question, he sees a way out of this mess. The Sanhedrin is clearly luring him into a political trap. But if Jesus is a Galilean, this matter is better suited for Herod Antipas. Galilee is the tetrarch's jurisdiction, and Antipas is staying in a palace just a few blocks away.

Pilate refuses to accept custody of Jesus. He dismisses the entire gathering and orders Jesus to be bound over to Antipas. Once again, Jesus is marched through the early dawn streets of upper Jerusalem. There is no sign of the peasant pilgrims from Galilee or of any of the other poorer class of Jews, for they have no reason to be wandering through this wealthy neighborhood at such an early hour. Slaves can be seen sweeping the porches of their masters' homes while, inside, the wealthy take their morning meal.

But if Pilate thinks he has escaped from Caiaphas's snare, he is wrong. For soon the entire Temple group, including Jesus, returns. Herod Antipas was most delighted to finally meet the Nazarene and spent a short time taking the measure of him. The tetrarch even requested a miracle for his personal amusement.

Antipas has no fear of Caiaphas or the high priests, for they have no power over him. So even as they launched volley after volley of accusation about Jesus, hoping to swing the tetrarch over to their side, Antipas refused to listen. Getting pulled into a power struggle between the Temple and Rome is most unwise. Besides, he is still haunted by the death of John the Baptist and the predictions by many that it will bring down his kingdom. The last thing Antipas needs is the blood of another holy man on his hands.

Even though Jesus refused to perform a miracle, Antipas saw no reason to condemn him to death. He let his soldiers have their fun, allowing them to taunt the Nazarene and ridicule him by questioning his royalty before placing an old military mantle on the prisoner's shoulders. It was purple, the color of kings.

†††

Now, once again, Pilate stands at his palace gates debating what to do about Jesus. He has underestimated Antipas, forgetting that the tetrarch was raised in a household where treachery and guile were as routine as breathing. Strangely, Pilate sees Antipas's decision as a quiet show of solidarity with him, for Antipas, a Jew, has clearly chosen to back Rome instead of the Temple priests. Pilate and Antipas were enemies until now, but they will count each other as friends from this day forward.

But Pilate must still deal with the wily Caiaphas, who has been coached in palace intrigue by Annas and again stands before him.

Pilate is running out of options. Clearly he cannot order the Jews to release Jesus, for that would be interfering in their religious law—and Emperor Tiberius has made it quite clear that Roman governors cannot do this.

Still, he doesn't have to accept the prisoner. He could order that Caiaphas send Jesus over to the Antonia Fortress, there to be held until after Passover—perhaps long after Passover, when Pilate has already left town. Above all, Pontius Pilate does not want trouble. So he finally sends Caiaphas on his way and reluctantly accepts custody of the Nazarene.

The fate of Jesus is now in the hands of Rome.

†††

Pontius Pilate is curious. "Are you the king of the Jews?" he asks Jesus. The governor is seated on a throne of judgment, looking down upon an open-air courtyard paved with flagstones. A small audience watches.

Pilate has chosen this location for many reasons. It is far removed from the center of the palace, near where his small personal garrison is housed. The courtyard is not actually in the palace but adjacent to it. Its unique architecture allows Pilate to address his subjects from an elevated position while also providing him a private entrance where he can come and go and where prisoners such as Jesus can be led out and tried, then quietly walked back to the prison cells.

Another advantage to the location, at the outer edge of the palace grounds, is that it's not actually inside the residence, and so Jews are permitted to enter on the eve of Passover. Hence the presence of Temple priests and Caiaphas's disciples, who are carefully monitoring the proceedings for their leader. They are there to ensure that the sentence passed by Caiaphas and the Pharisees is carried out.

"Is that your own idea, or did others talk to you about me?" Jesus asks in return.

"Am I a Jew?" Pilate asks. "It was your people and your chief priests who handed you over to me. What is it you have done?"

"My kingdom is not of this world. If it were, my servants would fight to prevent my arrest. But now my kingdom is from another place."

"You are a king, then!" says an amused Pilate. This is good news for the governor, for by declaring himself to be sovereign, Jesus has now committed a crime against Rome and the emperor. He is now a serious threat to public order. Whatever happens next can now be justified.

"You are right in saying I am a king. In fact, for this reason I am born, and for this reason I came into the world, to testify to the truth. Everyone on the side of the truth listens to me," Jesus responds.

"What is truth?" Pilate asks, now fascinated by Jesus.

But if the Roman was expecting an answer to that question, he is disappointed, as Jesus stands mute.

Pilate knows that preaching is not a crime—unless rebellion against Rome is a theme of that preaching. But any dissension from the powerful Sanhedrin will not help Pilate with Tiberius. So he turns his attention from Jesus to the disciples of the Jewish Temple who fill the courtyard. From his lofty perch, he can look down upon the group, measuring their reaction.

It is customary for the Roman prefect to release a prisoner at the time of Passover.* Now Pilate finds a simple solution to ease out of this politically volatile situation: he will give the crowd a choice between releasing the peaceful Jesus or the horrific Barabbas, a terrorist and murderer whose crimes truly deserve punishment.

"Do you want me to release the king of the Jews?" Pilate asks the crowd.

The response surprises him. For Pilate is not aware that the people he is speaking to have been ordered by the high priests and religious elders to make sure that Jesus is executed. It is not the Jewish pilgrims who want Jesus dead, nor most of the residents of Jerusalem. No, it is a small handful of men who enrich themselves through the Temple. To them, a man who speaks the truth is far more dangerous than a mass murderer.

"Give us Barabbas," they shout back.

✝✝✝

At the same time that Jesus is being judged, the business of Passover begins in the Temple courts. Despite their sleepless night, Caiaphas and the other priests cannot afford the luxury of a

---

*Matthew 27:15, Mark 15:6, Luke 23:17, and John 18:39.

morning's rest. Soon they walk across the bridge connecting the Upper City with the Temple and prepare to go about their day. Already, long lines of pilgrims are forming, and with them grows the incessant bleating of young male lambs.

The first sacrifices will take place at noon, in keeping with the law. Rows of priests are now assembling, some carrying silver bowls and others gold. These are for catching the blood of the lamb as its throat is slit. The bowls are then carried to the altar and the blood poured in sacrifice. A Levite choir is gathering as well, along with men who will honor this great day with blasts from their silver trumpets.

†††

Pontius Pilate does not care a whit about what is happening inside the Temple. The focus of his attention is the problem still standing before him. The Roman governor does not believe that executing such a popular figure as Jesus is a wise decision. Any unrest among the people following an execution of this sort would certainly be reported to Tiberius, and any fallout laid at the feet of Pilate.

So rather than crucify Jesus, Pilate sentences the Nazarene to *verberatio*. Perhaps that will appease the Sanhedrin. The Roman governor calls the high priests and church elders together to announce this decision. "You brought me this man as one who was inciting the people to rebellion. I have examined him in your presence and found no basis for your charges against him. Neither has Herod, for he sent him back to us. As you can see, he has done nothing to deserve death. Therefore, I will punish him and release him."

Within moments, the Nazarene is stripped and led into the *praetorium* courtyard.

The scourging pole awaits.

CHAPTER EIGHTEEN

Jesus endures. As with any other victim, his hands are manacled to the metal ring atop the scourging post, rendering him unable to move. Two legionaries stand behind him, one on either side. Each grasps a wooden-handled *flagrum*, from which extend three leather tendrils. Each thong is roughly three feet long. Today, rather than bits of metal or sheep bone, the executioners have affixed to the tips small lead weights known as *plumbatae*. The choice is strategic. These dumbbell-shaped implements do not rip away flesh and muscle as quickly as the sharper *scorpiones* tips. It is not yet time for Jesus to die.

A third legionary stands to one side. He holds an abacus so that he might keep track of the number of blows inflicted. The fourth member of the *quaternio* is the man responsible for tying and chaining Jesus to the scourging post. He now stands by to replace any member of the death squad who tires in his duties. Watching over all of them is the *exactor mortis*, the supervisor.

Jesus feels the lash. There is no gap between the blows. The instant one executioner pulls back his whip, the other unfurls his lash across Jesus's back. Even when the tendrils of leather and lead get tangled, the soldiers don't stop. The most lashes a man can receive under the laws of Moses are "forty minus one," but the Romans don't always trifle with Jewish legalities. Pilate has told these men to lash Jesus, and now they do so until the Nazarene is physically broken but not yet dead.

That is the order: scourge the Nazarene, but under no circumstances is he to be killed.

After the whipping, Jesus is unchained and helped to his feet. He has cried out in pain during his scourging, but he has not vomited or had a seizure, as many do. Still, he is losing a lot of blood, due to his severely lacerated back. The lash marks extend down to the back of his calves. And in addition to the dehydration that has plagued him all night, Jesus is in the early stages of shock.

The Roman death squad has clearly done its job. Striking at the Nazarene with surgical precision, they have beaten him almost to death. Pilate has made it clear that this will be the extent of their duties today. Yet they stand by for more, just in case.

Jesus's hands are still tied in front of him. He is slowly led back to the prison, where the Roman soldiers have their own brand of fun with this unique prisoner. Jesus does nothing as they drape that filthy purple cloak over his naked body, knowing it will soon stick to his wounds. The soldiers then make a faux scepter from a reed and thrust it into Jesus's hands, again mocking his claim of being king. Rather than take pity on a man who has just endured a scourging, the soldiers spit on the Nazarene.

If the soldiers stopped there, it would be a moment of low comedy by a group of barbaric men. But these brutes now turn their mockery into sadism. Up to this point it can be argued that they are merely soldiers, doing the job they were trained to do. Certainly, the Nazi death squads of World War II, who will pattern much of their behavior after the cold, heartless actions of the Roman *quaternio*, used that defense. The actions of Julius Caesar and so many other Roman warriors clearly show that unthinkably harsh punishment was a standard way to deal with enemies of Rome. There was even a certain pathological creativity to their methods.

But now the soldiers guarding Jesus up the ante. This is not a single death squad but an entire company of Pilate's handpicked legionaries. In an atrocious display, they begin to cut a tall white shrub. *Rhamnus nabeca* features rigid elliptical leaves and small green flowers, but its most dominant characteristic is the inch-long curving thorns that sprout closely together. The soldiers are more than willing to endure the prick of these sharp spikes as they weave several branches together to form a crown. When they are done, this wreath makes a perfect complement to the reed and the purple cloak. All hail the king!

Jesus is too weak to protest when the crown of thorns is fitted onto his head, and the spikes pressed hard into his skin. They brush up against the many nerves surrounding the skull almost immediately and then crash into bone. Blood pours down his face. Jesus stands humiliated in the small prison as soldiers dance around him—some punching him, others spitting, and still others getting down on both knees to praise their "king." Piling on, the soldiers rip the reed from Jesus's hand and strike him hard across the head, which pushes the thorns even deeper into that tight network of nerves. The result is an instant fiery sensation radiating up and down his face.

Much to the jailers' delight, they have contrived one of the most gruesome methods of torture conceivable.

But just when it seems that Jesus can't take anymore, the soldiers receive word that Pilate would like to see the prisoner. Once again, Jesus is led out into the public square, where the Sanhedrin and its loyal followers stand waiting.

Jesus's vision has blurred. Fluid is slowly building around his lungs. He is having a hard time breathing. He has predicted his death all along, but the details of his demise are shocking.

The high priests and religious leaders watch as Jesus steps forth, the crown of thorns still on his head. In him, they see the memory of a man who publicly humiliated them in the Temple courts just three days ago. They can see his suffering now, yet they have no sympathy whatsoever. Jesus must die—the more painfully, the better.

It is 9:00 A.M. as Pilate takes his seat again on the judgment throne. He tries one last time to release Jesus. "Here is your king," he snarls at the assembly of religious leaders and their disciples. These men should be in the Temple courts, for the slaughter of the lambs is soon to begin.

"Take him away," the religious leaders chant. "Take him away. Crucify him."

Pilate is tired of arguing. The Roman governor is not known for his compassion and believes he has done all that he can do. The fate of Jesus is simply not worth the effort.

"Shall I crucify your king?" he asks, seeking a final confirmation.

"We have no king but Caesar," a chief priest replies. If taken at face value, those words are an act of heresy, for in saying them the priest is rejecting his own Jewish God in favor of the god of the Roman pagans. Yet the followers of the Sanhedrin see no irony in the situation.

"What crime has he committed?" Pilate yells back.

"Crucify him!" comes the response.

Pilate orders that a small bowl of water be brought to Jesus. He dips his hands into the chalice and theatrically makes a show of a ritual cleansing. "I am innocent of this man's blood," he tells the religious leaders. "It is your responsibility."

But in fact the responsibility belongs to Pilate. Only the Roman governor possesses the *ius gladii*—"the right of the sword." Or, as it is also known, the right to execute.

So it is that Pilate orders his executioners to take control of Jesus. As they lead the Nazarene away to be crucified, Pontius Pilate prepares for an early lunch.

†††

The purple cloak is ripped away, but the crown of thorns remains. The death squad places a plank of unfinished wood on Jesus's shoulders. It weighs between fifty and seventy pounds, it is just a little less than six feet long, and its splinters quickly find their way into the open wounds on the Nazarene's body. The humiliation at Pilate's palace now complete, the procession toward the place of execution begins.

At the front of the line is the officer known as the *exactor mortis*. By tradition, this centurion holds up a sign written in Greek, Aramaic, and Latin. Normally, a man's crimes are listed on the sign, which will be nailed onto the cross above him. This way, any passerby will know why the man was crucified. So if treason is the charge, then that is what the sign should state.

But Pontius Pilate is changing tradition. In a last attempt to get the better of Caiaphas, the governor writes the inscription himself, in charcoal: JESUS THE NAZARENE: KING OF THE JEWS.

"Change it," Caiaphas demands before the crucifixion procession gets under way.

"It stays exactly as it is," Pilate replies, his condescension apparent.

So the sign leads the way as Jesus and his four executioners make the painfully slow journey to Golgotha, the hill used as the Roman execution ground. The trip is slightly less than half a mile, taking Jesus through the cobbled streets of Jerusalem's Upper City, then out the Gennath Gate, to the low hill on which a vertical pole awaits him. It is getting close to noon. A substantial crowd has gathered to watch, despite a blazing sun overhead.

As a former builder and carpenter, the Nazarene knows the proper way to carry a length of lumber, but now he lacks the strength to do so. The *exactor mortis* becomes concerned as Jesus repeatedly stumbles. Should Jesus die before reaching the place of execution, it is the *exactor mortis* who will be held responsible. So a pilgrim bystander, an African Jew named Simon of Cyrene,* is enlisted to carry the crossbeam for Jesus.

The procession continues. Despite the assistance, the Nazarene is constantly on the verge of fainting. Each stumble drives the thorns on his head deeper into his skull. Jesus is so thirsty he can barely speak.

---

*Not much is known about Simon of Cyrene, other than that he hailed from the city of Cyrene in Libya and had traveled almost a thousand miles from there to be in Jerusalem for Passover. Mark refers to him as "the father of Alexander and Rufus," and the legendary missionary Paul is later seen greeting a man named Rufus (Romans 16:13), suggesting that perhaps Simon's sons were so well known in the early Christian community that readers would easily recognize their names.

Meanwhile, just a few hundred yards away, in the Temple courts, the celebration of Passover is well under way, diverting the attention of many who revere Jesus and who might otherwise have rioted to intervene and save his life.

The execution site, Golgotha, is not a large hill. It is a low rise within a very short distance from Jerusalem's city wall. In fact, anyone standing atop those walls will be able to view Jesus's crucifixion at eye level and will be so close that they can hear every word he says if he speaks loudly enough.

But Jesus hasn't spoken in hours. As the procession arrives atop Golgotha, the soldiers send Simon away and hurl the crossbeam onto the dirt and rough limestone—"Jerusalem rock," some call it. The death squad takes control here. They force Jesus to the ground, laying his torso atop the upper crossbeam, the *patibulum*. His hands are then stretched out and two soldiers put all their weight on his extended arms, as another approaches with a thick mallet and a six-inch iron nail with a square shaft that tapers to a point.

The soldier hammers the sharpened point into Jesus's flesh, at precisely the spot where the radius and ulna bones meet the carpals of the wrist. He jabs the nail hard into the skin to stabilize it before impact.

Jesus cries out in pain as the iron pierces its mark. The Romans use the wrist location because the nail never hits bone, instead passing all the way through to the wood with just a few sharp swings of the hammer. The wrist bones, meanwhile, surround the soft tissue, forming a barrier. So when the cross is hoisted upward and the victim's body weight suspends from that spike, the bones keep the thin layer of muscle from ripping, preventing the person from falling to the ground.

The first wrist secure, the executioner moves on to the second. A crowd watches from the base of the hill. Among them are Jesus's devoted friend Mary Magdalene and his mother, Mary. She came to Jerusalem for Passover, not having any idea what would befall her son. Now she can do nothing but look upon him in anguish.

After Jesus is nailed to the crossbeam, the executioners hoist him to his feet. A careful balancing act ensues, because the weight of the wood is now on Jesus's back—not his shoulders. In his weakened state, he could easily fall over. Soldiers hold up both ends of the crossbeam, while a third steadies Jesus as they back him toward the vertical beam that will complete the cross.

The *staticulum*, as this in-ground pole is known, is close to eight feet tall. In cases where the Romans want a victim to suffer for days before dying, a small seat juts out halfway up its length. But tomorrow is the Sabbath, and Jewish law says that a man must be taken off the cross before it begins. The Romans want Jesus to die quickly. Thus, there is no seat (*sedile*) on Jesus's cross.

Nor is there a footrest. Instead, when the moment comes that his feet are nailed into the wood, they must first be flexed at an extreme angle.

One soldier grabs Jesus around the waist and lifts him up as the other two hoist their ends of the crossbeam. The fourth executioner stands atop a ladder that leans against the *staticulum*, guiding the crossbeam into the small joint that has been carved into the top of the vertical piece. The weight of Jesus's body holds the beam inside the groove.

And so it is that Jesus of Nazareth now hangs on the cross. Another moment of agony comes when Jesus's knees are bent slightly and his feet are lapped one over the other and nailed into place. The spike passes through the fine metatarsal bones on its way into the wood but, amazingly, none of the bones break, which is extremely unusual in a crucifixion.

Finally, in the spot directly over Jesus's head, the sign carried by the *exactor mortis* is nailed into the cross. Their physical work done, the death squad begins mocking Jesus, throwing dice for his once-fine tunic and calling up to him, "If you are the king of the Jews, save yourself."

The Roman killers will remain on Golgotha until Jesus dies. They will drink their sour wine and even offer some to Jesus. If necessary, they will break his legs to hasten his demise. For death on the cross is a slow journey into suffocation. Each time a victim takes a breath he must fight his own body weight and push his torso upward using his legs, thus allowing his lungs to expand. In time, the victim, exhausted, can breathe neither in nor out.

Three hours pass. The Passover celebration continues inside the Temple courts, and the sounds of singing and of trumpets resound across the city to the execution site. Indeed, Jesus can see the Temple Mount quite clearly from his place on the cross. He knows that many are still waiting for him. The news of his execution has not traveled far, much to the delight of Pilate and Caiaphas, who still fear the possibility of Jesus's supporters starting a riot when they hear news of his murder.

"I thirst," Jesus finally says, giving in to the dehydration that has consumed him for more than twelve hours. His voice is not more than a whisper. A soldier soaks a sponge in sour wine and reaches up to place it to the Nazarene's lips, knowing the liquid will sting.

Jesus sucks in the tart fluid. Shortly afterward, he gazes on Jerusalem one last time before the inevitable happens.

"It is finished," he says.

Jesus bows his head. The crown of thorns hangs rigidly. He lapses into unconsciousness. His neck relaxes. His entire body rolls forward, pulling his neck and shoulders away from the cross. Only the nails in his hands hold him in place.

The man who once preached the Gospel so fearlessly, who walked far and wide to tell the world about a new faith, and whose message of love and hope reached thousands during his lifetime—and will one day reach billions more—stops breathing.

Jesus of Nazareth is dead. He is thirty-six years old.

CHAPTER NINETEEN

JERUSALEM'S UPPER CITY
APRIL 7, A.D. 30
3:00 P.M.–6:00 P.M.

THE RACE IS ON. THE ROMAN DEATH SQUAD HAS HAD A HARD day, but there is still more work to be done. It is their practice to leave a man on the cross for days after he dies, perhaps to allow his body to decompose or even be eaten by wild animals. But Jewish law dictates that a body cannot remain on a "tree"* during the Sabbath, which begins at sundown today and continues throughout Saturday. So the *quaternio* must take Jesus down off the cross and throw his body into the communal grave reserved for criminals.

The *exactor mortis* now verifies Jesus's death by thrusting a spear into his chest. The pleural and pericardial fluid that have

---

*Deuteronomy 21:23.

built up around Jesus's heart and lungs for hours now pours out, mixed with a torrent of blood. Extracting the spear tip, the captain of the guard* then orders his men to remove Jesus from the cross. It is a crucifixion in reverse, with the men using ladders and teamwork to bring Jesus and the crossbeam back to the ground. Once again, Jesus is laid flat. But now the death squad works hard to remove the nails—unbent. Iron is expensive, and spikes are reused as much as possible.

Most who witnessed Jesus's crucifixion from a distance have departed. Mary, his mother, and Mary Magdalene are among those who remain. But as the soldiers now go about the hard physical labor of un-crucifying a man, a Sadducee named Joseph of Arimathea steps forth. This wealthy member of the Sanhedrin and secret disciple of Jesus was one of the few dissenting voices during the illegal trial. Another of those voices was that of Nicodemus the Pharisee, who now stands atop Golgotha with Joseph. They have received permission from Pilate to take the body, as the governor wants to put this execution to rest as soon as possible.

Somewhat shockingly, Joseph and Nicodemus are publicly declaring their allegiance to the teachings of Jesus. Joseph takes

---

*Jesus's *exactor mortis* goes unnamed in the Gospels, but legend says that his name was Longinus. He is considered a saint by the Roman Catholic and Eastern Orthodox Churches because many believe he converted to Christianity as a result of his brush with Jesus, which is said to have caused the soldier great remorse. His spear is often referred to as the "Holy Lance" and through the centuries it has been coveted by powerful men because of its alleged supernatural powers. The most recent of these was Adolf Hitler, who is thought to have gained hold of the spear prior to World War II, during the Anschluss. These same theories hold that General George S. Patton obtained the spear at the end of the war and returned it to the Hofburg Palace in Vienna, where it resides to this day in the Austrian Imperial Treasury. Other artifacts claiming to be the Holy Lance can currently be found in Armenia, Antioch, and Poland.

Jesus's body to his own private family tomb, a brand-new man-made cave carved out of the soft Jerusalem rock on a nearby hillside. The Jews believe that a criminal's presence in a tomb desecrates it. Even worse, for a member of the Sanhedrin to touch a dead body on Passover makes him unclean and disqualifies him from eating the Seder. By law, Joseph and Nicodemus will be declared impure and must undergo a seven-day cleansing ritual.*

No matter, these two bold members of the Sanhedrin demonstrate their role as followers of Jesus by carrying his limp corpse down off Golgotha and then to the nearby tomb. There is no time to perform the ritual washing and anointing of the corpse with oil. But they do make the extravagant gesture of coating the body in expensive myrrh and aloe, to overwhelm the coming smell of decomposition. Then they wrap the body tightly in linen, making sure to keep it loose around Jesus's face in case he is not really dead but merely unconscious. In this way, he will not suffocate. Jewish tradition dictates that all bodies be examined three days after apparent death.† Thus the tomb will be reopened and Jesus will be observed on Sunday.

But all this is merely adherence to ritual. For Jesus is clearly dead. The spear rupturing the pericardial sac around his heart left no doubt.

Nonetheless, the tomb will be reopened on Sunday. When death is formally pronounced, his body will rest inside the tomb for a full year. Then the bones will be removed from his decomposed body and placed in a small stone jar known as an ossuary,

---

*Numbers 19:11.

†Jewish tradition has offered the option of burial of the dead or interment in a tomb since ancient times. The wealthy were more able to afford a family crypt. Whether in a tomb or in the ground, the grave was considered a place of worship. Desecration of such a site was thought to be a grievous sin.

to be either stored in a niche carved into the tomb wall or removed to a new location.

The tomb of Jesus is in a garden outside the city walls. The stone that will cover its entrance weighs hundreds of pounds. It is already in position, resting atop a track that makes it easier to roll. The track, however, is engineered at a slightly downhill angle. Sealing the tomb today will be much easier than rolling away the heavy stone on Sunday.

Joseph and Nicodemus carry the body into the tomb and lay it down on the carved rock ledge. The air is dusty and laden with the smell of heavy perfume. The men say a formal good-bye to Jesus, then step outside the tomb.

Mary, the mother of Jesus, watches as the two men strain to roll the stone across the tomb entrance. Mary Magdalene also looks on. The shaft of daylight penetrating the tomb grows smaller and smaller as the rock rolls into position.

Jesus of Nazareth predicted his death and even prayed that God take the cup of sorrow from his lips. But now it is done. The silence of the grave is complete. Alone in the darkness of the tomb, Jesus of Nazareth finally rests in peace.

CHAPTER TWENTY

PILATE'S PALACE, JERUSALEM
SATURDAY, APRIL 8, A.D. 30
DAY

PONTIUS PILATE HAS VISITORS. ONCE AGAIN, CAIAPHAS AND the Pharisees stand before him. But now they are inside the palace, no longer fearful of being made unclean by the governor's presence, for Passover is done.

For the first time, Pilate notices that Caiaphas is actually terrified of Jesus's power. What was not so obvious in the Nazarene's lifetime is now quite apparent in death, for the chief priest is making an unheard-of request. Caiaphas tells Pilate directly, "That deceiver said, 'After three days I will rise again.' So give the order for the tomb to be made secure until the third day. Otherwise, his disciples might come, steal the body, and tell the people that he has been raised from the dead."

There is a certain logic to the request, for the disappearance of

Jesus's body might lead to an uprising against the Temple priests as his followers convince people that this man who claims to be the Christ has actually proven himself to be immortal. The presence of a Roman guard will deter any attempt to break into the tomb to steal the corpse.

Pilate consents to Caiaphas's request.

"Take a guard," he orders. "Make the tomb secure."

And so it is that a Roman guard is placed at the tomb of Jesus, just in case the dead man tries to escape.

✝✝✝

That should have been the end of it. The troublemaker and blasphemer is dead. The Sanhedrin and Rome no longer have any cause for concern. If the Nazarene's followers had any plans for trouble, there is no sign of it. The disciples have proven themselves timid, still stunned that their messiah is dead. They have gone into hiding and pose no threat to Rome.

Pilate is relieved. Soon he will be on his way back to Caesarea, there once again to govern without the constant interference of the Temple priests.

But Caiaphas will not go away. Wearing his expensive robes and linen, he postures before Pilate, not knowing how the Roman governor will report back to Rome. Caiaphas has much at stake and he is uneasy over Pilate's hand-washing display, which makes it clear that the governor is trying to distance himself from this proceeding. He will lose everything if Emperor Tiberius blames him for the death of Jesus. So Caiaphas stands firm, looking for any sign of approval from Pilate. But the Roman governor has had enough of this arrogant priest. Without a word, he stands and walks away.

CHAPTER TWENTY-ONE

JESUS'S TOMB
SUNDAY, APRIL 9, A.D. 30
DAWN

THE MORNING IS DARK. DAWN WILL SOON BREAK OVER JERU-
salem, marking the third day since Jesus's death. Mary Magdalene now takes it upon herself to perform the traditional task of
examining the dead body. She travels with another woman
named Mary, though not the mother of Jesus. Just as on the day
the Nazarene was executed, the streets of the Upper City are
quiet as the two women pass through. They exit the city walls at
the Gennath Gate and now travel in the Nazarene's last footsteps
as they walk toward Golgotha.

The vertical pole on which Jesus was crucified still stands atop
the hill, awaiting the next crucifixion. The two Marys look away
from the gruesome image and walk around the hill to Jesus's
tomb.

They have practical matters on their minds. Mary Magdalene has never forgotten the many kindnesses Jesus showed her during his lifetime. And just as she once anointed him with perfume and washed his feet with her tears, she now plans to anoint the body with spices. It is unconscionable to her that Jesus's corpse might molder and emit a foul smell. Perhaps a year from now, when she returns for Passover and is among those who roll away the stone in front of Jesus's tomb to collect his bones, the smell of sweet perfume will pour forth from the cave entrance instead of the stench of death.

But this presents another immediate challenge: Mary is physically incapable of rolling away the tombstone; she will require help. Yet most of Jesus's disciples are still in hiding. Since yesterday was the Sabbath, and she followed the mandate to do nothing but rest, she does not know about the Roman soldier ordered to stand guard outside the tomb.

But there is no guard. As the two Marys approach the tomb, they are stunned. The tombstone has been rolled away. The crypt is empty.

Mary Magdalene cautiously steps forward and looks inside. She smells the myrrh and aloe in which Jesus's body was anointed. She clearly sees the linen shroud in which the body was wrapped. But there is nothing else there.

To this day, the body of Jesus of Nazareth has never been found.

AFTERWORD

W HAT COMES NEXT IS THE VERY ROOT OF THE CHRISTIAN faith. The Gospels record that Jesus's body was not stolen. Instead, Scripture puts forth that Jesus rose from the dead and ascended into heaven. After his body was found missing, the Gospels state that Jesus appeared twelve times on earth over a forty-day period. These apparitions range from a single individual to groups of more than five hundred on a mountain in Galilee. Some in that large crowd would speak vividly of the event for years to come. A quarter century later, the disciple Paul included the mountain appearance in a letter to the Corinthians.

Whether or not one believes that Jesus rose from the dead, the story of his life and message achieved much greater status after his crucifixion. He would go down in history not just as Jesus or Jesus of Nazareth, but as Jesus the Christ, the Messiah. Roman writers of the period referenced his name, often preferring to call him *Christus*, the Latinized version of Christ. Unlike all other self-proclaimed messianic figures, Jesus became a noted personage in the history of Jerusalem and beyond. Theudas, the Egyptian prophet, and others such as Judas of Gamala were almost instantly forgotten. Only Bar Kochba (c. A.D. 132–35) retained as much Jewish interest. Followers of Jesus within Judaism are attested to well beyond the first century; the elite did not welcome them, but archaeological evidence and outside sources show that they persisted.

The Roman historians Pliny the Younger, Cornelius Tacitus, and Suetonius all mention Jesus in their writings. The secular Greek-speaking historians Thallus and Phlegon, the satirist Lucian of Samosata, and the eminent Jewish historian Flavius Josephus also mention Jesus. Not all the writers were kind. Lucian, for example, mocks the early Christians for putting their faith in a man who died such a lowly death. Indeed, for centuries, Christians were embarrassed by the cross, for it was considered a punishment best suited for slaves, murderers, and members of the lowest class. Those opposed to the new Christian faith mocked believers for worshipping "a criminal and his cross"* and parodied Christianity as a form of madness. However, Christians began crossing themselves on the forehead and chest ("the sign of the cross") as a way of warding off demons. By the fourth century, the cross was more commonly viewed with pride, as a symbol that Jesus had suffered a lowly death for the benefit of all mankind. The crucifix, that iconic image showing the body of Jesus affixed to a cross, was not a part of the Christian culture until six centuries after his death. The lack of representation of the cross may have been due to the Church's belief in his resurrection.

---

*Second-century Roman rhetorician Marcus Cornelius Fronto, as quoted in *The Octavius*, by Minucius Felix.

†††

After the crucifixion, the disciples of Jesus underwent a radical shift in behavior. They were quite positive that they had seen a resurrected Jesus and soon went out into the world and fearlessly preached his message. Known as the apostles, the men paid a tremendous price for their faith.

In A.D. 44, the grandson of Herod the Great, Herod Agrippa, who ruled Judea at that time, ordered that **James**, one of the sons of thunder,* be put to the sword. The beheading of James made him the first disciple to be martyred. Agrippa was violently opposed to Christianity and used his power to ruthlessly suppress the new theology of Jesus. For a time, he imprisoned Peter but did not kill him.

Peter's missionary work eventually took him to Rome, where he formalized the nascent Christian Church. The Romans were not amused, sentencing Peter to death on the cross. When he protested that he was not worthy to die in the same manner as Jesus, the Romans agreed—and nailed him to the cross upside down. The year is thought to be sometime around A.D. 64–67. There is good evidence that Peter is buried beneath St. Peter's Cathedral in Vatican City.

The deaths of most disciples are consigned to legend. **Andrew**, the apostle known for being optimistic and enterprising, preached Jesus's message in what is now the Ukraine, Russia, and Greece.

---

*The only other disciple to get a nickname was Simon, whom Jesus referred to as Peter ("Rock"), perhaps as a playful stab at Peter's impulsivity and less-than-stable personality. In both Latin and Greek, the feminine noun *petra* means "rock." Masculinized, it is Petrus. In time, however, Peter grew into this nickname, becoming the eminently stable "rock on which I will build this church" that Jesus speaks of in Matthew 16:18.

He was finally believed to have been crucified in Patras, a Roman-controlled region of Greece. Legend says Andrew was bound to an *X*-shaped cross, thus giving rise to the Saint Andrew's cross that adorns the national flag of Scotland to this day.

The often-pessimistic **Thomas** is thought to have been speared to death near Madras, in India. **Bartholomew** preached in Egypt, Arabia, and what is now Iran before being flayed (skinned alive) and then beheaded in India. **Simon the Zealot** was thought to have been sawed in half for his preaching in Persia. **Philip** evangelized in what is now western Turkey. He is said to have been martyred by having hooks run through his ankles and then being hung upside down in the Greco-Roman city of Hierapolis. The gregarious former tax collector **Matthew** may have died in Ethiopia, murdered just like all the rest for his fervent preaching.

Little is known about what happened to the others, except that each apostle spent his life preaching and was killed for doing so. It is a fact that the disciples of Jesus traveled as far as India, Britain, and even into Africa in their zeal to spread their faith, marking a vast sea change from their timid behavior during Jesus's life and in the hours after his death.

The last to die was **John**, the other son of thunder, who was taken prisoner by the Romans for preaching Christianity and exiled to the Greek island of Patmos. There he wrote his Gospel, and also what would become the final pages of the New Testament, the book of Revelation. John died in A.D. 100 in Ephesus, in what is now Turkey. He was ninety-four and the only apostle not to have been martyred.

Matthew's Gospel and the first book of Acts attributes **Judas Iscariot**'s death to suicide. Matthew writes that upon learning that his plan to force Jesus's hand had resulted in the execution order, Judas flung his thirty pieces of silver into the Temple and hung himself from a tree. Legend has it that he used a horse's halter to break his own neck. Whether or not this is true, Judas Iscariot was never heard from again.

The same is true for **Mary Magdalene**. After her appearance at the tomb of Jesus, she disappears from the story. She's very likely included among "the women" mentioned in Acts 1:14, as those empowered by the Spirit at Pentecost.

Mary, the mother of Jesus, is mentioned in the book of Acts and alluded to in the book of Revelation as "a woman clothed with the sun," but her fate goes unrecorded. On November 1, 1950, the Roman Catholic Church decreed that her body had been "assumed into heaven." Pope Pius XII noted that Mary, "having completed the course of her earthly life, was assumed body and soul into heavenly glory."*

✝✝✝

Six years after washing his hands of the Nazarene's execution, **Pontius Pilate** intervened in another case involving a messiah—and this time it cost him his job. The preacher was a Samaritan who had holed up in a mountaintop sanctuary in Gerizim. Concerned by the man's growing legion of followers, Pilate suppressed the movement with heavily armed Roman soldiers. This resulted in many deaths and led Pilate to be recalled to Rome to explain his actions. He thought his appeal would be heard by his friend

---

*On July 18, 1870, the Vatican issued a new doctrine that stated that the pope was infallible. In 1854, Pope Pius IX had issued a previous encyclical stating that Mary was pure and free from sin from the moment she was conceived in the womb. Pius XII's Munificentissimus Deus in 1950 decreed that the final moments of her life were not marred by the grave. It was issued as an infallible statement, an ex cathedra pronouncement, the first since the doctrine was enacted eighty years earlier.

Emperor Tiberius. But by the time Pilate reached Rome, Tiberius was dead, done in either by disease or by being smothered, depending upon which Roman historian is telling the story. No matter, the seventy-seven-year-old debauched emperor was gone. The fourth-century historian Eusebius records that Pilate was later forced to commit suicide, becoming "his own murderer and executioner." Where and how Pilate died is still debated. One report says he drowned himself in the Rhone River near Vienne, a city in modern-day France. There a Roman monument still stands in the heart of the city and is often referred to as "Pilate's Tomb." Another report says he hurled himself into a lake near Lausanne, in what is now Switzerland, where Mount Pilatus is said to have been named in his honor. There is also a rumor that Pilate and his wife, Claudia, converted to Christianity and were killed for their faith. Whether or not that is true, both the Coptic and Ethiopic Christian Churches venerate him as a martyr.

✝✝✝

Tiberius was replaced by **Caligula**, the twenty-four-year-old son of Tiberius's deceased adopted child, Germanicus. Caligula promptly squandered almost all the fortune he inherited from Tiberius—a fortune partially earned on the backs of Galilean peasants. He served for only four years before being stabbed to death in an assassination eerily similar to that of the great Julius Caesar. He was succeeded, in turn, by the emperors Claudius and Nero, who continued the ruinous policies that eventually led to the downfall of Rome. This occurred four hundred years later, in 476, when the Roman Empire was toppled by Germanic tribes. However, long before the empire's collapse, Rome turned away from its pagan gods and began worshipping Jesus Christ. Christianity was officially legalized throughout the Roman Empire in 313, with the Edict of Milan.

†††

With Pilate gone, **Caiaphas** was left without a Roman political ally. He had many enemies in Jerusalem and was soon replaced as the Temple high priest. Caiaphas then left the stage and disappeared into history. The dates of his birth and death are unrecorded. But in 1990, an ossuary containing his bones was discovered in Jerusalem. They are currently on display at the Israel Museum.

†††

Herod Antipas may have been well schooled in palace intrigue, but it eventually brought about his demise. His nephew Agrippa was known to be a close friend of the Roman emperor Caligula. The Jewish historian Josephus relates that when Antipas foolishly asked Caligula to name him king, instead of tetrarch (at the suggestion of his wife, Herodias, who continued to get him into trouble), it was Agrippa who lodged charges that Antipas was plotting to execute Caligula. As proof, Agrippa pointed to the enormous arsenal of weaponry possessed by Antipas's army. So it was that Caligula ordered Antipas to spend the rest of his life exiled to Gaul. His fortune and territories were handed over to the younger Agrippa. The former tetrarch was joined in what is now France by Herodias. The two lived in Lugdunum, which many believe to be the location of modern-day Lyon.

†††

The tension between Rome and the Jewish people did not abate after the unjust crucifixion of Jesus. In A.D. 66, the Jews waged war on the Roman occupying army and took control of Jerusalem. Taxation was a key component of this struggle. However, the Romans did not accept defeat. By A.D. 70 they had surrounded the city with four Roman legions (including the legendary Legio X Fretensis, which set up its forces on the Mount of Olives) and were laying siege. Pilgrims arriving to celebrate Passover were allowed into the city—then not allowed to leave, which put considerable pressure on Jerusalem's limited water and food supplies. Somewhere between six hundred thousand to one million men, women, and children were stuck inside the city walls. Those attempting to escape were promptly crucified, and their crosses left on the surrounding heights for the residents of Jerusalem to witness the fate that awaited them. Thousands were eventually nailed to the cross during the siege, so many that the Romans ran out of wood. Trees had to be logged and carried to Jerusalem from miles away in order to accommodate the tremendous number of crucifixions. Some of those who tried to flee were not crucified but were instead sliced open so that Roman soldiers could scour their digestive tracts because it was thought that many of Jerusalem's residents had swallowed their gold before trying to make their escape.

When the Romans finally breached the city walls, the destruction was total. Those Jews who didn't escape were put to the sword or enslaved. The Temple itself was burned to the ground, and much of the city was leveled. To this day, it has never been rebuilt.

Recent excavations have dug down through the rubble to locate some of the actual streets and homes of Jesus's time, allowing visitors to walk in his footsteps and examine what life was like in Jerusalem. Of note is that the Via Dolorosa* wasn't established until centuries later and was not in existence during Jesus's lifetime.

The real path that Jesus walked began at Herod's palace, near

---

*It is still cited by tour companies and souvenir sellers as the road to the crucifixion site.

what is now the Jaffa Gate. It ends at the Church of the Holy Sepulchre, which is thought to have been built atop the site of Golgotha and near Jesus's tomb. Today visitors can not only tour these sites, but also touch the place where the cross of Jesus is said once to have rested.

✝✝✝

In A.D. 132, with the city of Jerusalem still not completely rebuilt, there was a second uprising against the Romans known as Bar Kochba. The emperor Hadrian had originally been sympathetic to the Jews, allowing them to return to Jerusalem and rebuild the Temple. But he soon changed his mind, preferring to reinvent the Temple as a splendid pagan complex dedicated to himself and the Roman god Jupiter. Hadrian not only banned the Jews from rebuilding but also began deporting them to Egypt and North Africa. The Jewish rebellion grew to such proportions that Judea became a main focus of the Roman army's war efforts, with complete legions sent to suppress the revolt. Not only were almost six hundred thousand Jews slaughtered and almost a thousand villages leveled by its end, but worship practices such as reading the Torah, performing circumcisions, and observing Sabbath were outlawed.

For the next several centuries, the Jews of Judea were routinely persecuted, even as the Roman Empire embraced Christianity starting in the fourth century. In A.D. 637, Muslim forces defeated the Byzantine and predominantly Christian army that occupied Jerusalem. The Muslims later built a mosque on the site of the former Jewish Temple. As long as it remains there, Jewish hopes of rebuilding the Temple on the original site will remain unrealized. The Al-Aqsa Mosque and the nearby shrine known as the Dome of the Rock have stood since 705 and 691, respectively.

After its destruction by the Romans, Jerusalem became a run-down city. But over the centuries, the Jews have returned, despite several attempts to drive them out. As recently as 1948, the Jordanian army flushed every Jew from the old city, killing all those who would not leave. Finally, at the conclusion of the Six-Day War, on June 10, 1967, more than two thousand years after its destruction by the Romans, all of Jerusalem was once again in Jewish hands.

It is interesting to note that in many parables, Jesus of Nazareth predicted harsh things for the city of Jerusalem. There is no question those things came true.

POSTSCRIPT

Both Martin Dugard and I learned a tremendous amount while researching and writing this book. But one intriguing question and a profound statement of fact stand out. First, the question: Why did thousands of common people seek out Jesus of Nazareth? Most couldn't even hear him preach, as the vast crowds that surrounded Jesus were too thick for personal interaction. So why did they come? What was Jesus doing that prompted so many people to set aside their daily labor to be near him?

Christians attribute Jesus's popularity to his message of love, hope, and truth but also to his miraculous healings. But even nonbelievers must admit that something extraordinary was happening in Galilee.

Second, there is no doubt that Jesus of Nazareth is the most famous human being the world has ever known. But Jesus had no infrastructure. He had no government behind him. He had no corporation. He and his disciples depended upon the charity of others for food and shelter, and they had no organization other than a dozen faithful followers. In the history of mankind, no one has achieved worldwide fame with no outside resources whatsoever.

†††

Since his death, Jesus has played a continual role throughout history. The legalization of Christianity by the Roman Empire, in A.D. 313, soon led to its expansion into every part of the Western world. Not until the Prophet Muhammad began the Islamic religion in 610 did Christianity have any meaningful competition in terms of numbers of followers. Muhammad considered Jesus a prophet and is quoted in the Quran as saying, "When Jesus came with clear signs, he said: 'Now I have come to you with wisdom, and in order to make clear to you some of the points on which you dispute. Therefore, fear God and obey me.'"

In the United States, George Washington used Christianity as a rallying point for his colonial army, saying in his First General Order to his troops, "Every officer and man will endeavor to live and act as becomes a Christian soldier defending the dearest rights and liberties of his country."

Abraham Lincoln also referred to Jesus in a wartime setting: "When I went to Gettysburg and looked upon the graves of our dead heroes who had fallen in defense of their country, I then and there consecrated myself to Christ."

Dr. Martin Luther King Jr. of course based his entire ministry and civil rights struggle on the teachings of Jesus. Also, his nonviolent philosophy was adapted in part from the ordeal Jesus experienced. About enemies, Dr. King said the following: "Just keep loving them. And by the power of your love they will break down under the load. That's love, you see. It is redemptive and this is why Jesus says love. There's something about love that builds up and is creative. There is something about hate that tears down and is destructive. So love your enemies."*

President Ronald Reagan picked up on that theme: "He promised there will never be a dark night that does not end. And by dying for us, Jesus showed how far our love should be ready to go—all the way."†

✝✝✝

In the wake of writing *Killing Lincoln* and *Killing Kennedy*, Martin Dugard and I were excited to take on this project. But putting together *Killing Jesus* was exceedingly difficult. We had to separate fact from myth based upon a variety of sources, some of which had their own agendas. But I believe we have brought you an accurate account of not only how Jesus died, but also the way he lived and how his message has affected the world.

Thanks again for reading our book.

---

*Delivered at Dexter Avenue Baptist Church, Montgomery, Alabama, on November 17, 1957.

†Remarks to the Annual Convention of National Religious Broadcasters, January 30, 1984. The speech took place in the Grand Ballroom of the Sheraton Washington. His speechwriter at the time, Ben Elliott, noted that Reagan often went off message and inserted comments such as this on his own, to make it clear that he believed in the divinity of Christ.

SOURCES

Researching and writing a book about the life and death of Jesus was much more daunting than either of our past two efforts. There was no aid from YouTube, which, in the case of *Killing Kennedy*, made it possible to watch President Kennedy's speeches and many public appearances and then describe them in great detail. And there wasn't even media coverage, as in the time of Abraham Lincoln, making it possible to glean facts from newspaper depictions of events for *Killing Lincoln*. And while the Internet is a treasure trove of information about the life and times of Jesus, the information on most sites is contradictory, depending upon one's theology; hearsay is often quoted as truth; or information proved to be completely wrong, once double- and triple-checked against other sources.

So researching *Killing Jesus* required a plunge into classical works such as the four Gospels and the Jewish historian Josephus. These sources provided a jumping-off point, giving us the basics, and then demanded new levels of deeper research to tell the story in as much detail as possible.

The crucifixion, to take one example of this type of inquiry, is widely recorded. But telling the story of what it was like to die on the cross required looking into the type of wood that comprised the crucifix, the nature of men who did the killing, the physiological effects of crucifixion on the body, and the origins of this most grisly execution—and many other small details that eventually either were filed away as unnecessary background information or found their way onto the page.

The historical record may not have been as immediately accessible as that of more recent times, but the men who wrote the history of that period were very much concerned with getting their facts straight and telling the story as completely as possible. The Romans were very keen to chronicle their times, going so far as to publish a daily gazette known as the *acta diurna*, which was handwritten in Rome and posted throughout the city and distributed to Rome's many provinces. Its contents included information on such newsworthy events as crimes, marriages and divorces, and the upcoming schedule of gladiator battles. Sadly, not a single copy has survived to this day, but our knowledge that such a thing as the *acta diurna* once existed shows a commitment to the historical record.

This is a book that gives context to the life of Jesus, so it was also necessary to dig into a variety of other peripheral data in order to describe everything from the shape of a Galilean fishing boat to the type of roof on a Nazarene home. For these facts, like so many other details about that period, we are indebted to the men and women who spend their lives engaged in researching the historicity of biblical times.

And travel, as always, was a vital aspect of our research. Seeing the sights that Jesus saw, walking on the same streets (now buried beneath Jerusalem but accessible, thanks to recent excavations), and even climbing to the top of the Mount of Olives to view the Temple walls from that epic vantage point added immensely to the descriptions that you have read in this book. It is compelling beyond words to read a version of events, such as those found in the Gospels, and to then stand at one of those very sites to gain a new perspective on this most pivotal time in world history.

There are a number of different versions and translations of the Bible in existence, ranging from the time-honored King James Version to the New Jerusalem Bible. For the sake of consistency, we have used just one, Zondervan's New International Version Study Bible, which offers not just the words and depictions of Jesus's life but also detailed sidebars about everything from the height of the Temple to a time line depicting Jesus's ministry.

In addition to the Jewish, Greek, and Roman authors that have already been referenced in the text of *Killing Jesus*, what follows is a detailed list of the many sources upon which we leaned. While lengthy, this list is by no means exhaustive and is grouped by subject matter.

Rome: *Rome and Jerusalem*, by Martin Goodman, is eminently readable and highly recommended, as is *Rubicon*, by Tom Holland. Various other books were consulted for detailed information about life in the Roman Republic and among the legions. Chief among them were *The Complete Roman Legions*, by Nigel Pollard and Joanne Berry, and *The Roman Army*, edited by Chris

McNab, which offer amazing insight into not just the lives of soldiers and leaders but also the evolution of Rome from a fledgling city to a vast empire. *Roman Society and Roman Law in the New Testament*, taken from a series of lectures by A. N. Sherwin-White, provides a more academic view of those times, while *Jerusalem,* by Simon Sebag Montefiore, allows a great overview of the contentious relationship between Rome and Judea. *The Joy of Sexus*, by Vicki Leon, explores lust and longing in the Roman world. *Religions of Rome*, by Mary Beard, John North, and Simon Price, offers insight into the deity of Julius Caesar. *Caesar,* by Theodore Dodge, describes the slaughter of the Germans that made the Rubicon incident necessary. And Ralph Ellis's *Cleopatra to Christ* and Joann Fletcher's *Cleopatra the Great* provide many insights into Cleopatra.

And there's no better way to pass the time on a transatlantic plane flight than to immerse oneself in Martin Hengel's *Crucifixion* and its countless details about the many ways the Romans used the cross to torment their enemies.

Powerful Figures in Judean Politics: It's not going too far out on a limb to say that Helen K. Bond is the eminent authority here, delving into the life of both Pilate and Caiaphas with *Pontius Pilate in History and Interpretation* and *Caiaphas: Friend of Rome and Judge of Jesus?* Her scholarship is riveting and filled with valuable nuggets of insight and information. *Herod*, by Peter Richardson, is nothing short of monumental, fleshing out the life of one of history's most ruthless individuals. *The Army of Herod the Great*, by Samuel Rocca, offers not just minute details but also illustrations depicting everything from the robes worn by the Temple priests to the hairstyles and weapons of Herod's soldiers. Anthony

Saldarini's *Pharisees, Scribes and Sadducees in Palestinian Society* provides a detailed academic take on not just these complex individuals but also life in Judea and Galilee.

Historical Jesus: An entire field of study has been devoted to this viewpoint of the Nazarene, adding context to the Gospels in order to better understand Jesus's life. This focus has allowed a great number of modern advancements into the historicity of Jesus and a more complete understanding of the Gospels and their narrative structure. Recommended reading includes *Jesus Under Fire: Modern Scholarship Reinvents the Historical Jesus*, edited by Michael J. Wilkins and J. P. Moreland; *Studying the Historical Jesus: A Guide to Sources and Methods*, by Darrell L. Bock; *Will the Real Jesus Please Stand Up? A Debate between William Lane Craig and John Dominic Crossan*, edited by Paul Copan; and *The Historical Jesus of the Gospels*, by Craig S. Keener, who is also author of the two-volume *Miracles*. Another two-volume treatise worth a read is Raymond E. Brown's *The Death of the Messiah*. Also worth reading are *Jesus of Nazareth, King of the Jews*, by Paula Fredriksen, and *The Resurrection of Jesus: A New Historiographical Approach*, by Michael R. Licona. *The Sage of Galilee*, by David Flusser and R. Steven Notley, is highly recommended. A more theological take on Jesus can be found in C. S. Lewis's insightful and dense *Mere Christianity*.

The Crucifixion and Jesus's Last Days: In addition to the detailed and chilling version of events recorded in the Gospels of Matthew, Mark, Luke, and John, other recommended reading includes *The Trial of Jesus*, edited by Ernst Bammel; *Jesus, The Final Days*, by Craig Evans and N. T. Wright; and *The Final Days of Jesus*, by

Shimon Gibson. All are filled with nuance, detail, and unique points of view. And for a most graphic depiction of death on the cross, the reader is advised to wade into *The Crucifixion of Jesus: A Forensic Inquiry*. Among other clinical details, the text includes photographs of a crucifixion reenactment. Obviously, not for the faint of heart.

ACKNOWLEDGMENTS

Vast help is always needed in writing a complicated book. This time Makeda Wubneh, Rob Monaco, Eric Simonoff, Stephen Rubin, and Gillian Blake provided tremendous assistance, for which I am extremely grateful. And a special thanks to *O'Reilly Factor* producer Rob Monaco who helped me design the cover for this book.

—Bill O'Reilly

A great thanks to Eric Simonoff for his quiet counsel and literary genius. To Stephen Rubin and Gillian Blake at Holt. To Denny and Leesa Bellessi for the encouragement. To Bill O'Reilly, the world's best writing partner. And, as always, to Callie.

—Martin Dugard

ILLUSTRATION CREDITS

INDEX

Page numbers in *italics* refer to illustrations.

ABOUT THE AUTHORS

BILL O'REILLY is the anchor of *The O'Reilly Factor,* the highest-rated cable news show in the country. He is the author of many #1 bestselling books, including *Killing Lincoln, Killing Kennedy, Killing Patton, Killing Reagan,* and *Killing the Rising Sun.*

MARTIN DUGARD is the *New York Times* bestselling author of several books of history. He and his wife live in Southern California with their three sons.